Praise for *Blackwildgirl*

"Once upon a time/Before time could be counted/ Soft words were spoken/ Then a song was sung/ And a seed hearing those sounds followed them out/ To become a part of the newness/ To become a part of this warmth/To become . . . to become /To become a journey into/ Girlhood/ Menah Pratt follows/ That sound to/ That warmth to/ That possibility/ and invites us to travel/With her."
—NIKKI GIOVANNI, poet

"If there is one book every Black woman needs to read in her life, it's *Blackwildgirl*. Pratt invites us to find ourselves and our inherent power as she found hers. She shows how her journey from childhood to adulthood is also our journey and other women's journeys, from bearing the world to being the world."
—*READERS' FAVORITE*, 5 Star Review

"Menah Pratt has written a book that offers the chance to be empowered, to be educated, to be healed, to be liberated. Be ready to cry, to laugh, to mourn, and to celebrate. Most of all, be ready to have your eyes, heart, and mind opened."
—NAOMI TUTU, ordained minister and daughter of Bishop Tutu

"*Blackwildgirl* encourages all of us to reclaim our superpowers and be change-agents in life."
—KATRINA M. ADAMS, author of *Own the Arena* and former CEO of United States Tennis Association

"Part spell-binding memoir and part luminous teaching, this book shattered my complacency and opened my heart. Sensual and smart, dignified and vulnerable, Menah Pratt manages to simultaneously deconstruct white supremacy and celebrate the Divine Feminine as Black Woman. I haven't been this excited by an emerging voice in a long time. *Blackwildgirl* ought to be required reading for anyone longing to reclaim their own deepest, fullest humanity."
—MIRABAI STARR, author of *Wild Mercy* and *God of Love*

"*Blackwildgirl* starts like a strike of thunder a few hundred miles away, like a storm catching up to you. I was left gasping for air on several occasions. And at the same time, I felt enveloped with a warm hug. Once I got started, I could not stop. Be prepared to be moved!"
—PRISCA DORCAS MOJICA RODRÍGUEZ, author of *For Brown Girls with Sharp Edges and Tender Hearts*

"A gift to 'wild women' everywhere, Menah Pratt's *Blackwildgirl* makes an important contribution to the evolving field of Black Girlhood Studies, as well as Women's Studies, Black Studies, and Womanist Theology."
—BEVERLY GUY-SHEFTALL, founding director of the Women's Research & Resource Center, Anna Julia Cooper Professor, Spelman College, author of *Words of Fire: An Anthology of African American Feminist Thought*

"*Blackwildgirl* is a love letter to Black feminism and Blackwildgirls across the diaspora. A truly satisfying read, *Blackwildgirl* will leave readers breathless, while simultaneously providing space for critical reflection. This is one memoir you will want to read time and time again."
—LETISHA ENGRACIA CARDOSO BROWN, Assistant Professor, University of Cincinnati

"Menah Pratt sets new precedents in her writing of *Blackwild-girl*. All would benefit from reading this almost sacred and critical text. She reminds us of Toni Morrison, Maya Angelou, and Oprah Winfrey. Her visionary and spiritual voice meld into one, going from a Moonlight Sonata to hip-hop and the Psalms. In her feminist hands the act of crying becomes an act of transparency and empowerment; it rises to healing and refurbishing the spirit on the table of our consciousness, not in the closet."

—GABRIELLA GUTIÉRREZ Y MUHS, Professor, Seattle University, author of 8 books of poetry

"Every now and again a poet comes along and allows her reader a peak beyond the veil. *Blackwildgirl* takes us on a journey across time and geographies through the eyes of a determined spirit. The book is in conversation with every precarious daughter who dared to live free. Pratt boldly, yet delicately, reveals the warrior spirit within!"

—VENUS E. EVANS-WINTERS, author of *Black Feminism in Qualitative Inquiry: A Mosaic for Writing Our Daughter's Body*

"*Blackwildgirl* breathes life into the bones of Black women and girls everywhere."

—RENATA FERDINAND, Chair and Full Professor, New York City College of Technology (CUNY), author of *An Autoethnography of African American Motherhood: Things I Tell My Daughter*

"*Blackwildgirl* is a valuable resource for parents, daughters, women, husbands, partners, and lovers of women, as it sheds light on the challenges faced and the strength required to embrace one's true self and stand as a warrior in the world."

—SHARON TETTEGAH, Director, Center for Black Studies Research, Professor, University of California, Santa Barbara

"*Blackwildgirl* takes its readers on a mythic, iconic, revelatory journey, opening the pathway for other would-be wildwomen and their allies to step up, speak up, and stand up. This poignant, multi-layered, mixed genre story is a must read for those interested in what it means to be a father, a mother, a daughter, a professional, a human being."
—VALERIE LEE, author of *Sisterlocking Discoarse: Race, Gender, And The Twenty-First-Century Academy*

"Dedicated to wildgirls and wildwomen, *Blackwildgirl* is essential reading for anyone who wants to live in the fullness of creativity, wisdom, and joy."
—CORINNE FIELD, Associate Professor, University of Virginia, co-editor of *The Global History of Black Girlhood*

"The breadth and depth of Menah Pratt's soul journey to uncover Blackwildgirl and Blackwildwoman is not just inspirational, but the most unselfish revolutionary act I have experienced in book form maybe ever!
—GINA L. CARROLL, author of *The Grandest Garden*

"A must-read for those committed to Black girls' and women's non-negotiable liberation and for Black women journeying to reclaim their wildness and freedom."
—DOMINIQUE C. HILL, Assistant Professor, Colgate University

"This Black feminist/womanist gift will no doubt have a profound impact on the lives of all the Black women who engage this love offering: a wake and an awakening, a sunrise and a libation."
—ANDREA N. BALDWIN, Associate Professor, University of Utah, and author of *A Decolonial Black Feminist Theory of Reading and Shade: Feeling the University*

"This work is a beautiful and perfect mirror for young girls and women, especially those from diverse backgrounds, as they explore their own positionality in becoming bold and powerful humans in our rapidly transforming society."
—JOHANNA B. MAES, Faculty, University of Colorado Boulder

"Truly a triumph of the spirit!"
—ANTONIA DARDER, author of *A Dissident Voice: Essays on Culture, Pedagogy & Power*

"*Blackwildgirl* creates new entry points to hear, see, and love on Black girls."
—COREY J. MILES, author of *Vibe: The Sound and Feeling of Black Life in the American South*

"*Blackwildgirl* is a vivid example of what Maya Angelou describes in her poem, *Still I Rise.*"
—V. JEAN RAMSEY, Retired Professor, Texas Southern University, co-author of *Teaching Diversity*

blackwildgirl

blackwildgirl

A Writer's Journey to Take Back Her Superpower

Menah Adeola Eyaside Pratt

SHE WRITES PRESS

Published 2024
Printed in the United States of America
Print ISBN: 978-1-64742-632-3
E-ISBN: 978-1-64742-633-0
Library of Congress Control Number: 2023915519

For information, address:
She Writes Press
1569 Solano Ave #546
Berkeley, CA 94707

Interior Design by Tabitha Lahr

She Writes Press is a division of SparkPoint Studio, LLC.

Names and identifying characteristics have been changed to protect the privacy of certain individuals.

This book is dedicated to wildgirl, revealing Herself to all who seek Her, and the angels and ancestors who help us to find Her. Journal and journey along with the Blackwildgirl Companion Journal: Finding Your Superpower *on Amazon.*

Contents

List of Photographs and Images

Prologue

Stage is set.

Lights. Camera.

Revolution.

THIS IS THE STORY OF A LITTLE BLACK GIRL (Blackwildgirl) who knew she was a queen and, in her innocence, shared her knowledge too soon. The world dethroned her, burying her spirit, expecting to asphyxiate her. But the world didn't know that she was a seed. Germinating underground in the bowels of the earth—almost suffocating—the seed miraculously survives, nourished by nutrients submerged in composting decay. Drinking from dew drops and snatching heat from sunlight, the seed sustains herself, rooting and grasping on to small grains of dirt offering their hands to her. With a fierce, fiery, and feisty determination, she births herself from her seed-coat womb, detangling from the weeds and the wily ways of the world attempting to sabotage her divine destiny. Pushing through the muck and the mire, bursting forth and rising up, she announces her above-ground presence: her arms, like branches, outstretched and her breasts, like buds, boldly baring themselves. Her willow, palm-tree spine, bending but never breaking, sways unassuaged in the glorious air of her reclaimed throne. Regal, resurrected, and refusing to be denied her rightful role as an African goddess, Blackwildgoddess blossoms and blooms, radiating rays of love, joy, and hope for other seeds on their journeys. Her journey begins with libations.

SCENE ONE: **Libation**

When Mama and I visited Freetown, Sierra Leone, in West Africa for the first time in 1989, Mama Pratt (my father's mother) and Aunt Dorothea (my father's stepsister from a different mother) took us shortly after our arrival to a seemingly ancient, weed-covered cemetery. Mama Pratt carried a traditional African meal of jollof rice, chicken, beef, and vegetables in a large brown paper bag. She also had a bottle of rum. Slowly, bending down, moving away weeds and debris with her old Black worn and weathered fingers, she paused at certain headstones. Brow wrinkled, she turned to Aunt Dorothea to ask her to read the barely visible name. Hearing it, she slowly shook her head, mumbled in frustration, looked around, and gradually moved to another grave. The process was repeated until the name called was the one she'd been listening for. Once the ancestor's name had been called, Mama Pratt got on her knees in front of the headstone and began a conversation.

The conversation went something like this: "Ancestor, how are you doing? We are here today with Menah, my grand-daughter, and her mother, Mildred. This is Ted's child, my son's daughter. They are from America. Menah is in college now, a big girl. They have come here to meet you." She then turned to my mother and me and introduced us to the ancestor: "This is Ancestor So-and-So, your father's such-and-such. So, they are your such-and-such (great-great-third-cousin-in-law)." My mother and I nodded in respectful acknowledgment, to either her or the ancestor or both.

After the introductions, my grandmother reached into her bag of food, placed some food near the headstone, poured a little liquor near the food in reverence and remembrance, and resumed the conversation: "I ask you to bless them, and help them to be prosperous and healthy." Silent for a bit, she mumbled a bit more and poured a little more liquor. A libation. Standing up, she picked up the brown bag of food, grabbed the liquor, and started wandering, pausing, and searching for the next ancestor. For the next hour, she repeated the ritual, confirming the name, making introductions, asking for blessings, and pouring libation. When we finished, she drank the remaining liquor. It wasn't a lot, but it was as if she was rewarding herself for a job well done. I remember feeling reverence and confusion, all at once. Obviously, a sacred moment, but I didn't know the ancestors, and I wasn't sure the ancestors knew me. It was many years later before I could fully appreciate the power, importance, and significance of visiting ancestors at their grave sites.

Five years later, I returned to Sierra Leone alone, without my mother. Again, shortly after my arrival, Mama Pratt, Aunt Dorothea, and I made the ritual cemetery visit. And again, my grandmother walked us around to the grave sites of the ancestors, introduced me to them, asked for their blessing, and left the African meal of jollof rice, chicken, beef, and vegetables. Again, she poured the liquor in front of their graves in reverence and remembrance. A libation.

On that visit, we celebrated Mama Pratt's eightieth birthday with a big party. Generations of aunts, uncles, cousins, and friends, numbering close to fifty, all showed up to her two-story, always-under-construction apartment building. She lived in the small cluttered downstairs unit with chickens running around, in and out of her house. Around midday, we began to set up a makeshift kitchen in the yard out front. Big pots of stews and soups were placed on top of fire and rocks. Simmering stews, sweating women, and scintillating aromas revealing sacred secrets attested to the culinary expertise of the cooks. Games and storytelling across generations gradually led to a hungry restlessness. Hours later, it was time to eat.

I remember Mama Pratt calling several men and boys to her side. She asked them to dig a large hole. She went to all the pots of food, prayed over them, and asked the sister-cooks to create plates with rice, meat, and vegetables. Not initially satisfied, she often would tell them to add more meat, more vegetables, and more rice from the steaming pots to her plates. Eventually, she was satisfied, and she went to the large hole. With a bottle of alcohol, kneeling down, she began to talk to the ancestors, mumbling. We couldn't understand what she was saying, and perhaps we were not meant to. It seemed to be a private conversation between her and those down below. Reverently, she began to share the meal with the ancestors, spooning and scooping large portions and placing them into the hole, as if she was literally feeding them. As cousins in our teens and twenties standing around, we shared subtle side glances, smirks, and snickers, wondering to ourselves, *How much food is this strange old lady going to give to these dead folks? Here we are alive, and we are hungry.*

We were a little shocked and slightly horrified at how much Mama Pratt seemed to be giving the ancestors. We were too young in the knowings of an African Blackwildwoman to understand why the ancestors deserved so much. I learned over the years that a libation is so much more than giving ancestors food and drink. It is an act of pouring out gratitude to ancestral energy. It is an act of humility to those who have gone before. It is a call for assistance and protection. It is an act of acknowledgment of the interconnected spirits of those above ground with those on whose ground we are living.

And so, like Mama Pratt, I am taking time to create a symbolic libation—a pouring out of gratitude in reverence and remembrance to the women who have inspired this work: Lorraine Hansberry and Leanita McClain. It is a libation to two Black women who died in their thirties, never fully actualizing their potential but inspiring and calling on Black women to write as if our lives depended on it—because they do.

On August 18, 2019, I wrote in my journal about the challenge of being a Black woman writer:

> *Two days ago, I was in despair. I didn't think I could write this book about my life. I was tired of fighting invisible ghosts of racism, sexism, and hatred. I was tired of the energy of those who are jealous, of those who are dismissive, and of those who make me question everything. I cried and cried and cried. I called upon the God I believe in to rescue me, to save me from what I don't even know—then or now. Maybe it was just the sinking feeling of my constant struggle. I woke up in the morning, surprised I fell asleep. I must have cried myself to sleep.*
>
> *I look at the outline for this book. It is rough. I'm struggling to write about my life as a Black woman, for our lives are not singular lives, but intertwined with others. Our stories are part of their stories, and their stories are part of ours. In telling the intertwined stories, I have been experiencing an internal battle about what to share, what to reveal, and what to allow to remain hidden. My brother, Awadagin, an internationally renowned classical pianist, conductor, and full professor of music, reminds me that sanitizing protects no one and that something has to explain how we got to where we are in the world.*
>
> *In working on this manuscript, I've been asking myself questions: What do I say? What do I omit? How do I not harm? How can I be authentic and honest?*

What will people think? What do I share about myself? How much of myself do I share? Do I actually share how much I weigh and that I have been fighting my weight for decades, not quite willing or able to accept that perhaps this is where it is, and what it will be? Do I share my financial struggles of always worrying about money, of never having enough, of living paycheck to paycheck, of being a primary breadwinner (or the sole breadwinner), and of living with credit card debt with interest at 27%? Do I share about all the times I wrote to my supervisors begging them to pay me what I knew others were paid with less education and less time in the office than me? Do I write about the times I have cried and cried from the racism and sexism and meanness in the world? How do I write about the lonely journey of being a young, gifted, and Black girl in the world? How do I share how hard it was and is to be a Black woman scholar-activist?

In *To Be Young, Gifted, and Black* (Nemiroff and Hansberry 1970, 148), Lorraine Hansberry wrote that what makes us "exceptional" inevitably also makes us lonely. She wrote of the pain and perhaps shame of being lonely and alone at a typewriter in her journal entry on the Saturday evening before Easter in 1962. Like Lorraine, on August 16, 2019, I wrote in my own journal: "I felt very lonely just now and today. . . . My legs felt very dry and old today just now." Yet I am committed to the almost indescribably lonely path of a Black scholar (Franklin 1989, 304). It is indeed a lonely road and a precarious journey to be a Black woman scholar-activist, with a commitment to being revolutionary.

On June 17, 1964, in the midst of the Civil Rights Movement, Lorraine interrogated her own commitment, asking the question: "Do I remain a revolutionary?" She decided that she needed to travel to the heart of the Civil Rights Movement to "find out what kind of revolutionary" she was (Nemiroff and Hansberry 1970, 256–7). Unfortunately, she died six months later at the age of thirty-four from pancreatic cancer.

Almost twenty years later, in 1984, another Black woman writer and journalist, Leanita McClain, also died in her prime at the age of thirty-two. She committed suicide. I saved the May 31, 1984, newspaper article about her death in my childhood journal. It said she was too sensitive for an insensitive world (Balamaci and O'Driscoll 1984). Like her, I, too, felt I was too sensitive for an insensitive world, and attempted suicide in 1984; I was seventeen. Having graduated from high school at sixteen, I was pursuing a professional tennis career. Traveling across the country to tournaments and practicing tennis six to eight hours a day with my father, who was my coach, I was miserable, lonely, and suffering under expectations that I could not meet. Opening the medicine cabinet and finding my father's high blood pressure pills that he had stopped taking, I took several and then—sobbing, crying, and heaving—vomited. Unsuccessful at suicide, I researched death and suicide and learned that people choose suicide when the fear of living is greater than the fear of death. I understood why Leanita could choose suicide, and throughout my life, like Leanita, there would be seasons where I didn't think I could live another day.

Leanita had married and divorced Clarence Page, another Black journalist. In his reflections on Leanita, Clarence said she was clinically depressed and bipolar (Holleran 2011). It may be that we label people clinically depressed and bipolar when it might just be that they are sensitive and human, that the world is too insensitive for them, and they are impacted differentially because they care so deeply. That does not mean something is wrong with them; rather, something is wrong with the world. In an interview with Clarence, the interviewer noted that Leanita's obituary said that she "carried the weight of the city [Chicago] upon her shoulders" (Holleran 2011). The interviewer asked Clarence, "Should she have shrugged?" And Clarence responded, "I think so."

No—I think quickly and angrily. Some of us cannot shrug our shoulders. This is who we are. We come into this world, we care deeply, we have a calling, and we do not shrug our shoulders. We cannot shrug our shoulders. We must not shrug our shoulders. We must, like Lorraine, find out what kind of revolutionary we are.

Lorraine left behind a plea and exhortation for those of us who are young, gifted, and Black. She urges us to "write about the world as it is and as you think it ought to be and must be—if there is to be a world" (Nemiroff and Hansberry 1970, 262–3). And so, Lorraine and Leanita, I will write. I will write about the world as it is and as I think it ought to be and must be. I will not shrug my shoulders. I will carry the weight of Black womanness. And you two will be my inspiration. I will write for you and for the years you couldn't write. Through this libation, I call upon your ancestral energy to come to my side to write for and with me. And I will find out what kind of revolutionary I am. *No, I will show the world what kind of revolutionary I am.*

SCENE TWO: **Excavation**

*I*n 2010, as part of the introduction to my first book, *Critical Race, Feminism, and Education: A Social Justice Model* (Pratt-Clarke 2010), I wrote: "I see myself as part of a long line of revolutionary Black feminist scholar-activists" (Pratt-Clarke 2010, 7–8). More than ten years later, I am still working to fulfill that calling as a revolutionary Black feminist scholar-activist. I am still working to turn around the world, in the meaning of the Latin root for revolution—*volvere*. As Black women, we have to work to have the world turn and face us, face to face, eye to eye. We cannot have the world continue to turn its back to us and cause us to feel invisible. To cause it to turn around, we must engage in revolutionary writing.

For our writing to be revolutionary, we must engage in the work of revelation—revealing parts of ourselves to the world that we have had to hide to survive. Paul Lawrence Dunbar (1895) reminds us, "We wear the mask." It hides "our tears and sighs," "our torn and bleeding hearts," and "our cries to Christ" from our "tortured souls." As Black women, we symbolically wear masks—invisible veils, hiding, protecting, and shielding not only our most fragile selves but also our powerful spirits from the outside world. When we write about ourselves, we remove the mask. That delicate work of removing must be done with care. For not only are we removing masks, but we are also unearthing elements of our essence.

Gardening is an apt metaphor for the work of excavating the buried and submerged spirits of Black women and girls. Gardening involves tilling and turning up soil, weeding and watering, and giving birth to seeds. It is about creating new life from that which has been pressed down and buried. Garden growing for Black women is revolutionary. As enslaved women and sharecroppers, we planted our gardens in addition to the master's. Rising early and working late, we cultivated life for ourselves and families. Garden growing empowers us to be creators, to bring forth brilliant and colorful life from the womb of the earth. Because Black women have been relegated to the sidelines, thrown to the underbrush amid the thorns and thistles of life, and into the bowels and basements of society, we often live desert lives. We are rarely allowed to live an enormous life above ground. But through our gardens, we bring those submerged parts of ourselves above ground, where we can bloom and blossom, even if tattered, torn, and weather-worn.

Like gardening, to unearth the self and spirit requires tending and cultivating, with carefully selected tools—sickles, scythes, spades, shovels, trowels, and shears. If we are not careful, we damage and destroy the root. Like archaeologists, we must try to preserve the ancient artifacts of our spirits waiting to tell their story from shreds and pieces of memories. Before we garden, we must prepare the ground with our libations and gather our tools.

Estés (1995) provides a wonderful guide for exhuming the hidden parts of ourselves as women. She uses the ancient Indigenous tale "The Handless Maiden" and the maiden's initiation in an underground forest to illustrate the path our spirits and psyches must take to reclaim what was buried. The handless maiden's journey has seven stages. The first stage (The Bargain Without Knowing) is about a father's terrible bargain that leads to the second stage (The Dismemberment), where the father has to cut off his daughter's hands. In the third stage (Wandering), the handless maiden wanders until she finds love, marries a king, and becomes a mother in the fourth stage (Finding Love in the Underworld). Experiencing challenges in the fifth stage (Harrowing of the Soul), she is separated from the king and wanders again in the sixth stage (The Realm of the Wild Woman). In the final seventh stage (The Wild Bride and Wild Bridegroom), she is reunited with the king.

"The Handless Maiden" is an allegory for the development of endurance, resistance, grit, and knowledge in the pursuit of our divine feminine and goddess energy, our Blackwildgirl. It is that essential element of our power as women that was dismembered and buried so that men could live without the conscience and power of the feminine force. When we start this initiation journey, we must ask: What parts of ourselves have we lost? How, when, and by whom was our Blackwildgirl silenced and crucified? And most importantly, how can we find, resurrect, and breathe breath into that which was suffocated?

This book is about my journey and search for my childhood goddess self, Blackwildgirl. Blackwildgirl, a little Black
girl, was five years old in 1972. She was acting grown and
sassy, being womanish in the Alice Walker (1983, xi–xii) way
with "outrageous, audacious, courageous or willful behavior,"
behaving like Blackwildgirl should and must be in the world.
However, her way of being in the world enraged her father.
Towering over and peering down, he shouted so loud it almost
shattered her soul: "Who do you think you are?" With tears
streaming down her face, Blackwildgirl said, "Queen of Sheba."
Seemingly out of the wild, out of nowhere, she claimed to be
the biblical, powerful, beautiful, and wise queen of an ancient
African nation. This story, almost lore, was often shared with
me by my parents, like a joke, accompanied by hearty, and
maybe even haughty, laughter: "How dare a little girl say she
was Queen of Sheba?" But I did, because I knew I was.

Blackwildgirl knew the secret of her soul and claimed it,
spoke it, and owned it. And because the world is never ready
for Blackwildgirl, who knows she is a queen, it metaphorically
dethrones, dismembers, and buries her. Yet Blackwildgirl can
never fully be silenced, so Blackwildwomen undertake treacherous and difficult underground initiation journeys to reclaim
and resurrect their crowns and their superpower—the African
queen spirit of knowing, sensing, dreaming, and divining.

When Blackwildwomen reunite with their Blackwildgirl
spirit, they become a Blackwildgoddess. A Blackwildgoddess
is uniquely aware of her "wildness" and her original goddess
energy. She is serious and in charge, she loves the Spirit and the
struggle, and she loves herself (Walker 1983). She appreciates
the emotional flexibility of women and the interconnectedness
of tears and laughter; she is committed to humanity and its
survival (Walker 1983). She is a warrior who is able to wield
her wildness as a weapon. She has wisdom born from centuries
of lessons learned and strength from having moved boulders

through valleys and over mountains. She moves through the world with confidence, conviction, and courage. When she speaks, her words bring life into being; her voice shatters silences. She is not timid or afraid. She moves fearlessly and fiercely, like an impetuous child stomping in her own power, marking her territory, sashaying, and dancing to her own beats and rhythms. No longer restrained, now wild and unruly, her revolutionary role transforms and liberates.

This is the story of one Blackwildwoman's search to find and reclaim her Blackwildgirl superpower, so that she could become a Blackwildgoddess. Through a twelve-stage initiation journey documented in forty-five years of journals, letters to Love, and letters to God, beginning at the age of eight, my earnest, challenging, and revealing mission unfolds like a theater performance, with acts, stages, and scenes. In the spirit of African diaspora cultural storytelling, the audience-readers are invited to come into community and conversation with the writer-performer; they are also invited to enter into dialogue with themselves, to reflect, reveal, and share moments of meaning and mystery in their own lives.

It is time for Act I. The curtain is rising, and the main characters are stepping from the shadows onto the main stage. Get ready for a breathtaking journey of bargains, battles, and burials.

Photographs and Images

On the next page is a photo of the poem in my journal that I wrote on August 17, 2019, struggling to write about my life journey as a Black woman in America.

8-17-19
Last night I cried—
Many years
Tears from ancestors
that they had left
uncried
I cried for them, too
Deep sorrow for
the pain of blackness,
womanness
black-womanness
& then today the
lord strengthened
me.
Reminded me if we want to blaze a trail
we will get burned
But like Shadrach Meshack a Abenego
we will emerge unscathed
I ans being prepared to lead 1000s
It is a war, a battle of principals &
principalities—
when you get knocked down, tighten gloves
Get back in the ring
Don't give enemy more power than they have—

Poem written by Menah Pratt, August 17, 2019.
Photo credit: Menah Pratt

Reflection Questions

1. What does excavation mean as you think about your own life?
2. Who would you pour libation to as you think about the ancestors, guardian angels, and perhaps even other writers that have inspired you?

References

Balamaci, M., and P. O'Driscoll. 1984. "Acclaimed Chicago Journalist Takes Life." *Chicago Tribune*, May 31, 1984.

Dunbar, P. L. 1895. *Majors and Minors: Poems*. Hadley & Hadley Printers and Binders.

Estés, C. P. 1995. *Women Who Run with the Wolves: Myths and Stories of the Wild Woman Archetype*. Ballantine Books.

Franklin, J. H. 1989. *Race and History: Selected Essays, 1938–1988*. Louisiana State University Press.

Holleran, S. 2011. "Clarence Page on Leanita McClain." *Scott Holleran: Writer* (blog). May 31, 2011. http://scottholleran.com/culture/clarence-page-on-leanita-mcclain/.

Nemiroff, R., and L. Hansberry. 1970. *To Be Young, Gifted, and Black: Lorraine Hansberry in Her Own Words*. The New American Library.

Pratt-Clarke, M. 2010. *Critical Race, Feminism, and Education: A Social Justice Model*. Palgrave.

Walker, A. 1983. *In Search of Our Mothers' Gardens: Womanist Prose*. Harcourt Brace Jovanovich.

Act I: Seed

Ground is shattered.
Spirit descends.
Silenced.

THE FIRST STAGE—Bargains

WE COME INTO THE WORLD AS BABIES, vulnerable and hapless, birthed through parents we perhaps unconsciously chose in the great world of unknowing. Inevitably at their mercy, we can only trust that they have our best interest at heart and are able to raise, guide, and steer us to be our best selves. We have no say in the matter, for we are in the world because of them, and we cannot survive without them. Like little seeds, our lives are completely dependent on them, and we become victims and beneficiaries of bargains—life-altering decisions by our parents, often influenced by their own childhoods, their own adulthoods, and bargains they made or were made in their lives. These bargains, often without consent or consultation, set us upon a course that could become a curse, a blessing, or both. It behooves us, then, if we can, to try to understand the bargains in our own lives and in our parents' lives, especially if their lives were circumscribed by the harsh realities of the American devils of racism, legalized segregation, discrimination, and poverty.

SCENE ONE: **Papa's Bargains**

My father's life was defined by bargains made without his consent. My father, Theodore Allantantu Emmanuel Cyril Pratt, was born in Freetown, Sierra Leone. Freetown has a powerful history for formerly enslaved people. It was initially named Granville Town after Granville Sharp, a British abolitionist who came to the coast of Sierra Leone in 1787 with 411 former slaves known as the Black Poor (Knight and Manson 2007; Flynn 2007). The town's name was changed to Freetown in 1792 when almost 1,200 newly freed former slaves arrived. These former slaves—the Black Pioneers—were originally settled in Nova Scotia by England (Jeffries, n.d.). They had been granted freedom for fighting for the British in the American War of Independence. Due to the petition and efforts by Thomas Peters, an escaped slave from North Carolina, England agreed to relocate the former slaves to Freetown (Jeffries, n.d.). Eventually, Freetown became the destination for thousands of liberated Africans (Walker 1992). Collectively, these liberated Africans, African Americans, and West Indians are known as Krios or Creoles. Theodore was a descendant of the Creoles, part of the ruling elite and educated class. His name reflects that dual identity with a combination of traditional American, British, and Creole names.

Theodore's father, Daniel Gershon Pratt, was a government accountant and a senior officer on the Freetown City Council. He married Elizabeth "Lizzie" Jean Horton, whom we called Mama Pratt. She was from a prominent Creole family. They

only had one child together—Theodore. Theodore's relationship
with his parents was complicated. He kept journals about his
life in very small books in which he often only wrote one or two
sentences about his day. Some of the entries in the eight journals
from 1952 to 1962 were written in an undecipherable code. His
journal from 1952 (when he was fifteen years old), however, was
not in code. He wrote about studying and homework; his faith
and church; his physical and mental health; and enduring trials
and indignities, often from his father, who frequently did not
come home in the evenings or was "a nuisance" when he was
home. In the last journal entry about his father, dated October
9, 1952, he wrote: "Mr. D. G. Pratt disgraced my mother and
me by putting our things out of the house. And closing the house
to us." He didn't even refer to him as his father.

At some point, his parents divorced, and apparently
Theodore had to testify at his parents' divorce hearing against
his father. The divorce created a new harsh financial reality
for Theodore and his mother. I remember hearing stories of
my father walking around barefoot because his mother could
not afford shoes. I never knew my grandfather, who had three
daughters (Dorothea, Theodora, and Frederica) from another
relationship, because he died at the age of forty-six. Mama
Pratt, however, was a significant presence in my life.

I first met Mama Pratt when she came to America and
to our house in Illinois. I was two or three years old, and I
remember she pierced my ears with a needle, an African/Afri-
can American tradition (Massaquoi 2004). Although Mama
Pratt only stayed a few months during that visit, my mother
shared that it was a contentious visit. At one point, my mother
and Mama Pratt were having an argument, and my mother
said it was one of the few times she saw my father cry. He
told my mother he would have to choose his mother over her
if she didn't apologize to his mother. My mother apologized.
Many years later, Mama said the argument was over something

petty involving the laundry, and apparently, my grandmother expected my mother to do her laundry daily. During that visit, Mama Pratt visited my mother's mother, Eula Sirls, who lived in Los Angeles. It was her only visit to the United States.

Although Mama Pratt never visited the United States again, she seemed almost omnipresent because twice a year, she sent a large package of African food: bitter leaf, cassava, dried salt fish, egusi, ginger cookies, and coconut cookies. My mother cooked Sierra Leonean food—jollof rice, peanut soup, and other dishes—for weeks from those packages. My father had taught her how to cook his food, and since he never cooked any meals, my mother had to cook his food for him and our family.

My grandmother also wrote long airmail letters almost monthly. The letters were quite detailed. They described her life in Freetown and her struggles to survive as a single woman: building an apartment building; needing money; and seeking protection from soldiers, civil wars, and thieves. In one of her letters in 1982, she wrote about the meaning of my name: Menah Adeola Eyaside Pratt. She said that Menah Adeola means "talented gift from God." Eyaside is the name of her grandmother, and when I was born, she saw a vision of her grandmother in her dream. Eyaside means "grandmother returns." So, my full name means "talented gift from God and grandmothers." Several years later, I found a piece of paper from my grandmother with African names on it and their meanings. Next to Adeola, it said: *"The Crown of Honour."* I was named and crowned, like a queen.

Each visit to Freetown included significant time with my grandmother, though I always stayed with Aunt Dorothea and her husband, Uncle Joe, who was a minister of finance. They were well-to-do and had a house staff that included a cook, a driver, and a maid. Aunt Dorothea was a tall, thick-boned woman, always wearing beautiful African clothes and jewelry. She was extraordinarily generous, kind, and gracious. Her driver chauffeured us around Freetown, but Mama Pratt didn't like the idea of being chauffeured. She said I needed to walk the streets of Freetown with her because I could learn more and see the people and community better. And she was right. The streets were full of people and cars and bicycles and carts, with mothers carrying babies on their backs and bundles on their heads, vendors selling wares, and children playing games next to food stands along the side of the road. It was a colorful city with buildings in oranges, reds, blues, and greens, contrasting with the people with dark black skin in colorful African prints, glistening with sweat from the heat of the sun. Freetown was teeming with life and energy.

Because Mama Pratt and I spent a lot of time together, I learned a lot about her. She was an argumentative woman, always fussing at and about people. She seemed to be a loner, without any close friends or any real community. She was very stubborn and wanted everything her way; there was an inflexibility about her. She was also not an affectionate woman. She never once said "I love you" to me. I waited and hoped to hear those words, at least once, during my visits. But I waited in vain. She never said them, and she never hugged me. Each time I left to return to America, I gave her a hug, and each time, she was as stiff as a board.

I suspect she never hugged Theodore either. My mother told me that after the divorce, my grandmother essentially abandoned her son, and he began to spend most of his time with aunts and uncles from her family, prominent Creoles with a long history as government officials, professionals, and educators. As a result, Theodore was shaped and influenced by the cultural values of Creoles: fundamental unwavering beliefs and commitments to education, excellence, and achievement. He was raised to be a Renaissance man: he played the organ and piano in church; he composed music and submitted a composition for the national anthem; and he played tennis and helped create the Sierra Leone Tennis Association. Theodore was the traditional African Creole man, and he benefited from being raised by his aunt and uncle.

While privileged as a Creole, he still had to overcome significant personal health and financial challenges to pursue his educational dreams, as he documented in his journals. Finishing school, he briefly studied in Durham, England, and at Fourah Bay College in Freetown before being sponsored to come to America. He got his bachelor's degree in physics from Hampton Institute in Virginia and his master's degree and PhD in nuclear physics in 1968 from Carnegie Mellon Institute in Pittsburgh. He met and married my mother in 1964, while she was pursuing her doctorate at the University of Pittsburgh. My brother and I were born in 1966 and 1967, and my parents both accepted tenure-track positions at Illinois State University (ISU) in 1969. With my brother, Awadagin (age three), and me (age two), they moved to Normal, Illinois.

Theodore's faculty career would be short-lived when he took an approved leave of absence from ISU to teach graduate students at the Federal University of Rio de Janeiro in Brazil in the fourth year of his contract. While on leave in Brazil, he was notified by the Physics Department at ISU that his contract would not be renewed. After 1973, my father never taught again. He never conducted research in a lab again. He never wrote or published another physics article, even though he had published articles in numerous international physics journals. His career as a nuclear physicist and professor was over. The painful reality was that he was forty years old with no job, and a wife and two young children. He was at a crossroad. He needed to quickly decide what he was going to do with his life, what career he was going to pursue, and how to support his family as a father and husband.

Growing up, I had occasionally overheard muffled stories between my parents about what happened at ISU; these were stories involving racism and discrimination by the university. Many years after Papa transitioned to the spiritual realm, my mother showed me boxes and boxes of legal documents related to his discrimination lawsuit against the university and his fight for justice. One of the documents was a law firm's letter dated March 26, 1975, that states, in part: "It appears to me that there is substantial evidence of racial discrimination against this man from the first year of his employment at Illinois State University right down to the date of his termination while he was on sabbatical leave in Brazil" (Pratt-Clarke 2018, 170). After Mama showed me the letter, we hugged one another, still feeling the pain and sorrow buried in those boxes after all those years.

As a child, I knew there was something funny about our lives. I knew Papa did not go to "a job." Unsuccessful with the lawsuit in regaining his position as a faculty member, and unable to find another faculty position in the United States, my father's job became managing the three rental properties that my parents slowly accumulated in Bloomington and Normal. One building had six townhouses (4 Larry Court), another had eight apartments (104 Shelbourne), and the third was a house with three units (606 East Taylor). His life revolved around these rental properties: cleaning them, shoveling snow, and mowing yards. He was also his own lawyer: going to court and filing papers to evict tenants; fighting the mortgage company for incorrectly charging interest; and fighting the city to keep a parking structure he erected that they said violated building codes. His world was one of ongoing battles against injustice and racism, and regular confrontations with tenants.

Papa was a victim of a bargain made without his consent—a bargain resulting in the theft of his career and livelihood. It was a bargain that influenced his decision to create a bargain for his children's lives, unwilling to have them become victims of the same racism that decimated his career. His partner in the bargain was my mother, a woman also impacted by bargains.

SCENE TWO: **Mama's Bargains**

my mother, Mildred Inez Sirls Pratt, spent her life fighting bargains made without her consent. She was born in 1928 in Henderson, Texas, on the cusp of the Great Depression as one of eight siblings. Her parents were sharecroppers, living and working on another's land, barely eking out a living, just one generation removed from slavery. My mother's grandmother, Rosa Hubbard, was enslaved on a plantation in Alabama. She met her husband, George Thirkill, and they decided to move to Texas to have access to land, with their only child, my mother's mother, Eula. Distraught when Eula married RP Sirls, a "good for nothing" sweet-talker, after her mother died, George left Texas, eventually settling in Arizona, where he was buried. With only a sixth-grade education, Eula struggled to raise her eight children, as RP was often absent and in jail.

Barely subsisting and often dependent on the leftovers her mother brought home from the big house where she worked as a maid, Mildred and her siblings picked cotton and often made daily pilgrimages to a garbage dump to find scraps they hoped were food. Once they unknowingly ate "gum" from car batteries, only realizing years later that it was not gum but corrosive material. They ate birds, caught by their mother with a net she fashioned outside the kitchen window, and snow as ice cream. Despite the dire and desperate conditions of her life, Mildred held on to a dream that there was something more, something better, something different, even for her, who, as a little Black girl, was raped by her own brother.

In the hospital, just weeks before she died at age eighty-three, she turned to me and proceeded to tell me about being raped by her brother at the age of eleven or twelve. She was an adult before she learned that there had been a witness—her younger sister, Bernice. When they were both adults, Aunt Bernice told Mama, to her utter shock and surprise, that she had seen the rape. Mama also did not know that Aunt Bernice had told me about the rape several years before Mama did. I was visiting Aunt Bernice in Los Angeles, and she was telling family stories and family secrets. One of the secrets was about their brother who was a child molester. Talking about him, she shared that he had raped Mama. She said, "I saw him take Mildred under the mound, beat her, and make her submit to him. I bent down and peeked and saw him rape Mildred" (Pratt-Clarke 2018, 94). I didn't tell Mama that I knew when she told me in the hospital. I just listened and told her that I would honor her request to include the rape in a book I agreed to write about her life. I felt it was important for her to be able to release the secret shame that she had carried all those years.

Mildred didn't allow this theft of innocence—this bargain without her consent—to define her. Instead, she used it as fuel to prove that a little Black girl could do anything she set her mind to, even if it meant constantly challenging the status quo and the racism, classism, and sexism in the world. It was a world where she wasn't supposed to challenge and talk back to a postman who called her a boy, but she did anyway, telling him that she was not a boy, but a girl. Though her mother told her never to do that again, Mildred's spirit could not be silenced and confined. She had a purpose to fulfill, and her life would be dedicated to speaking up, challenging the status quo, and fighting for justice. In a world where it was a school's custom to nominate all valedictorians to be class president, but because she was a girl, a teacher refused to nominate her, she still questioned and challenged the teacher. In a world where she, as a poor Black girl and daughter of parents who didn't finish high school, wasn't supposed to graduate from high school or earn a bachelor's degree, two master's degrees in religion and social work, and a doctorate in social work, she did, under extraordinarily difficult circumstances.

It was a world where she was not supposed to start her career as an assistant professor of social work at Illinois State University, but rather as the director of a Black student support program in the bait and switch the university attempted. Overcoming odds after odds, Mildred not only fought to retain her tenure-track position but fought for tenure, writing the president of the university and challenging the delay in her tenure promotion. It was a world in which she was not expected to become part of the 1 percent of Black female full professors in the 1970s, but she did. And it was a world in which the life stories of one hundred elderly Black people in her community were not supposed to be told, but they were because Mildred founded the Bloomington-Normal Black History Project and sat down with each of them, learning, listening, and documenting their fight for dignity despite the daily injustices caused by their skin color.

She was a woman who was not supposed to sing at her funeral, but she did, almost seeming to defy death. A few years before she died, while fighting Alzheimer's, she took voice lessons and created two DVDs. One was of her singing folk songs and spirituals; the other was of her reciting poetry. She instructed me to play the recordings at her funeral, which I did. Mama was a fearless, strong, and powerful Black woman who overcame inconceivable odds and bargains made without her consent. She was a dynamic role model for me, demonstrating the incredible fortitude and strength of character one must possess to succeed as a Black woman in America. Yet Mama was not just my mother; she was also my father's wife, and she was often sandwiched in and conflicted by these two roles, because she, too, was part of a marriage bargain she did not anticipate.

SCENE THREE: **The Pratt Bargain**

My parents were two highly educated Black people in America, raised by single mothers with absent fathers, often in poverty. They met in Pittsburgh as graduate students and married a few months later in 1964. My brother, Awadagin, was born in 1966 and I was born in 1967. Ambitious and credentialed, my parents moved to 1405 West Hovey in Normal, Illinois, and started faculty careers at Illinois State University. Once my father's career was sabotaged in a bargain without his consent, he became the mastermind of a bargain in his children's lives—without our consent.

The Pratt Bargain was a systematic and scientific strategy for raising successful African American children. The foundations of the plan were discipline and hard work. The objectives were self-reliance and independence. The cost of the bargain required a sacrifice of the traditional American childhood: socializing with friends, going to movies, attending parties and dances, having sleepovers, and exploring life at one's own beat and rhythm.

Papa masterminded the bargain, and Mama acquiesced. Papa was determined that his children would never be dependent on the "system" that had decimated him and stolen his livelihood. Unsure as a child what the "system" was that he spoke about so regularly, I later learned as an adult that the "system" was the "imperialist white-supremacist capitalist patriarchy" that bell hooks (2006) coined. If the bargain was well executed, the children of Theodore and Mildred would be independent from that system, and the resulting success would also be Theodore's redemption.

Because Papa was no longer a physics professor, he transferred his scientific acumen to parenting. The house became his lab, parenting his profession, and my brother and I were his research subjects. Papa was a relentless disciplinarian and a perfectionist. Always a physicist, he saw the world through the lens of science and math. For him, it was a world of precision. There were right answers, correct equations, and logical steps that produced anticipated outcomes. Deviations were not acceptable. There was an expectation of efficiency with no room for error.

The implementation of the bargain began in 1974. As young children, my brother and I began playing piano at ages six and seven, and a few years later, we started violin. At the ages of seven and eight, we started learning tennis with our father as our coach. As children, we woke up at 4:30 a.m. and made Papa's coffee. We would lift weights and stretch in the basement from 5:00 a.m. to 5:30 a.m. At 6:00 a.m. (or 7:00 in the winter), we were on the tennis court until 8:00 a.m. After tennis, we ate breakfast in the car on the way to school. After school, it was usually piano or violin lessons, depending on the day of the week. In the evening, it was eating dinner that Mama always prepared; practicing piano and violin for at least an hour; doing homework with the expectation we would get A's; and then bedtime.

Mama was a quiet, yet ever present, partner in the plan. Loyal and dedicated to Papa, she supported this disciplined and demanding lifestyle. She, too, had been a victim of the system and was committed to the bargain as a tool for dismantling the potential effects of America's racism. She actually did most of the work of the bargain, as women often do. Not only was Mama a full-time professor working to get tenured and then promoted to full professor, but she also had second and third shifts. The second was as a mother and housewife. Cooking every meal, she cooked breakfast at 5:00 a.m. for my brother and me to carry to tennis practice. Breakfast was a toasted sandwich of sausage or bacon, with a hot thermos of apple juice from apples she had canned from our fruit trees.

She also made our lunch for school, and because Papa didn't cook, perhaps because of sexist beliefs about a woman's role, Mama cooked and left his lunch on the kitchen table or in the refrigerator before going to work. After work, Mama would make dinner.

Mama was not only the chef but also the chauffer and seamstress, driving us to every piano and violin lesson twice a week and sewing our clothes when we were young, sitting at her sewing machine with patterns, scissors, and threads. She did the laundry and hung clothes out to dry on the clothesline. It was fascinating to watch how fast Mama could hang clothes, systematically, almost machine-like in her precision and efficiency.

Her third shift was apartment owner, manager, and maintenance worker. With my father as the overseer and self-proclaimed "supervisor," Mama did most of the work on the apartments. She painted the walls and baseboards; cleaned the floors, kitchens, and bathrooms; mowed the yards; and shoveled snow off sidewalks and driveways.

As my brother and I got older, we became more responsible for maintenance, and just like my mom, we painted, cleaned, shoveled, and mowed. We were also traveling to tennis tournaments and performing piano and violin recitals. It was a grueling and isolating childhood. There was little time or space for laughter. We were taught that life was serious. There was no room or time for fun and being frivolous. There was only space for tennis competitions and music performances, for practices and lessons, for yards of grass and driveways of snow, and for painting and cleaning apartments. My father occasionally quoted scripture, and one of his favorites was "When I became a man, I put away childish things." We did not have childish things.

While we had the trappings of a middle-class lifestyle, our family's financial circumstances were often precarious. Dependent on the inconsistent occupancy of the rental units and my mother's faculty salary, which was barely $30,000, Papa negotiated discounted rates for the indoor court time at the local tennis club, and discounted rates for the private piano and violin lessons with university professors. We never bought new clothes or went to the mall. When we got older, we had to darn our socks, learning how to thread a needle and sew. It was a rare treat to go to Ding-a-Ling, a local consignment store that smelled of old White people's clothes, old stuff, and old people, to buy something old for ourselves. I only remember one dress that I wore as a little girl to church; there was rarely an occasion to dress up or to feel beautiful and precious.

My parents owned our home at 1405 West Hovey, in an all-White neighborhood in Normal, Illinois. It had three bedrooms, two bathrooms, and a full basement. My room was in the corner of the house, next to my brother's. His had nice wood paneling; mine had green wallpaper, and I was a little jealous of his dark brown aura of a cabin in the woods. We shared a wall and developed a knocking communication system. One knock meant that we wanted to talk. We talked through the wall, listening closely for footsteps signaling a parent was coming down the short, narrow hallway. Two knocks meant good night. Because our time and lives were so regimented, we rarely had time to even talk to each other, and when we did, Papa accused us of conspiring against him. And sometimes we were, devising horrible plans for our parents' demise and our eventual escape and freedom from the rigid discipline. Our parents' room was across the hallway from my brother's, next to the main-floor bathroom. It was large with a huge bed, a big dresser with a mirror, Mama's sewing machine, and a desk, always cluttered with paperwork and bills.

In the living room, there was a chair that only Papa sat in, a green-yellow plaid-covered La-Z-Boy. Not only did he sit in that chair, but it was also where he ruminated, remembered, reminisced, and repeatedly reinscribed the trauma into his soul. He sat there, brooding, alone in his mind. It was where he sat after his afternoons and evenings of soothing his tortured soul with liquor stashed under the kitchen sink and cans of beer that were a never-ending presence in the refrigerator. It was like he and the chair were one, yet his spirit was so powerful that his presence in the chair cast a large shadow of domination over the entire house, reaching even into the recesses, cracks, and crevices.

The living room also had a matching green-yellow plaid-covered very long couch pushed back against the dark brown wood paneling, facing a large picture window. That was the couch for the children. It was where we sat and received lectures and instructions from Papa. Along another wall by the front door was a plush multicolored cloth chair that didn't match the couch. Mama would sit on the floor in front of it, grading papers and doing her professor's work. Just a few feet from the chair was a corner, next to the front door. It was the corner of shame, where we had to stand for hours when we were being punished. Across the room from Mama's chair, on the far wall toward the kitchen, was the 1912 Cable piano that my parents had bought for $100, where we practiced piano for hours each week.

Next to the living room was the kitchen and two doors. One led outside to the two-car garage and the other to a large full basement with a ping-pong table and a pool table. The pool table was rarely used and was covered with plastic cloth, papers, and dust. The basement had bookcases filled with my father's physics books and publications from his aborted career, monuments silently testifying to a sabotaged dream. There were also cupboards filled with jars of canned fruits and vegetables. We had a large number of fruit trees, mostly apple but also pear, plum, and peach in the backyard, with two more apple trees in the front yard. Mama regularly canned fruit from these trees and vegetables from her garden.

Almost every year, Mama planted a garden on the two

sides of our house. One side of the house had a large plot. It was by my bedroom window. I remember occasionally looking out the window and seeing her on her hands and knees in old Black woman's clothes—ragged baggy pants, a big blouse, and a bonnet—bent over, with her worn and weathered hands fingering the dirt, pulling weeds, and planting seeds. The other side of the house was a little rocky and rough. It didn't seem like much sun ever shone on that side. It was a very narrow sliver of land, close to the neighbor's house. I didn't think a garden should be there, but like Alice Walker's (1983) mother, she could make anything grow, even on rocky soil. She planted onions, peppers, watermelons, tomatoes, carrots, mints, and herbs. She did whatever it took to bring forth and sustain life in her garden. Perhaps she was trying to breathe life into the inside of our little house, which looked like sunshine with its yellow siding on the outside but was as dark and black as the night inside.

Mama also had flower gardens. She planted four-o'clocks in the front of the house by the steps leading to the front door and tulips, marigolds, and moss by the sidewalk of our house and alongside the driveway. She loved her four-o'clocks and so did I. They came in all kinds of colors: red, pinks, yellows, and blues. They were bright and vibrant, and they bloomed in the morning and then closed up by midday. The next morning, they were back at it. Ritually, Mama pulled dead flowers off to make way for new ones.

I remember that Mama habitually brought flowers inside the house, placed them in vases, and set them on the small kitchen table with four chairs, where my brother and I ate. Mostly, it was just the two of us, because our parents rarely ate with us. They often did not eat together either. But whoever sat down at the table was the guest of the flowers sitting silently and softly, performing their revolutionary role of being beacons of light and beauty in the midst of darkness and sadness.

I was never in the garden with Mama. I never asked and she never invited. I think it was because she needed these spaces for herself, for her quiet time of solitude and solace from a world and household in which she often had to hide her light. I felt she intentionally hid her light and kept her light from shining too bright, so that it could not overshadow Papa's lightless, dimmed shell. My father cast such a strong shadow with his haunting sadness that almost no one's light could shine. His angry, aggressive, and abusive demeanor was fueled and stoked by an unquenchable appetite for alcohol that could never numb the raw nerves of pain and sorrow etched on his almost always frowning brow.

They were a team. They struggled together. Mama had a deep loyalty and compassion for Papa. As a wife, she had watched her husband's career evaporate. I think she sometimes felt guilty that she still had hers and so made herself smaller so he wouldn't feel so small with her greatness. Mama acquiesced to the shadowing and submitted to his dominance. She, too, was a victim of a bargain in her marriage. She had married one man on her wedding day—a funny, intelligent, and jovial man with a delightful laugh and sense of humor. Just a few short years later, she had a bitter, sullen, impatient, and frustrated shell of one. Yielding to the consequence of the bargain, my mother remained committed to my father.

I believe she really loved him. She single-handedly cared for him in his illness after he had a stroke, driving forty-five minutes every day to the hospital and sometimes twice a day. I never remember them showing affection, kissing, embracing, or holding hands, except for a Valentine's Day picture at a dance they went to seven months before he died of pancreatic cancer at age sixty. In the picture, they are actually holding hands. I don't know if it was natural or staged for the photo. But they are both smiling, looking happy. Mama actually looked regal, almost like an Egyptian queen. She was wearing a gorgeous, silky off-white dress with detailed gold embroidery and a matching scarf on her head. Papa was wearing a black suit with a white shirt. Even his hair was combed, which was rare. Papa had invited Mama to that Valentine's dance at a local hotel. They had never gone to a dance together before; it's the only formal picture ever taken of them together other than their wedding day.

The bargain with America that my parents made for our family—that they could raise their children to be independent of the system—came at a great cost to them, my father in particular. In the last letter my father wrote to me in January 1996, nine months before he died, he referenced and named the bargain and described its impact on him. Still recovering from a massive stroke from two years earlier, his letter was typed with a confusing combination of capital letters and lowercase letters, provoked by his frustration at a late payment by me on a loan from my parents. I was twenty-eight years old and married when he sent the letter. In part, the letter said:

> Dear MENAH,
> You do not know what PREOCCUPATION WITH SUCCESS FOR YOUR BLACK CHILDREN in this country means. It was a 24hrs job—NO SLEEP—LYING IN BED OR NOT.
>
> THE FACT IS THESE WERE/ARE CHILDREN OF PARENTAGE, highly EDUCATED IN THE UNIVERSITIES and on the streets but with inadequate FINANCIAL MEANS desirous of MAKING AN EASY and COMFORTABLE LIFE for everyone in the FAMILY. PARENTS WHO DID NOT HAVE ANY INHERITANCE OR initial financial family lift.
> . . .

*I DO NOT HATE YOU BUT I FEEL DEEPLY
BETRAYED—maybe I had been living a LIE (WITH
ALL THIS HARD WORK AND PREMATURE GREY)
about FAMILY and FAMILY MATTERS within the
PRATT–SET-UP.*

. . .

*THERE ARE NONE OF THOSE NICETIES as I love
you.*

*THE FACT IS—YOUR BIOLOGICAL FATHER."
"TAECP."*

The bargain I was born into had a name; it was called the
Pratt Setup. It was a bargain made with the devil of America's
racism; it was a bet that Black children born in the 1960s in
the middle of the Civil Rights Movement and the fight for
equality for African Americans could be raised in America in
such a way as to be successful and independent, in spite of the
presence of racism, bigotry, and discrimination. The bargain
had great benefits, but also great costs.

SCENE FOUR: **Goddess Wisdom**

Each stage of an initiation journey leaves its mark, and
we have an opportunity to engage in revolutionary
work, by turning around and looking again at our
paths with different eyes and through a different lens, to extract
goddess wisdom—gifts of insight and lessons learned about
ourselves, our relationships with others, and our lives.

One of the lessons is the importance of understanding the
cost of the bargain. The Pratt Setup was designed to prepare me
for life in a country steeped in racism and sexism by giving me

two survival tools—discipline and a commitment to excellence. Discipline and excellence were a virtue and value to help me, as a young Black woman, persevere—no matter what. In spite of all obstacles, in spite of any challenges, discipline and excellence were my guides. They would be guideposts to ensure that my feet remained on the straight and narrow road of life. Discipline and excellence would ensure persistence, resilience, and endurance. Hard driving forces, pushing me forward against all and any odds, excellence required setting almost unachievable goals, and discipline helped me achieve them.

The Pratt Setup was consistent with a poem from Henry Wadsworth Longfellow (1880) that my mother's mother, Grandma Eula Sirls, sent me and that I referenced in my June 6, 1982, journal: *"Poem from Grandma Sirls: The heights that great men reached and kept were not obtained by sudden flight, but those while their companions slept, were toiling upwards through the night."* The Pratt Setup, as my father wrote, was a *"24 hours job. No sleep lying in bed or not."* It was always about toiling. When one is toiling *"with all this hard work and premature grey . . . there are none of those niceties as I love you."* There was no time for love or being loving or showing love. I have wondered if the burden of surviving America's racism precludes love from flourishing like it could and should. Love has to fight to survive because the struggle and suffering from racism causes such intense psychic, spiritual, emotional, and financial pressure and pain. It is a world where love becomes contorted, trying to bend and adjust to an unnatural world. It is a world in which saying "I love you" is a nicety and not a necessity.

The relationship between my parents was one of pain, sorrow, and sacrifice. It was as if Mama was willing to sacrifice her joy because of my father's pain. Perhaps as so many Black women do, in trying to compensate for the hate and racism in the world that affects Black men so profoundly, we sacrifice our own need for love, affection, care, compassion, and support. Although we, too, experience not only racism but also sexism, including Black male sexism, we, as Black women, often give all, expecting little in return, knowing that some Black men have little to give and are just struggling to survive and not go "mad," as James Baldwin said of his father (Baldwin and Giovanni 1973, 44). Because, as Black women, we have often seen and experienced so much abuse and neglect and the men appear to be "mad," we have been socialized not to expect much. But we should expect and demand more. We deserve more.

Baldwin, in his interview with Nikki Giovanni, spoke about the impact of America's racism on Black men, particularly his father (Baldwin and Giovanni 1973). Recognizing his father was always angry and difficult to live with because his manhood was continually decimated by racism, Baldwin almost justified his father's abusive behavior in the home. Nikki, however, challenged the notion that because of America's racism, it was acceptable for Black men to mistreat their children and wife, asking how Black men "could be mistreated and then come home and mistreat someone in the same way" (Baldwin and Giovanni 1973, 45). She argued that it was unfair to expect a woman to "walk ten paces behind" her husband in order for him to feel like a man, saying, "If that's what the black man needs, I'll never get far enough behind him for him to be a man. I'll never walk that slowly" (Baldwin and Giovanni 1973, 45).

My mother, in fact, like many Black women, was willing to walk that slowly. Mama was often conflicted, standing in the middle of my father and me: loyal to my father, who was suffering, but also knowing that she needed to be loyal to me, who he was causing to suffer. In the archetypal journey, the mother can represent a lack of awareness and an inability to protect her daughter. This reality of her lack of awareness and inability to protect me was most profoundly demonstrated during one of the most important moments in my life—the onset of womanhood and my cycle.

When my period came around age thirteen, in the midst of the operation of the Pratt Setup, I remember waking up one morning and seeing blood on my panties. I told my mother, and for some reason, she did not go to the store with me. I had to go with my father to get maxi pads. I don't know why my mother didn't go with me. She should have been there. Instead, it was me and my father. I put a bunch of toilet paper in my panties and got into the car to ride to the store with him. When we walked into the store, he told me to find "them," and when I looked confused, he said "something to go down there." I didn't even know what "them" were. There were so many choices of pads and tampons and so many different brands. Nervously scanning rows and shelves, becoming overwhelmed and almost paralyzed, suddenly and startlingly, I heard my father's voice from the front of the store. I was taking too long. "Menah! Menah, hurry up! Hurry up!" His voice seemed to boomerang and echo through the store with his heavy British African accent. Embarrassed, I grabbed a bag of pads and started running. Harried and humiliated, trying not to cry, I laid it on the checkout counter in front of the male checkout clerk.

When I got home, I put on the pad. At that time, pads didn't have an adhesive strip; they just had long ends. I didn't know how to put it on. It moved around. I guess at some point, my mother told me I needed pins and got me some. But the damage was done. This transition to womanhood was traumatic. My mother failed to be present for me, and I had a horrific experience. I felt like a gross, disgusting little girl, with blood flowing between her legs, who didn't even know how to put a pad on. I felt ashamed, and I was angry at my mother for making me go with my father on a deeply feminine and personal rite of passage.

Mama, perhaps recognizing the tension and trials of the Pratt Setup, and perhaps her own shadowiness, tried at times to compensate for the inevitable cost of the bargain and the expectations of discipline and excellence. This was evident in her first letter to me, presumably from both my mother and father since she used *"us"* and *"we,"* though she signed it *"your mother."* The letter was dated December 18, 1980:

Dear Menah:

I think this is the first letter I have ever written to you. I wanted to write this letter because it has occurred to me that you will be graduating from high school in about three years and leaving home. These three years are very important to you and us—your family.

You are 13, a big girl now—a teenager, but I still remember the morning when you were born and how happy your father and I were to see and welcome you. You were just as special to us as Awadagin and just as special to us now.

You are not only special to us (your family) but also to your Grandmother Pratt, your aunts and uncle, and all of our White and Black friends who like us want the best for you.

You are special—you are a Pratt. You are African— part of one of the oldest cultures in the world. Remember that and never take a backseat to anyone. You are some- body special.

You are special also because you are very bright. You are strong. You want to be the best. You have a nice smile, a sense of humor, and you are a lovely young lady. Aspire to be the best that is in you to be. Don't let anyone set low goals for you, and don't set them for yourself.

Menah, when I think of you, I think of myself growing up. I was strong and determined to achieve—even though there was no "women's lib" then (smiles).

I know things are not easy for you. You may sometimes think of us too demanding. I am sure that I sometimes had such thoughts when I grew up, but deep down inside, I'm glad they helped and disciplined me, because I know I could not have managed to get to where I am now. I know a lot of girls with whom I grew up did not even go to college, let alone get a PhD.

You are somebody! We love you very much. We want you to be happy. We want you to be the best so that you can like and be proud of yourself.

Your mother.

"You are a Pratt." It was confirmation that I was, indeed, an African queen and a gift from goddesses and grandmothers crowned with honor. The Pratt Setup was designed to continue a destiny associated with one of the oldest cultures in the world. My life had been designed without my consent and had set me on a path that would have me dancing between discipline and excellence on one hand and suffering and sorrow on the other hand. The bargain had taken my independence, my autonomy, and my ability to explore the world at my own pace and rhythm. My brother and I had been placed upon a predefined path, not of our own choosing, by parents as complicated and as challenging as the path itself. We would be the burnt offering and the sacrifice for what had been taken from my father. Perhaps through our lives, our father would achieve revenge against racism and what it had snatched from him—his manhood and the opportunity to fulfill his talent and destiny.

Letters from my mother were a constant pattern throughout my life as she attempted to mitigate the inevitable cost and consequence of the Pratt Setup: a consequence that involved a life dedicated to searching earnestly, intensely, and sincerely for the love I rarely felt as a child and the hugs I rarely received. I needed her letters more than I realized, savoring them throughout my life as evidence that I had always been, and always would be, loved by her.

Reflection Questions

1. Have you experienced anything that might resemble a "bargain"—a loss or removal of a core element of your childhood self? What was it and how did it impact your life?
2. What is a defining childhood memory that you have or a childhood experience that was shared with you in which you felt an affirmation or awareness of your own unique spirit or power? Have you been able to use and channel this power?
3. Are there any early memories in which components of your identity were very salient, perhaps around race, gender, economic background, or religion? What stands out for you and why?

References

Baldwin, J., and N. Giovanni. 1973. "A Dialogue: Ten Paces Behind the Man." *The American Poetry Review* 2, no. 4: 44–45.

Flynn, D. 2007. "Krio Heritage Rich but Crumbling in Sierra Leone." Reuters. September 9, 2007. http://www.reuters.com /article/2007/09/10/us-leone-krios-idUSL0684532820070910

hooks, b. 2004. "Understanding Patriarchy.".

Jeffries, L. 2018)n.d. "Thomas Peters—Symbol of the Struggle for Freedom." In *The African-Americans Search for Truth and Knowledge.*

Knight, J., and K. Manson. 2007. "Sierra Leone Draws Americans Seeking Slave Roots." Reuters. March 22, 2007. http://www

.reuters.com/article/2007/03/22/us-slavery-leone-idUSL185
7050920070322

Longfellow, H. 1880. "Ladder of Life." In *The Liberal Hymn Book*, edited by E. B. Burnz, Burnz & Co.15.

Massaquoi, R. 2004. *The Wind Within: A Novel*. iUniverse.

Pratt-Clarke, M. 2018. *A Black Woman's Journey from Cotton Picking to College Professor: Lessons about Race, Class, and Gender in America*. Peter Lang.

Walker, A. 1983. *In Search of Our Mothers' Gardens: Womanist Prose*. Harcourt Brace Jovanovich.

Walker, J. 1992. *The Black Loyalists: The Search for a Promised Land in Nova Scotia and Sierra Leone, 1783–1870*. University of Toronto.

THE SECOND STAGE—Battles

BARGAINS OFTEN LEAD TO BATTLES—emotional, psychological, and spiritual. When bargains require the sacrifice of precious gifts—childhood innocence, curiosity, and independence—there is a need to grieve. Though it is a time for tears, it is not a time of powerlessness, but of processing. Journaling and writing about our sorrow can be empowering. Often it is the only place to acknowledge and affirm the legitimacy of our feelings. It is a place for our anger and pain and our frustration and confusion to have their say. It is a place for our smothered sounds to have voice, allowing us to call out in written words with all our might for the goddesses of the world to come to our side, to hold and to hug us.

SCENE ONE: **Sixteen and Sadness**

*T*he Pratt Setup, the bargain in which love was a nicety and discipline and excellence were necessities, created a deep sadness in my spirit. My tears were documented in a diary that Papa gave me when we returned from Brazil. The whole family had moved to Brazil in 1972 for my father's one-year faculty appointment. I was five years old, and my brother was six. We both went to school, I took ballet lessons, and Awadagin took judo lessons. We all spoke Portuguese fluently. It was a time my mother told me was wonderful, and my parents were part of an amazing community of friends.

My father taught graduate students in Brazil, and the journal he gave me was legal size, with a light green swirled cover and the Portuguese word "*Doutorando*" (translated "doctoral candidate") on the front. The pages inside were colored white, yellow, pink, and green. One of my first entries was on March 1, 1976. I wrote, "*8 going on 9, 4th grade. I started violin lessons and I think I'm doing a good job. I started with Mrs. Sompong (my first piano teacher) when I was 6 and I'm rolling along just fine.*"

Seven years later, the entries were radically different. The journal became a friend with entries addressed to "Love." My journal created a protective circle for my sorrow journey, documenting my cries to the universe for Someone or Something to know and see and understand my suffering. As part of the Pratt Setup, I graduated from high school in three years at the age of sixteen and began pursuing a full-time professional tennis career with Papa as my coach. I was alone with my parents, without the routine and friends of high school and without my brother. Awadagin had also graduated from high school at sixteen the year before I did, and he was attending college at the University of Illinois in Champaign-Urbana, about forty-five minutes from Normal. He was on a music scholarship and pursuing degrees in piano and violin. He rarely came home, and it was a period of tremendous sadness and isolation.

As I shared in a college essay, my daily life was regimented and isolating:

> *After I graduated from high school, I would play tennis from 6 a.m. to 10 a.m. and write down all the day's drills and document all my "messiness" to make sure there would be no repeat. I would have to review the reason I lost to such-and-such [person] four to five months ago, for at any moment, my father could say, "I've been thinking about your tennis situation" and whatever the fuck he had been thinking would flow out like diarrhea for an hour.*
>
> *I swear his life motto had to be "reduce all errors." He was an extreme perfectionist, not only of himself but for others as well. He would say, "Don't forget, I am a nuclear physicist. One error and explosion." He took social life, social interaction, social skills away. It was family and family alone. It was discipline—strict discipline—like the beat of a metronome. He was in control and there was no doubt about it at all. My life was put together with the precision of architecture.*
>
> *Papa, a man who cared way too much, was too obsessed with precision and discipline to feel, see, or notice emotions. So, with the same precision, we were punished with sentence writing, spankings, and standing*

in corners. Sentence repetitions of 1000 to 5000—no trial, no attempt of justification, defense, explanation. Misunderstandings were not possible, errors were not allowed, and lack of respect and back talk was unheard of. One learned to accept, continue, and unfortunately, to hate.

To hate the one who did it all out of love, and yet could not express, show, or make you feel loved. I was alone—alone amidst many—and lonely. Alone with his pressure, his weight, his disciplined love. Alone with him, his dream, his preaching, his thoughts. It was as if he became me, or I became him. We became each other. I lost myself, was engulfed into him, like how a yawn seems to engulf, absorb, and encompass all. From the age of 16, I remember clearly the sadness that fell like dew upon me when I graduated and was told that because of my tennis potential I should take advantage of an opportunity to be my very own boss, my own manager, and be responsible for myself, as a tennis player. I had no rights as long as I was in his house.

I could sense the danger, the fear, as the dew was falling. I was being stifled. My support system of school was disappearing. I had no outside support, no phone, no dates, nothing but me and Dad and tennis. Music died and I was left to my thoughts and my poetry. I thought about suicide, what death was, and what God was; religion, life, and meaning.

This college essay summarizes much of what I was journaling as a teenager. My thoughts, my poetry, and my search for meaning were chronicled in *Doutorando*. On June 3, 1983, I wrote the following on the inside cover:

Dear Love,

I shall confide in you my utmost secrets, feelings, and thoughts. You shall know of all my experiences, whether they be happy, sad, full of anger, full of love, or full of hate. I shall tell you things which I could tell no one because I know that you will not judge me, you will not degrade me, you will not hate me, you will not humiliate me, and that you will always be my LOVE. Only you and I shall ever know these and if anyone else reads between these pages you and I will both perish. You and I will destroy ourselves. When I die, you will be buried with me. I want to express my deepest and most profound gratitude to you and your secrecy. I'm glad you're mine. You're the best!! I will care for you as I have cared for nothing else. You're my life, breath, and love. I know you will always be there.

And Love, my journal's name, was a safe haven. In 1983, after graduating from high school, it was a place for thoughts that wavered between hope and despair. A song of optimism was followed by a poem, partly in French, on pessimism. There were also entries on depression and suicidal thoughts:

May 31, 1983

Song Composed of Optimism

Dit-moi, qu'est-ce que tu vas faire?
Tell me, whatcha gonna do
Tell me, whatcha gonna do
Dit-moi, qu'est-ce que tu vas faire?
Dit-moi, qu'est-ce que tu vas faire?
Tell me, what are you gonna do when you get down?
We know that life is rough

You know you gotta be tough
The question is, are you strong enough
to go out in the world and do your stuff?
So, tell me, what are you going to do when you
get down?
Well, you can wet your eyes
and you can blow your nose
and you can have your sobs
and you can sit and stare and watch the world
with your life go by
or
you can talk to friends
and you can seek some help
you can sit and think
and you can get off your feet
go out in the world
and do whatever it takes to survive.

Poem of Pessimism

Life; Success.
Death; Failure.
Happiness; Sadness.
Joy; Depression.
Opposites to be found in the world.
Equal Opportunity for all? No.
Discrimination? YES.
Life is too rough and tough.
One may die trying for success.
One may die coping with failure.
One may laugh a beautiful laugh in happiness.
One may laugh a bitter laugh in sadness.
One may cry with joy.
One may weep with depression.

Life is too rough and tough.
Life is for a selected
And well-picked few.
Not for me; not for you.

June 3, 1983

Becoming depressed. Worked hard yesterday at apartments cleaning floor behind stove and refrigerator and painting baseboards. Yelled at in the morning. Also raining, as yesterday. I lack self-esteem. I am also lazy. Yelled at constantly. Feel so low and degraded. Feel literally like a piece of shit. Noah and Wilander in French Open final. Evert-Lloyd and Jausovec. Martina Navratilova and Ivan Lendl of Czechoslovakia are my favorites. Also, love Evonne Goolagong, Yannick Noah, Mats Wilander. Do people care?

Suicide note of October 23, 1983

I may kill myself someday and I will because I feel like a total idiot and feel that I will never be successful in life because all my years, I got the feeling that I am an ass who cannot think or function like a normal person. I have done nothing right and give no one happiness so my death will be all the better for you and then you two can enjoy your lives without the burden of me.

You all need not worry about your "FAILURE" because I'm no longer anyone's FAILURE. The arrogant, conceited, immature FAILURE is gone from your lives forever. The failure could not handle all the pressure to succeed in tennis. Can't be a surprise to you because after all I'm a baby. A baby who can't handle pressure. So instead of being a burden to you and wasting all the family's resources— time, money, and energy—I'm gone. Please give my savings account to Dagin. My other things—clothes, shoes, etc.,

*may be disposed of at will. Best to all. I'm sorry but I didn't
seem to create much besides chaos and argumentation.*
—Menah

November 16, 1983

Questions

*Life
living
breathing, and being
Is it worth suffering for?
Death
dying
ending by one's own hand
Is it right?
Sorrow
sadness
depression
Are they why we exist?
Happiness
pleasure
Joy
Are they worth waiting for?
Friends
family
others
Do they deserve this?
Why does it matter?
Why do they care?
Why are there rules?
Let them all go
And let me be free*
—MAEP

A February 1, 1984, journal entry reveals the magnitude of my father's efforts to drown and deaden his own sorrow, our complicated relationship, and the depth of my fear, anger, and apprehension:

> *I have come to the conclusion that dad is an alcoholic. He drank 10 cans of beer yesterday from 3:00-7:30 pm, plus he also drank wine, vodka, whisky, and bourbon. Yesterday was the first day I counted because I had started saving beer cans so they can be recycled so there were ten cans. I knew he drank lots of beer, but I never counted, but he doesn't act like your typical drunk, but he is a lot fiercer and angrier at me during the night. Last night he came in my room and must have yelled for 20 minutes about the tennis practice. With all this, I get mad at myself because I take it and I don't do anything about it and then I hate myself for being such a coward. I continue to do all the housework and cooking like I'm a housewife. It's like I'm married to him because I spend more time with him than mom. He's around me the entire day except when I go to bed. The other day he told me that he doesn't joke and laugh with me because I would interpret it as a sign of weakness. Come on. It's insane. . . . All I think about some days is killing myself. I wish I could kill my folks and then I wouldn't have to worry about them. . . . I cannot travel and perform properly if I'm afraid of the only person I'm around. . . . I hate the man and I am so scared of him.*

Two days before my seventeenth birthday on April 5, 1984, my journal entry reads: *"I'm so tired and sad. Tournaments here and there. Symphony. Religion. Race. Frustrated. Don't know. Just fucked up."* I was reading books about suicide and death. I learned that people choose suicide when the fear of living is greater than the fear of death. I was trying not to fear death. My only interaction with other people was during rehearsals and concerts with the Bloomington-Normal Symphony, where I played violin. I was the youngest musician, and everyone was older than me. I did meet another Black woman violinist who was a Jehovah's Witness. Since I had very little exposure to religion, I was curious about different religious beliefs. She gave me their religion's red "Bible."

When I was a young girl, my parents had a Black couple take my brother and me to Mount Pisgah Baptist Church. The husband was a local barber in Bloomington. Despite my parents' very religious upbringing, my father in the Methodist Church and my mother in the Baptist Church, they did not go to church with us. But this couple religiously came to our house every Sunday and took us to church. I remember the only dress that I owned was a very pretty yellow dress, the yellow of a bright sun. I loved wearing that dress to church and I loved going to church, especially listening to the music and watching the choir in the purple robes singing and swaying. I liked the love I felt in the church and the way Black church women can make you feel special; the way they greet you with "hey, baby" and hug you with their entire souls, the way I imagine Jesus himself would hug me.

The church was like a theater with different characters—the ushers, the deacons, the choir, the musicians, and the preacher. They all had parts and roles to play. Sometimes the women would "get the spirits" and appear possessed by joy or sorrow, shouting and jumping or running. That chaos was followed by ushers, holding, fanning, and consoling. It was an exciting show. One day the show was even more dynamic than usual, and it seemed like everyone was "getting the spirits." This time, though, it was actually a domestic dispute that led to fighting and yelling in the church. And that was it. We never went to church again. My father said that our church was 1405

West Hovey. And I think the Pratt Setup was church for him. It was almost like a religion.

Because I no longer went to church after I was about seven, I was left to my own imagination about religion and spiritual matters. This started a lifelong journey, searching not only for love but also for Love. My journal entries would continue to be addressed to Love as I turned seventeen.

SCENE TWO: **Seventeen and Struggling**

I turned seventeen on April 7, still pursuing a tennis career, and journal entries continue to reflect the struggle and the ups and downs of wins and losses. The entries vacillate between hope and despair, between happiness and sadness, between strength and weakness, between feeling accomplished and feeling like a failure.

The journal entries in the summer of 1984, often addressed to Love, reflect on the complexity of the tennis relationship with my father. Mama was often gone, working as a faculty member at the university; and I spent hours with my father, being lectured on the green-brown plaid couch or alone in my room. I had pages of notes and notecards. I documented coaching advice and having to watch *How to Play Your Best Tennis* and the importance of fundamentals: consistency, accuracy, depth, spin, power. I noted that in order to improve concentration, I should think *"only the ball."* I wrote, *"Think of the present only, not future or past."* I admonished myself to play only one point at a time and reminded myself that each point is most important. My father sketched out diagrams of my tennis career and wrote a note that I still have: *"It is absolutely imperative that I do my very best to have a meteoric rise to the top."* My life was defined by tennis practice and tennis tournaments:

April 23, 1984

Love,

I won the Cincinnati tennis tournament. I want to run forever through a field of wildflowers or any flowers: tulips, moss, marigolds, blossoming apple trees. Total bliss. Hello, by Lionel Ritchie. So touching.

June 19, 1984

Love,

Can you believe it's June 19 and I've hardly spoken to you? Well, I'll inform or at least attempt to inform you on the progress of my life. I played the Olympic Qualifying and lost first round indoors which was a real bummer. It was real hot outdoors—so hot I almost fainted. Anyway, I rode subways for the first time. Sometimes I believe I would like to just ride the subway forever, drift away. Well, then it was off to New Jersey. I love the countryside but I don't know. Not many Blacks. However, it seems the majority of tennis players are very stuck-up, conceited. Leanita McClain committed suicide. May 31. "Too sensitive in an insensitive world." I believe no one really cares. The world, life all so insensitive uncaring and harsh. It's awful.

Mom is real nice. Dad says she spoils me. I say maybe but it feels like love. No moss [in the front yard] this year. Too bad. Going to bed early. Did lots of cooking on the trip. Racial identity is very puzzling. Almost want out of America, out of life. Too cruel, harsh, and unfair. So much pain everywhere. If school—which majors? I want to help people and yet survive myself happily. Yet a man with riches will find difficulty reaching glory. With Dad, I seem to vacillate between fear and love. Life is so complex. Want out of life. Too complex. Song Title: Suicide's for me. All for now!

Love,

Menah

July 17, 1984

What Happened?

What Happened?
The tennis court
My home, domain
Habitat for many victories
Location of
Serenity, Happiness
Enjoyment, and
Stability
Is no longer a place of
Comfort, Peace
Ease, or
Control.
What happened?

On July 28, 1994, I wrote a letter to a friend in my journal about my dad, tennis, and my sadness, called "Words of the Heart and Mind":

I have just returned from a three-week tennis excursion with moderate success. I should have done better but mentally, my mind seems out of the court when I'm on the court, and that circumstance does not promote consistent match wins.

Life's so tough and complicated. I have not had a piano or violin lesson since April 1983 and haven't practiced since the end of May and I miss them dearly. I have been writing poems and songs and occasionally, a few lines of musical notes that resemble a tune comes to mind. I write them down but they're not on a manuscript. I probably won't play [in the Blooming-ton-Normal Symphony] since Dad's been saying it takes too much time away from my tennis.

My tennis is another soap opera. Talent and potential are very evident but so much pressure dwindles my interest. Dad's my coach, my hitting partner, my dad, my traveling companion, my everything. He's practically merged himself into me totally and I have no outlet from his obsession—his driving obsession—with my tennis and potential and my ability for success. I swear I could do so much better without him around constantly watching my every move and sans all this mental, physical, social, and emotional control.

I've become the sole target for the release of Dad's frustrations. I have no right to look sad, no right to pass up opportunities because I'm a Black female and they always say Blacks don't get opportunities and here I am wasting it. I lose and he thinks everyone blames the coach for a player's loss and so he yells at me to sufficiently erase any feeling of responsibility he may have ever had. I "don't have any rights and that is how democracy is maintained in the house."

My dad is firmly against college tennis, and it hurts even more now that I received two offers for scholar-ships—Memphis State and Lee College, a junior college in Texas—but I can't go. But life's tough and the strong survive even if they may be dominated by the weak who believe they are strong. I hope I'm strong and that I can leave this environment soon, have a chance to develop my personality, learn right from wrong, and learn from my mistakes, which may be caused from inexperience in dealing with freedom which I have never had, although Dad seems to believe I have unlimited freedom.

I hope happiness from sunshine will spotlight on me very soon and for a very long time and I hope this is a very realistic and achievable desire.
Words from the heart,
Menah

A month later, I wrote a letter to my father, genuinely sharing my emotions and feelings about recent losses and suggesting a possible break from tennis. I tried to counter comments he frequently made about me not having the right to say things, about me being a "stereotypical woman," and about my head being "shitty":

August 1984
Dear Papa,

I want to apologize for my actions, in word and deed. I have never meant to insult you but I'm a very confused girl. I try my best in tournaments but something's missing. In practice, I think that since I played tennis for 10 years, I know a great deal and I don't want any corrections. Most of what you say I already know, and I just don't execute correctly.

I have trouble conveying my feelings to you because I feel they are wrong, and I get frustrated. I know I can play better tennis than I have been and I suppose my mentality is preventing me from achieving. All the losses have lowered my confidence and self-esteem. But I still feel I can do great things in my life even if I fail in tennis. I'm not sure what a "stereotypical woman" is but I am someone who wants to achieve. I believe if I don't go far in tennis now, I appreciate all the work you've done for me and I don't believe I'm ungrateful. You've helped me develop my talent and skill but somehow things haven't been going well for the last one to two years.

I don't know if I have the right to say what I feel because you always say my head is shitty. I'd like to think my problems are all part of growing up and maturing and that soon I'll be a stable person mentally. I don't know why some other 16- and 17-year-olds are succeeding but I guess either they are more mature or have their heads on straight. I think that if I don't succeed now, I can try to pick it up on my own in two to three years and possibly be successful.

I don't expect anyone to hand me a living. I intend to work for it and although I may not have the right to say this, I feel I can succeed outside of tennis in some academic field and still be functional in the world knowing that I'm Black and female. I feel I'll be able to control myself and not go to a mental institution, prison, or become bankrupt. After all, you and Mom succeeded outside of the athletic field, Dagin's outside it and will succeed, and I too can succeed outside tennis.

I know I've insulted you and I don't know if it is forgivable, but I hope that our relationship can begin again and if not in the tennis field, then perhaps as friends in life. My personality still in the developing stage. Maybe it has changed from the calm, cool tennis personality of younger ages to another one that is trying to develop, understand life and the world, and find out "who I am" so that I can be happy and successful in a few years.

I love tennis and I'm not afraid of hard work, discipline, and dedication but maybe I need time off to clear my head, see life clearly, and in the meantime pursue other interests and perhaps later resume tennis on my own and become financially independent that way, or set up my own tennis business. I firmly believe that I will be happy and successful in or out of tennis. . . .

I'm not seeking for the whole world to love me because it's not necessary. I want to be happy and when I'm not happy with my tennis, it affects my whole personality.

I know you've done a great deal for me which I seemed not to appreciate. But I do and know that my experiences and relationships with you will always play an important role in my life.

I'm at the stage of going mentally and emotionally from a girl to a woman and I guess that's not an easy time for me. I'm a Black woman in a male-oriented, White society but I can achieve in tennis possibly or anything else. I won't let failing in tennis carry over to other aspects of my life.

I love you as my father but our relationship concerning tennis seems to be where it all falls apart because of my attitude. I never meant to insult you and I'm very sorry. I feel utterly disgraceful but maybe our relationship can blossom in other areas and we both can be happy and feel good about each other. I think now that everything is out in the open, I will be a better person and freer with myself. I also apologize for any marital problems my actions may have caused.

—Menah

I gave the letter to my father, and he told me I had no right to write it. I was lectured and humiliated for even thinking that I could challenge the Pratt Setup. I was proud of myself, though, for being courageous enough to write it. At the same time, I was sad that my world was not going to change. It was the season I attempted suicide. My parents were working at the apartments, and I was alone and distraught. I went to the medicine cabinet in the hallway bathroom and took some of my father's high blood pressure medicine. Throwing up immediately, I remember sobbing uncontrollably on the floor next to the toilet. I remember feeling like an even bigger failure; I couldn't even kill myself.

My mother, however, must have sensed my sadness and surprised me with a letter a few weeks later:

> *My dear daughter Menah,*
>
> *Let me first say that I love you unconditionally. I want you to be happy. I think you are a lovely young lady, attractive in many ways, not the least of which is your delightful laugh and sense of humor. You are also a highly intelligent young lady with tremendous potential.*
>
> *I hope you will be able to fulfill your highest dreams and potential for you, to make you happy and feel good about yourself. You are also a kind, sensitive person with great writing talent. Don't give up on yourself. I will not [give up on you] and will help you all I can.*
>
> *Whenever you want just to talk or pour out your thoughts and feelings, I am here for you.*
> *Sweet Dreams.*
> *—Mom*

Mama must have given this letter to me in the evening or put it on my bed. She knew the Pratt Setup had a cost, and that cost was feeling loved. She sought to reassure and reaffirm that she loved me unconditionally, perhaps to counter my father's conditional love. This was not a letter from both of them, like the earlier letter; this was from Mama to me. Despite this affirmation, the sorrow journey continued as I tried to encourage myself, despite countless disappointments. My journal continued to include poems, short notes, and reflections about my ambivalence around a tennis career:

September 17, 1984

The Odds Are in My Favor

I never can win.
No matter how hard I try
In spite of my seemingly endless attempts
I never can win.
I toil with obsession
I apply myself to the limit
but the odds always increase beyond my reach.
I never can win.
I dedicate myself to my dream
I strive toward my best
it's not enough
I never can win.
However, after defeat
after defeat
After insult
After insult
My pride and esteem will remain intact
And I will eventually win.
And I will be pleased.
MAEP

October 22, 1984

Religion is so puzzling. So confusing. Totally lost.
Totally guilty. Totally sinful. Prince is King of Charts.
Want album and Tina Turner. Am I wrong to wish for
happiness? Am I wrong to wish for death? Lost in life.
Must escape before suffocated by confusion.
—MAEP.

Best Approach to Winter Circuit

(1) Recognize that I have all the necessary equipment to succeed. I am going to play one match at a time—play the draw. I am not inferior to anyone. No one is superior to me. We are equal. I have an equal chance to win. I must not lose the first round. (2) There is no need to be nervous or timid. I must remain aware of my capabilities and see to it that every one of them is used to the best of my abilities.

Goal: Play the best possible tennis I am capable of and still maintain a desire to win. Keywords: Calm and relaxed, but not apathetic. Think Points, Patience, and Win.

Tennis was a dominant part of my life, and I was frequently punished in a variety of ways for losses. Consistent with African Creole culture, Papa was a strict disciplinarian who believed in corporal punishment since he had been beaten as a child. Other punishments included standing in the corner by the chair and the front door for hours; not being allowed to eat meals; and being assigned sentences to write. Assignments included writing five hundred to a thousand sentences.

Once, after I had won a tournament, my father was upset about a comment I made about form and told me to write one thousand sentences saying the following: *"Form is important in tennis. I cannot cheat and deceive myself and my father."* Sentence writing was a routine part of my life. Some of the sentences that I had to write said: *"Emotions are not part of the tennis game"*; *"I will not be defeated before I enter a match"*; *"I have to stop taking too many aspects of my life, including my parents, for granted,"*; *"I will not be defeated before a match and bring disgrace to myself and my father"*; *"I will not act like an ass"*; and *"I will not disrespect my father in more ways than one."* These sentences, which he rarely read, were often not only about tennis but also about him and his *"little and bruised ego,"* as I wrote in my journal. I saved these sentences for decades in my journal until I started writing this book—papers that were quietly bearing witness to hours of imprinting into my psyche a sense of worthlessness and helplessness.

I was struggling for air, literally and psychically. So was Awadagin. My parents, unhappy with his experience at the university, had decided that Awadagin would have to live at home and commute to Champaign that fall school year. Mama was driving him to Champaign every morning for school, and he was catching the bus back home in the evening. After he missed the bus one day, my mother had to drive to Champaign to pick him up and bring him home. Papa was incensed when Awadagin and Mama walked into the house. After hours of yelling and arguing, my brother left the house. Although my parents tried to persuade or bully him to return, he never did. And for years, he never returned to 1405. My parents and I would celebrate Thanksgiving and Christmas without him for years. He had decided that he would make his own way in the world. That evening, I had an asthma attack. I couldn't breathe. Awadagin's sudden departure amid the chaos and confusion had taken my breath away.

SCENE THREE: **Goddess Wisdom**

The battles were brutal and were the inevitable result of the bargain. A bargain had been made. My father's physics professor career loss would be replaced with my brother's career in music and my victories in tennis. Papa's dreams would be fulfilled by us. The expectations were not unreasonable because we were both tremendously talented.

Awadagin was an extremely talented musician, and I had won over fifty trophies by the time I was seventeen. I was nationally ranked in the USTA Amateur Circuit; I was having some success on the Avon professional circuit; and I had been selected to compete in the Olympic Tennis Trials in 1984 in New York. Despite these successes, I was continually beaten down, physically, emotionally, and mentally, and I was made to feel inadequate, insufficient, and worthless.

In my sorrow journey, my journal provided a space to process and grieve and to document and validate my sadness. My writings created a hedge of protection around myself to save myself from dying. They were literally a cry for Love and an insistence on the legitimacy of my sorrow. It was a space where my words and thoughts had power and could not be challenged. It was a space for self-preservation and affirmation, and it became a place of empowerment for the next stage of the initiation.

I wanted out: out of the Pratt Bargain; out of the Pratt Setup; out of the house; out of the loneliness; out of Papa's lectures; out of the corner by the chair and the front door; out of the imprisonment of my room; and out of the sadness, suffering, and sorrow. I wanted my breath back. I wasn't the only one who wanted me out. Mama did too.

Reflection Questions

1. Have you experienced anything that might resemble a "sorrow journey" or a period of sadness during your childhood? What was the experience? How did you adjust to it?
2. What memories and emotions stand out for you about your junior high and high school years? Do you remember any key life lessons or experiences impacting your self-identity?
3. If you had siblings, did their experiences impact you? In what ways?

THE THIRD STAGE—Burials

BATTLES ARE FIGHTS FOR CONTROL. Though there can be a victor, often everyone loses something in a battle. There is usually a cost when we are attempting to gain control by wresting authority and power from another. It is similar to the relationship between a parasite and a host. Because a parasite needs a host to live and survive, parasite relationships can often damage the host. Conversely, separating the parasite from the host can kill the parasite if the host is not replaced. Extricating ourselves from complicated entanglements inevitably results in sacrifices of important parts of our spirits.

SCENE ONE: **The First Burial**

*P*apa had unlimited control and influence over my life. His power, in effect, had to be neutralized. He had become a parasite, living and feeding off my success and failures on the tennis court. The complicated intertwined relationship of my mother, father, and me required an intricate extrication to sever our entangled ties. My journal, with its entries, letters, and poems, bears witness to acts of separation and severing.

Our lives have turning points, and February 3, 1985, was a transformational day in my life. It was the day I buried my tennis career. I so vividly, even as an adult, remember this moment. It was about 6:00 p.m. I was waiting for the dishwasher to finish so I could unload the dishes, which was one of my many household chores. I decided to go downstairs and fix my tennis shoes. I rarely got new shoes, and those were for matches, so I had to constantly fix and repair the holes in my practice shoes with glue. That day, for some unknown reason, Mama came downstairs to watch the TV show *60 Minutes*. She rarely watched TV, and especially not downstairs, so I think she wanted to be near me. After I finished my shoes, I remember Mama suggested I stay and watch *60 Minutes* with her. We sat on the small green couch together in the dark basement. This was a rare moment for us to be together. After a few minutes, I noticed Papa standing at the top of the stairs, and I remember feeling my heart skip a beat. Suddenly, he called my name: "Menah." It always felt like he shouted my name. I got up from the couch and, as I always did, said, "Yes, Papa," and started running up the stairs. I only reached halfway before he angrily shouted, "What are you doing?"

"Watching *60 Minutes* with Mama," I said.

"You have other things to do besides watch TV."

I heard and felt my mom getting up from the couch, and out of the corner of my eye, I saw her moving toward the staircase. Standing at the bottom of the stairs, she said to my father: "What exactly does she need to do? Why can't she watch TV?"

Her questioning enraged him and shocked me. He said, "She needs to get ready for tennis tomorrow." To my absolute surprise, Mama calmly said, "She may not want to play tennis, and there are other things to do besides play tennis. Ask her." I was still standing in the middle of the green indoor-outdoor carpeted staircase, in between my mother at the bottom of the staircase and my father at the top. I didn't know which way to look or who to look at. It was almost an out-of-body experience; I was paralyzed, standing on the staircase, sandwiched between my parents, but felt that something important and life-changing was about to happen.

Papa, in a harsh voice that almost assumed the answer, asked me if I wanted to keep playing tennis. I paused a long time. I knew the answer, but I was afraid to say it. In the long silence, I was trying to gather the courage to speak truth to power. During my silence, my mother moved up a few steps on the staircase, closer to me, and quietly said, "Tell the truth. What do you want?"

I remember rarely hearing my mother's voice as a child. My father's was so dominant. But I heard her voice that day, and from the middle of the stairs, in between my parents, I said, "I want to go to college." After I said that, my parents began yelling and shouting at each other, and then I was sent to my room.

Incarcerated and imprisoned in my bedroom cell, I heard my parents still arguing. Mama threatened not to sign the passport form for the winter tennis tour in Brazil that was about to begin. Unexpectedly, I was called out of my room and asked again what I wanted to do. I repeated myself and said, "Attend college." There was more arguing and yelling, and I was sent back to my room. The next morning, the house was strangely and eerily quiet. Sitting in my room, I didn't know if I was supposed to get ready to play tennis or not. My mother came to my room and told me that tennis was over. I never went to another practice, and I never played another tournament. I was relieved yet also confused and scared. I didn't know any other way to be in the world other than playing tennis with Papa.

I wrote about the aftermath of this moment in my journal, referencing the incident leading to quitting tennis and reflecting on what might be next, including getting a job and planning for college:

February 12, 1985

Golly gee—been so long since I've written here. So much has happened. Should have written before. Hopefully, I'll get as much down as I can. I am going to the University of Iowa this fall. Current plan for major is philosophy, in preparation for law school. This summer, some classes at ISU [Illinois State University]. Job at McDonald's starts tomorrow—only a few hours. Looking for another job with more money.

Total rejection by Dad. Not speaking at all. Needs Mom, not me.

Mom is exercising every morning. Overweight, almost 200 but down to 182 now. Slight susceptibility to diabetes. I just need someone to hug. Going around hugging pillows with all this loneliness and guilt. Really tentative and unsure about myself. Hopefully will out-grow. Priest in Wisconsin killed. What a shame. God, where are you? Such tragedies all over everywhere. Is the world really coming to an end? Need some personal sense of direction, purpose, and meaning. I really haven't found it yet.

Unsure of college—perhaps. All the tennis balls and all the worn and torn tennis shoes I have! This deep-down desire for love and attention, especially with this recent all-out rejection by Dad isn't being matched by Mom. Her love, personality—everything—is great. I admire her more than anyone else and she is my inspi-ration, but somehow without Dad, part of me seems missing. I will hope and hope and pray and pray. Things must work out and somehow, I have to feel that they will, no matter how small the chance or likelihood. Got to get my act together and hopefully it will be soon, and I can feel whole totally again. Individuation? Will write more often. Promise.

I love you, Menah.

The parasite had been severed, and the severing was pain-ful. Because Papa was so connected to me, I was feeling the acute loss. At the same time, I was liberated and excited to explore my individuation. I got my first job at McDonald's and also worked at Arby's. My journal entries in February reflected this new reality. I gave my dad a Valentine's Day card that he returned. I saved the card in the journal in between the punishment-writing sentences. In the card I wrote:

February 14

I bought this before the fallout so I hope you'll accept it now. I also hope that someday in the near future we can be friends again. I know that one day soon, you will see that I will have excelled far beyond your ideas and beliefs. Whatever the case, I still love you now and will continue to love you until the day I die. Much, much love, Menah, your daughter.

A few days later on February 23, I wrote a poem called "At Last, Inside My Grasp":

Happiness,
Like a blooming tulip
A budding rose
A flowering fruit tree,
Is so beautiful.
Grabs me so suddenly and sensuously
Lifts me high above the ground
Leaves me floating on air
Suspended with excitement
Never to fall, but only to rise
Higher and higher every day.
A new, never before seen sparkle
Appears in the white of my black eyes.
A spontaneous giggle
A gorgeous grin
A mischievous smile
Seem insuppressible.
The heart so warm
The spirit so fresh
The soul so clean
The mind so open
And life so wonderful.

May it last forever.
But for those who have not
What I have
Do not despair.
The law of life dictates that
One must reach, touch, and live at the pit of Hell
To truly appreciate the greatness of heaven.
And once the unknown surge of joy appears
Treasure the feeling forever—as long as you can
Because
Although it is not extinct
It is rare.

The next day, I wrote about the poem, the Valentine's Day card, and my excitement at my new journey:

February 24, 1985
Hey Love,
Today is February 24 and for the last few days at least I seem to have hit one incredible, emotional high and it's wonderful. Working at McDonald's and Arby's. Wrote "At Last Inside My Grasp." So beautiful.
Dad is speaking to me to some extent. Dad liked my Valentine's Day card. Gave it back but appreciated it. . . . Lately, just feeling really full of energy—life—good thoughts, enthusiasm. Really wonderful. New shoes, Ding-a-Ling. Glasses tomorrow. Braided hair. Really like just on top of the world. So much love for everything and everyone. Hope it continues for a long time. Love you. Thanks for being here for me.
—Menah

For several years, even while in school, I had been struggling to see, but my father refused to believe I needed glasses.

Once I quit tennis, my mother took me to get them. Wearing my new glasses, I exclaimed, "I can see," as soon as I put them on. The glasses were big on my face, with thick lenses, but I didn't care. Not only could I see the material physical world, but I was also going to be able to see the spirit world and past the immediate day-to-day reality to envision a different future. This led to a poem about my search for God:

April 22, 1985

God. Where is He?
I can't see Him.
I can't feel Him.
I can't hold Him.
I can't hear Him.
Where is He?
And from those who claim to know
"You must have hope . . ."
"You must have faith . . ."
"You must have trust . . ."
"You must believe . . ."
So much honest confusion
Uncertainty
Unknown hesitancy
I know, though, that as long as the doubts and
unsatisfactory responses remain,
I will and must continue to search, seek,
And ask for the acceptable answers and the
Real and true meanings and explanations
And hope that in my wanderings that
I may stumble upon the way which leads
To peace of mind,
Heart, and
Soul.

And thinking . . .
Wondering . . .
What if we all showed Kindness, Concern,
Tolerance, Patience, and a Special Spiritual Love
For others, and not only ourselves,
Would not the whole world, perhaps, be a much better
place for all?

This entry reflects my deep desire to understand God. More importantly, it begins the shift outward, as an eighteen-year-old, to thinking about others and how to make the world a better place. As the second separation happens, I continue to write to Love and explore my purpose in the world.

SCENE TWO: **The Second Burial**

When I symbolically buried my tennis career, I didn't know that I would also be burying a part of my spirit. The consequences of the severing of the parasite were not yet complete. Papa was angry and still fighting for control, and I would not be prepared for the humiliating consequence of his anger.

Even today, I still remember one of the more traumatic events of my teenage years. Permanently imprinted like a tattoo on my mind, I will never forget that day. I was returning home from working at McDonald's. Just like every other day, I used my house key to enter the house. Papa met me at the front door and refused to let me come inside the house. He told me I didn't have a right to be in his house and I needed to wait until my mother came home. He had disowned me and wanted nothing to do with me. I was told I couldn't live in the house if I wasn't going to play tennis. And so, I just sat on those steps, with my little Black butt in my brown McDonald's uniform, right on the hard concrete. I was stinky from the early morning shift, smelling like biscuits and burgers. It was summer and hot. And there I was—on my own front porch, embarrassed and humiliated.

I remember trying to decide which of the four steps of the porch I should sit on. Sit high on the top step. Sit low on the bottom step. Sit in between. Waiting for my mother. I remember trying to be strong, to look cool, like I belonged there—on the steps—in case anyone walked or drove by. I remember working on not crying. I remember fighting back the tears of hurt and confusion and just telling myself to be strong. I thought and wondered and worried about what was going to happen. I looked all afternoon at the flowers my mother had planted. I looked at the four-o'clocks, wondering if I could see them open and close. I looked at the apple trees in the yard. I looked at the marigolds. And I just sat there, on the steps, like a lost and abandoned child, until my mother came home from the university.

As soon as I saw her, I told her what had happened. She started to go inside the house and kept telling me to come with her, and I told her that Papa told me that I couldn't come in. She went in and talked to my father, and they began arguing. Eventually I was allowed to come in and was sent to my room. I don't know what was said in the conversation between my parents. That night, Mama told me that we were going to move and that they were going to get a divorce. I remember being told that we were going to start our own lives.

Just as my father, as a teenager, and his mother had been put out of his house by his father, my mother and I were now put out of our house by him. I remember packing up my few clothes, all my many trophies, and other belongings for the move, including one of my most prized possessions—a little black bear stuffed animal. I was excited to be leaving the house

of so much trauma, but also apprehensive. I was tired of tiptoeing and trying to be invisible, but I almost felt guilty that after
twenty years of marriage, my parents were going to divorce,
seemingly because of me.

I was shocked, disappointed, angry, and embarrassed when
just three days later, we moved back to 1405 West Hovey, with
the same movers. I realize now that my parents had something
deeper that connected them than me. They had their shared
experience of America's racism and journeying together to
survive. At the time, my mother only shared bits and pieces of
the long conversation that led to our return. During their talk,
it was only the second time that she had seen him cry. The first
time was when Mama Pratt visited and argued with Mama;
he had been caught in the middle of his mother and his wife.
And now, he was in the middle of his daughter and his wife.

Because Mama had such love and compassion for him,
another bargain was made: Mama would return to him, and I
would go to college. She also got more power in the marriage.
I knew even as a child that my father controlled all the money,
including my mother's salary. Though perhaps not unusual for
that generation, I always felt that since Mama was working,
she should be able to control or have access to her money. As
part of the negotiated return, my mother gained a certain level
of financial freedom. She got her own bank account and was
able to manage half of her salary. Her financial bargain with
my father enabled her to pay for me to go to college, at least
for the first year. I was also going to be able to go to summer
school. I wrote in my journal about the separation:

May 7, 1985

Mom and I moved out on May 3 to 1608 Bryan and now we are going back. Nothing wrong with the apartment. It's really nice, but Dad needs us I suppose. Guess it's all for the best. Was rather depressed originally. Mom got the wrong end of it all. Worst car, half salary. But now, half of the assets, money each month. $2,000 to do with as we please. Don't want to move again. Mom told me about the time he cried, having to decide between Grandma and her and that he would choose Grandma if she didn't apologize.

Still wonder what he is going to do the rest of his life? Is he really so vulnerable, gullible, and dependent? Difficult to believe. Did he just use us—being nice? But everybody is different. Not just him. But all men can't admit their vulnerabilities and use others for their pleasures. Not considerate.

More freedom with Mom, but still disciplined. Some uncertainties. Starting school session on Monday. Looking forward to something else to dig into.

We as humans are so vulnerable, dependent on one another for love, support, guidance, disapproval, and approval. It is to a certain extent frightening, but perhaps good if we all realize it and try to be considerate of others and not hurt them. Life: is it just a stop on a long journey, or is this all that there is? You are here and then you are gone. Why do some lives seem to be laden with one heartache after the other, or do all lives have ups and downs and it's our duty to try and create as many ups as we can for ourselves but for others as well?

During my childhood, I had many mixed feelings toward Mama. She represented an energy that attracted me and also repulsed me. I remember her silence and almost invisibility much of the time in the house: quietly grading exams, writing papers, and working on the Bloomington-Normal Black History Project. She seemingly silently cooked, did laundry, hung it on the clothesline outside, and gardened. I often wondered if she saw my suffering and, if she did, why she didn't say something sooner. She was a social worker, for heaven's sake, a career that focused on protecting the vulnerable, and here I was, vulnerable, fragile, and abused. When, if ever, was she going to stand up for me? I was often angry with her, and I resented the level of her loyalty to my dad and not to me.

Decades later, I asked my mom why she hadn't done more sooner. She acknowledged that my father was cruel and that she should have done more. That was all I needed to hear. She shared with me that she had found *Doutorando* and my letters to Love, and it was then that she realized that she needed to become my advocate, and she did. I remember feeling, at one point before I quit tennis, that Mama had read my journal. It felt out of order, as if someone else had seen it. I had left it out instead of hidden. I just resolved to make sure that I hid it better. It may have been then that Mama read it. Something clearly moved her to action.

As a child, I never saw my mother cry. Yet she must have cried during her marriage. She must have cried for all the love she desired and must have rarely received. She must have cried for the treatment of her children by her husband. She must have cried for the cost of the Pratt Setup. It wasn't only me who suffered. Awadagin did too, and she did as well. And perhaps her suffering and witness to my suffering, and maybe her silent and invisible tears, eventually led her to act boldly and challenge my father's dominance and power. She secured my ability to go to college, and that was a defining marker in my life.

After that incident, I spent the rest of the summer working at McDonald's and trying to stay invisible. My father rarely spoke to me, and I rarely came out of my room. I was just waiting for the day Mama was going to drive me to Iowa City in August. On the day we left for Iowa, my father yelled at me over something simple related to picking apples in the yard. He was upset. He was being disentangled from his host, and he needed to try to regain control in some way. I remember carrying out the last of my belongings from my room to the car. On the very top of a box was my little black bear—the special stuffed animal I'd had for years. He saw the bear and laughed, almost a laugh of derision, surprise, and confusion. I think for a moment he saw me as the little girl who said she was Queen of Sheba, and he realized I was still his daughter, a little, tender-hearted girl. I was embarrassed by his laugh, and embarrassed that I still valued that stuffed black bear of my childhood, remembering all the nights I held it and it felt like my only friend. Fighting back tears, I said goodbye. He extended his hand. I put my box down and shook his hand. We never hugged. The handshake was big for him. It was almost an act of conciliation and concession. I got in the car, and my mother drove me to college. I thought I carried all of myself to college. I didn't. Unknowingly, I left behind, buried, a big part of myself.

SCENE THREE: **Goddess Wisdom**

The extrication of our entangled lives created scars for all of us. I have realized over time that I left much more behind when my mother drove me to Iowa than just my bedroom of sorrow; the living room corner of shame; the kitchen with its flowers performing their revolutionary role; the morning coffee-making routines; the piano and violin lessons; and the aborted tennis career. As part of this writing journey, I have reflected that though I had symbolically dethroned my father as king over my life, I had also experienced being dethroned from my identity as Queen of Sheba, Blackwildgirl, the one crowned with honor.

Who was she? Blackwildgirl was my childhood self—a child that felt unwanted, unloved, abhorred, and hated. She was the child who could never be perfect. She was the child who could not win tennis matches. She was the child who was always punished and had to write one thousand sentences chastising and demeaning herself. She was the young woman who was disowned from her own home and put out on the front steps, wearing her stinky brown McDonald's uniform and waiting for her mother to reclaim her. She was the child who sat in her room in fear. She was the child that was depressed, that thought about and attempted suicide. She was a Black girl on the verge of womanhood who was humiliated by her father in her mother's absence at the store getting maxi pads. It was this tender, innocent little Black girl who just needed and wanted love so badly she wrote letters to Love. It was this precious and beautiful spirit that was treated so harshly as part of the bargain that she needed to retreat, perhaps for her own protection, so that she could not be completely annihilated.

Blackwildgirl was figuratively shoved into a backpack and zipped up, hidden and invisible. Though she accompanied my adult self, Blackwildwoman, literally and figuratively on her back, Blackwildgirl remained invisible, silent, and mute for many years. Like a seed, she would need to experience the treacherous journey of burial, growing roots, experiencing weeds, and eventually rising above the ground to become a strong tree, bearing fruit. This initiation journey is about Blackwildgirl—trying to find love and to be loved excellently. Despite her burial, she had the spirits of her ancestors, her grandmothers, and her great-grandmothers, all the way back to the Nubian empire. This "Queen of Sheba" was fiercely determined to rise up, to speak, to share her story, to find Love, and then to share that Love with the world.

Though buried and zipped up, she would not remain hidden. The ancestors would be her guide so she could emerge and reconnect with Blackwildwoman. Blackwildwoman would begin exploring and wandering in the world at the University of Iowa. She would unknowingly carry with her a reminder of Blackwildgirl, her little black bear, symbolizing resurrection and hibernation. Before Blackwildgirl can emerge, Blackwildwoman first must figure out who she is with her Blackness and womanness and learn to honor, love, and cherish herself. She would start her own journey, separated from the parasite, as the host of her own life, looking for Love and drinking from the fountain of knowledge in the world.

Though I had physically left my father behind and metaphorically dethroned him from his controlling and dominating authority in my life, his energy, his values, and his way of navigating the world continued to influence me. The lesson from the Pratt Setup was that life in the rough world of American racism required excellence, perfection, sternness, inflexibility, and rigid discipline. These were values implanted and imprinted from my father. In this life, there was no space for softness, gentleness, tenderness, weakness, fragility, or even love.

And perhaps, that is the ultimate tragedy of American racism. Racism singes, marks, and brands us. Love that is mixed with the bile of racism does not feel like love. It is love without joy, an on-guard love, a distant love. This love is harsh and heavy, tinged with bits of anger, pain, frustration, and hurt from the bitter sting of racism in America. Many generations of African Americans know this love from their parents, especially from their fathers. bell hooks, Viola Davis, Alice Walker, Nikki Giovanni, and many other Black women wrote about it. It is like the father in August Wilson's *Fences*: a love, if it can be called that, with no niceties such as "I love you"; a love that is "I do not hate you." No love and no hate. It is about parents sacrificing for their children. It is not about love; it is about Black children's success. It is about pursuing a career to be financially independent and self-reliant, building an impenetrable fortress against racism. It is only about excellence and perfection, twin shields against the hatred of America. There is a standard that has to be met, and there are always consequences for failing to meet the standard.

As Blackwildwoman, I spent many years hoping that if I excelled, I would feel loved. Only later, much later, I learned that there is no correlation between love and excellence, unless one can love and be loved excellently. I began to learn these lessons as I started looking for Love anywhere I thought I could find Her and trying to understand what it means to be a Black woman in America.

A seed had been buried. Like an acorn, she would need to break forth from her protective and sheltered shell and start growing roots.

Photographs and Images

Photographs tell their own story. These photos capture some of the salient moments in Act I. They include photos of my parents and grandparents, excerpts from the first letter my mother wrote to me; my father's tennis coaching advice; my Olympic Friendship Medal; and my high school tennis team photo. Some of my early journal writings are also included.

Grandma Eula Sirls, my mother's mother (left), and Mama Pratt,
my father's mother (right), circa 1970. Photo credit: Unknown

The first letter my mother wrote to me on December 18, 1980, where
she reminded me I was from the oldest culture in the world, Africa.
Photo credit: Menah Pratt

Menah Pratt, Normal Community High School tennis team photo,
Normal, Illinois, circa 1981–1982, with my favorite tennis racket
and inspiration, Evonne Goolagong. Photo credit: Unknown

Doutorando (translation, "Graduate"), my childhood journal from Brazil that my father gave to me; this is the inside cover note written on June 13, 1983. Photo credit: Menah Pratt

Friendship Medallion of the 1984 Olympic Games

This 1984 Olympic Medallion has been issued jointly by the Organizing Committees of the Games of the XXIII Olympiad in Los Angeles, California and the XIV Olympic Winter Games in Sarajevo, Yugoslavia.

1984 Olympic Tennis Trials Friendship Medal from my participation in the Olympic Tennis Trials at USTA National Tennis Center, Flushing Meadows, New York, from May 28 to June 2, 1984.
Photo credit: Menah Pratt

My parents, Mildred and Theodore Pratt, at a Valentine's Day dance in February 1996, seven months before my father died. Photo credit: Unknown

My father, Theodore Pratt, wrote a tennis coaching note, circa 1983–1985. Photo credit: Menah Pratt

You all need not worry about your "FAILURE" because I'm no longer anyone's FAILURE. The arrogant, conceited, immature FAILURE is gone from your lives forever.
The failure could not handle all the pressure to succeed in tennis. Can't be a surprise to you because after all I'm a baby — A baby who can't handle pressure.
So instead of being a burden to you a wasting all the families resources, ie time, money & energy.
I'm gone.
Please give my savings account to Dagen
My other things — clothes shoes etc may be disposed of at will
Best to all. I'm sorry but I didn't seem to create much besides chaos a argumentation.

Menah.

A suicide note I wrote on October 23, 1983. Photo credit: Menah Pratt

FEMALE
OMOTOLA   A Child is Sufficient honour.
ADEBISI   my Crown increases
OLABISI   my Honour
EBUN   The Gift of God or gift.
OLUTOYIN   The Lord is to be Praised
Olufunmike The Lord gives me to Care.
OMOLADE   Child is my Crown.
ADEOLA   The Crown of Honour

Mama Pratt's suggestion of names for me, including the
explanation of one of my middle names, Adeola, as
"crown of honour." Photo credit: Menah Pratt

Reflection Questions

1. Our lives often have defining moments, where there is a radical shift in our worlds. What shifts have you experienced in your life, particularly during your childhood or early adulthood?

2. What memories stand out for you about turning eighteen and finishing high school or gaining some type of independence? How did you transition to the next stage of your life? What worked and what did not work? What lessons did you learn?

3. Do the photos generate any emotions in you? What are they and why? What photos are important in your own childhood?

Act II: Roots

Spirit thirsts.

Dirt.

Water.

THE FOURTH STAGE—Marooned

THE SPIRIT-LIKE SEED HAS COMPLETED its descent and burial. There were bargains, battles, and burials. The parasite has been severed. Marooned, it is time for the host to be on its own. It is a time for pushing out small tentacles, like roots, into the world and trying to find something to hold on to in the midst of the ungraspable, ephemeral, and elusive energy of life. It is a time for the host to begin both an inward journey of self-exploration and an external journey of wandering in the muck and mire of life, being initiated into womanness and Blackness.

SCENE ONE: **Womanness**

As Blackwildgirl, I had led a very protected and shielded life in Normal with my parents. As a host, I was rarely alone, almost always with my parasitic, omnipresent father. Marooned in the cornfields of Iowa, my eighteen-year-old Blackwildwoman was ready to taste life in all its fullness of spices and sweets. As Blackwildwoman, I began exploring my womanishness and my Blackness in the meadows of Iowa, as part of my search for Love—that unconditional love that I could feel, touch, hold, and cherish. It was the Love that I knew existed; I just needed to find Her and seize Her with all my heart.

I realized early in my life that something was different in my world as a Black girl. Since my father was raised in Sierra Leone, he had some very traditional ideas about women, their roles as wives, and their responsibility for cooking, cleaning, and household duties. At the same time, my father acted like I could do anything a boy could do. I was not raised to be feminine or to feel like a woman or a girl. I did hard manual and physical labor, including moving railroad ties, mowing yards, shoveling snow, and cleaning apartments. I never wore dresses and never wore makeup. I never had my nails done or a manicure or pedicure. I never socialized, dated, went to a school dance, or went to a sleepover. I wasn't even allowed to talk on the phone.

I was curious about what it really meant to be a woman. I was curious about sexuality. I had even written in my journal on July 2, 1985, *"Many questions about sexuality. Notions of being gay—meaning? So confused."* I remember that confusion because I had torn out and saved a picture of a naked woman from a girly magazine my brother had thrown away after he was caught with them. I distinctly remember feeling an attraction to her energy. I remember exploring my own body in the darkness of my room, trying to understand what it was that made me a woman and why I felt drawn to the naked pale White woman's folded-up photo hidden in the pages of my journal. Yet, while working at McDonald's the summer before college, I had met two older men, both of whom invited me to their houses on separate occasions. We kissed and made out. I liked the attention and the feeling of being desirable and attractive. It was thrilling to be exploring my sexuality. It was also scary because they were older men, at least in their midthirties, and they tried to convince me to have sex with them. Able to resist, I was still a virgin when I went to Iowa.

In my gullible search for Love and the feeling of being cherished and desired as a woman, I became a victim of predatory men and boys, without advice, protection, or guidance from my mother, family, or friends. In an article I wrote in 2018, I reflected on my experience at the University of Iowa as a young college Blackwildwoman:

> *In August, she [my mother] drove me to the University of Iowa. Despite my intense longing for freedom, I did not realize that I was not ready for a college campus. My mind and my spirit were in a state of disharmony. I had tried to convince myself that hearing "I love you" didn't matter. My body was used to moving through life with disciplined routines, and my mind was accustomed to a life focused on excellence and achievement.*

My spirit, however, refused to cooperate with my game of self-deception. It was as if she—my spirit—was on her own journey. She knew what she needed, and she was being guided by a deeply rooted and almost imperceptible desire to hear the words "I love you" from the universe. And, in 1985, that universe was the University of Iowa.

Like other naïve and emotionally immature girls, I was vulnerable to emotionally immature boys. I was prime prey for boys. I was curious. I wanted to know what sex was and what sex felt like. I had secretly read romance novels and felt the excitement of the woman, often simultaneously running away and running toward the "rough" man. The rough man often initially took the woman violently, though the woman seemed to yield and eventually enjoy the ride. These images made me feel that perhaps love could be rough, but acceptable. The books portrayed romance and love in explicit, vibrant, and vivid language; they created a yearning for that experience in me. I wanted to be that woman in those novels. I wanted to be a Harlequin woman and I was in a co-ed dorm with rough Harlequin boys.

One of those Harlequin boys was a dashing, handsome, and sweet-talking athlete from New York. He had a beautiful name with Jamaican ancestry. His first and last names seemed to run together as one. I loved his accent. He had a slender build, a cute face, a flashy personality, and beautiful Black skin. He was short (like me), and I felt a connection. I was thinking connection and he was thinking conquest.

He was my first experience. It took about 15 minutes. When it was done, I remember saying to him, "Is that all there is?" He said, "Yes." We both soon realized that I was bleeding from my hymen breaking—confirming my loss of virginity. While I felt embarrassed by the visible blood, I also remember sensing internal bleeding— spiritual bleeding. I didn't feel right; I remember feeling an emptiness as if something was missing. I didn't feel the romance of the Harlequin woman, but because I so earnestly wanted to believe it was special, I tried to convince myself that our encounter was love. My spirit knew it wasn't, but my mind and body ignored my spirit. Confused, I headed back to my dorm room.

Over the next few weeks, we had several more encounters. At the same time, my roommate's boyfriend and alcohol became constants in our room. "Invitations" to be with my Harlequin man became an opportunity to escape my room and convince myself that I, too, was wanted, desired, and hopefully, loved like my roommate. When the "invitations" came, I always obliged.

Thus, I could never have anticipated that one day the familiar invitation would become a nightmare. He had called me to ask me if I wanted to come to his room. I went. While I was lying with him and having sex, I was shocked to hear and see other Black boys— athletes and friends of his—enter the room. For what seemed like hours, different athletes came in and out of the room to rape me. When I was finally alone and able to leave, I was raw, shattered, horrified, embarrassed, and confused.

I moved out of the dorm. I never told my parents. I survived by using the only skills I had. Ironically, these were skills that my father taught me: discipline, persever- ance, hard work, and self-reliance. Thus, I studied hard, I worked hard, and I focused on literature, philosophy, and the writings of African-Americans in my major and double minors. I thought I could mask, dull, hide, and ignore the pain and hurt through academic excellence. I could not. Though I excelled academically, I continued to struggle emotionally. I could not manage the emotions on my own.

I knew I needed help, and I began what was the first of many years of on-and-off counseling. I wanted answers about myself and about sex. I wanted to connect with my spirit who was on her own journey. My parents had never talked about sex to me, and I was under the dangerous impression that sex was love. Unfortunately, my counselor was an inexperienced and ineffective young White male intern at the university's counseling center. Interns, I believe, should not be interning on a college campus when the lives and experiences of students require skilled and experienced counselors. In addition to his inexperience, the race and gender difference felt real. I didn't feel I could trust him so I left professional counseling and sought my own.

I sought to comfort and counsel myself through a new search. This search to hear "I love you" from a man was earnest and intense. I am convinced that men saw my vulnerability, perceived my fragility, and sensed the intensity of my yearning. I continued to find myself having largely unsatisfying sexual encounters with men—older men who were five to fifteen years older than me. These were men, not boys, and I believe these were men who were also seeking conquests. I had sex with these men thinking it was a precursor to a relationship. The emptiness and void inside me grew as did the blood of invisible and internal bleeding. The encounters included professionals and non-professionals. Some were Black and some were White; most were American. There was one African.

The man from Africa was from Freetown, Sierra Leone. His connection to my father's ancestry was initially *comforting and exciting. He picked me up at my apartment in his car, and after dinner and a movie, he invited me to his house to show me some African art. He calmly showed me the art in his living room. A wedding-like picture with him and a White woman caught my attention, and I asked him about it. He said it was his wife, but that they weren't really together. He then said he wanted to show me some art in his bedroom. I felt anxious but convinced myself to ignore the feeling. I hesitantly began to follow him to the bedroom.*

Suddenly, his behavior changed. He became sinister and evil. He violently grabbed me, dragged me onto his bed, stripped me of my pants and underwear, and raped me in front of a picture of his White wife while telling me to shut up and be quiet. When he was done, he angrily handed me my pants and underwear and told me to put them on and that he would take me home. Frightened and trembling, I silently sobbed during the car ride to my apartment. I showered for hours. Since that day, I take long showers twice a day. In some way, I believe I am still trying to wash off the hideousness of that day.

My response to this rape was the same as before. I resorted to the only coping mechanism I had: maintaining a disciplined life of achievement. I continued to study hard, and I continued the search for the "I love you." Addicted to soap operas and scheduling my class schedule around All My Children, One Life to Live, *and* General Hospital, *I continued to feed my spirit ideas about love, sex, and romance (Pratt-Clarke 2018).*

Feeding my spirit ideas about love, sex, and romance was a critical part of my Iowa wandering. I was looking for Love, conflating a man's desire for sex with love. I was yearning for intimacy and the attention of men and father figures, perhaps to assuage the absence of affection, love, and hugs from my father in my childhood. During my college years, I had sex with at least ten different men and was asked to marry four other men. Some of the men who came across my path included an older White coworker in a restaurant who bragged openly about the conquest at work; a White classmate in a philosophy class who abruptly ended our short-lived time with racist comments; a Black ex-con who attempted to physically assault me when we were living together after he proposed to me; a medical student who was Catholic and ashamed every time we had sex so proposed to me to mitigate the guilt; a military man who proposed after a few short weeks; and a writer from Harlem who was in the Writers' Workshop.

I wrote about the writer in my journal. I met him in my freshmen year, in the spring of 1986. Ten years older than me, he was worldly and street-wise. In February 1986, I wrote in my journal:

Love,

Met The Writer today. He is a writer in the Iowa Writer's Workshop here and he's from Harlem—the slum of the Black ghetto in New York. I was playing piano at the student union and the music caught his ear. He peeked around the movable barricade and listened and then we began to talk. We talked first about music and the fact that I played classical music. He mostly listened to jazz but could listen to anything and welcomed the fresh romantic-sounding music. We talked about how music may relate to writing. I talked to him about the themes, subthemes, diversions, and key changes in music and he tried to relate them to his writing and the different themes, voices, and styles. We talked about what it was like being artists in a university system. I found out that artists truly desire freedom from society, societal restrictions, and beliefs about making money and the importance of a steady job. They want to reject college and its imposition of general education courses—classes which in no way relate to their field and expertise. We talked about their constant need to be working at their field, trying to improve, and having to deal with the time and energy-consuming activities of other classes.

*We then began to talk about society. He spoke to me about Harlem and told me briefly how he happened to arrive in white Iowa City and the adjustment. He told me about jealousy and competition in the Writers' Workshop environment. He spoke about finding a mentor to guide him independently of the chaos and discontentment of the workshop environment. Told me he thinks he is a king sitting high atop a mountain and the only book he brought with him—*To Be Young, Black, and Gifted (sic). *Told me of his disdain of money. Carries money all balled and wadded up in his pocket. Spends it frivolously and suffers, takes it all in stride until he inherits more. Told me of his Harlem friends and how his goal is to tell their story, show people that they are sensitive, and shatter some stereotypes. Told me that someone like me is a dream—being Black, talented from family background.*

He was a very interesting person—brilliant, edgy, pensive. We began a sexual relationship, but it was short-lived, because he told me he was waiting for his dream woman, and it wasn't me. Realizing my gullibility and innocence because I felt connected to his call to be a writer and his background from Harlem, he began to use me as a parasite. Unknowingly, I became his host, full-time benefactor, and source for his food, shelter, clothes, and drugs for seven years.

Contrasting with this street-smart, conman writer, a few months later I would meet Gordon. Gordon was thirty-eight years old, tall at six one, with sunburned cocoa brown skin and mystical green-hazel eyes that radiated a charming combination of kindness, curiosity, and playfulness. He was walking across the United States in support of nuclear disarmament and stopped in Iowa City. Somehow our paths crossed, and we became pen pals for four years, writing long letters back and forth. Like a gardener, he was a force of regeneration, always encouraging me even from a distance in his letters and cards. Throughout those tough college years, Gordon replenished my depleted spirit, often sending affirmations in his letters, reminding me that I am powerful, able, successful, whole, and complete, supported by the universe, and able to be Love.

His letters were affectionately addressed "hey baby," and in one of his last letters to me, he wrote:

So, what do we have to do my dear distant friend but hang in there and keep getting up. If we hang tough enough and get up high enough, we'll get through these passages we've set before ourselves. And somewhere down the road, we'll come round on each other again and remember.

We lost touch with each other after four years, but true to his promise, thirty years later we would "come round on each other again and remember." Gordon was a light in an increasingly dark journey of trying to understand my womanness.

At the University of Iowa, majoring in English and minoring in philosophy and African American studies, I took Black Poetry in the fall of 1985, in my first year. Two poems, written in that class, sum up the hopes and the hurts in my search for my womanness:

Untitled (November 1985)

Tired,
Frustrated and
Lost.
All the dejected parts of me stop.
My soul
Waiting, crawling, like a child.
Stopping, complaining, tired, crying,
Waiting to be picked up and held.
My heart
Stumbling along through the forest of life.
Tripping, falling, trying to rise and go on to the end.
My mind
With its nerves all entangled like a ball
Of string, looking for someone to
Wrap it up neatly again and play with it.
Friendly and fun
My body
Possessor of all the pieces of me
Desiring to be puzzled together
By loving hands.
The key to the puzzle—a rainbow.
The many colors
The red-hot love and happiness with
The beauty of orange marigolds in full bloom with
Yellow sunshine radiating all over.
Sprouting green grass from the sun-launched
High above in the
Blue-violet background of life.
Here we are, all of me
Waiting for all the rainbow puzzle pieces of life
To be pierced together by love.

Untitled (December 8, 1985)

Don't reject me
Any part of me
My poems
Speech
Laughter
Tears
Body
And love
Just don't
Don't hurl them like rocks
With full discus force
Or fling them aside for fireplace fuel
Don't slash at them as waves
Do surfers at sea
Or toss them back
Into my sea as fish not fit for a feast
Don't pretend to plead
While towering over me
Proud and erect in your tweed
Or stoop so low as to
Pout and implore.
Accept me
Dripping with blood
Drenched in sweat
Streaming down tears
And stinking with the stench of confusion
In the mistying fog-filled forest of existence
Accept
My poems, with or without sounds and imagery
My speech, with or without dialect
My laughter, nervous or real
My tears, with or without purpose

My body, pure or used
My love, fresh.
Don't shove back my poems
Engulfed with red marks of
Hatred and coolness
Don't stare back my tears
With a questioning, blind
Idiotic look of disdain
Don't beat my body back
Battered by bruises
Don't disown my love
Don't hand it back
Untouched
Don't

I was wandering and waiting for my womanness to be acknowledged, found, and respected. I was looking for acceptance and unconditional Love. I just wanted to be picked up, held, and cherished. Vulnerable, naive, and innocent, I was in a crash course of life: learning rough and hard lessons about dating, sex, and relationships with men. I was also learning about what it meant to be Black in America, in college, in Iowa.

SCENE TWO: **Blackness**

*I*n 1977, when I was nine years old, my parents made me watch the entire *Roots* TV miniseries. The eight-day historical drama reenacted the African American experience from slavery to freedom. The violent scenes of beatings imprinted the trauma of Blackness into my soul. It also provided a point of connection with my own Africanness and Americanness. I knew that I was very different as a Black person. I was a true African American—with both African and American roots. As the only Black student in my high school graduation class of 388, my life had been immersed in White culture. My exposure to Black culture ended when I stopped going to the Black church, Mount Pisgah Baptist Church, as a child. All my friends in high school were White; I knew I was Black and different.

Through poems, I began exploring race and Blackness, but also my anger at the cost of having Black skin in America:

Untitled (December 8, 1985)

Ominous clouds of Black and White
Circulating
Surrounding
Blending
Merging
Combining
Torrential outputs of filth
Full of their filth
Their perceptions of
My Whiteness
My Blackness
The non-dialect is White
The lack of Black friends is White
The lips too thick
The hair Black textured
The skin African tar black
Being checked out
My credits
My debits
The balance . . .
The bottom line . . .
Too White-oriented

Too Black-featured
Sometimes
Oreo cookies
Don't do good
With
Fudge or Cool Whip

Untitled (February 1986)

When you're Black
and things don't work out
You wonder, sometimes
"Is it me, my skin, or them?"
One can't ask
'cuz they'll deny the two
And point it all to you.
You know you're getting
The rotten, bottom end
But think you can't speak 'cuz
They'll say "You're paranoid . . .
Causing trouble when none exists."
They think you're too stupid and dumb
To see the subtleness
They lack the courage to boldly display
So,
It's either suffer in silence
Growing bitter
Always wondering
Is it me, my skin, or them?
Or
It's speaking out
Growing stronger
Knowing it's not you
But your skin and them.

I was wrestling with the reality of my "skin and them" and struggling with the daily reality that I did not fit the stereotypes associated with that Black skin. I wasn't always accepted in the Black community because I wasn't "Black enough," and I wasn't accepted into the "White community" because no matter how Black I wasn't, I still had Black skin. I was an outsider and didn't fit in.

I began studying the African American experience through classes in literature, deciding to write an honors thesis on five novels by William Faulkner. I was also learning about Nikki Giovanni, Alice Walker, Toni Morrison, Gloria Naylor, and Maya Angelou. I was learning about powerful Black women writers who were writing texts that talked about Blackness and womanness. These works resonated and helped me understand the complexity of being a Black woman in America, being Black in a White culture, and being a woman in a male culture. An undated poem reveals the anger and bitterness I was experiencing as I developed a deeper awareness of my Black womanness:

Untitled (Undated)

I am black—coal black, mind you.
It bothers me.
Should the distinction be made?
I am a woman.
It doesn't bother me.
The distinction must be made.
I am defined by my color.
I hate it.
I also hate the words
Black
Negro
Nigger
White

Whiteness
Purity
Cleanliness
I hate all of them.
I am bitter.
Women
Weak
I hate them.
Men
Black
White
Egos
Insensitivity
I hate them.
America
Forgotten dreams
Lost chances
Ignorance
White
I hate it.
Me
A woman
African descent
In
America
I hate it.

SCENE THREE: **The Goddess Wisdom**

"**M**e / A woman / African descent / In / America / I hate it." Although learning about my identity as a Black woman in America, as Blackwildwoman, created tension, frustration, and anger, it was also a catalyst for thinking about how to make a difference in the world as a Black woman. Though marooned, I was not completely abandoned. Mama continued to be close by my side. She wrote me letters almost every week. She always asked about how I was doing, and she always encouraged me. She also called me. Because Papa remained ambivalent about me, I couldn't call the house to speak freely with Mama when he was home. So, Mama and I developed a clandestine relationship. She let me know when her office hours were so I could call then. And she called me from pay phones or her office when she thought I was in my dorm room. There were no cell phones then, and so we had to coordinate our conversations. I was grateful for my evolving relationship with Mama, although there were so many constraints on our relationship because of Papa. I did know that she loved me, cared about me, and wanted the best for me.

Mama could only afford to pay for my first year of college, so I became financially independent from my parents after the first year and started working two and three jobs to pay for college. I worked as a waitress at Golden Corral; I worked as an office assistant in the Special Support Services office; I worked as a tutor in Upward Bound; I worked in summer orientation; I worked in an after-school program for Black sixth-grade girls; and I played piano every Sunday at the Unitarian Universalist church. Mama knew that I was struggling, and so she often put a little money for me in the envelope with her letters. Her help wasn't enough my last year, and I almost dropped out of college, until the director of the Honors College, Sandy Barkan, loaned me $5,000. She told me to pay her back as I was able, even if it was $5 a year. I have never forgotten her sacrifice and kindness.

The Pratt Setup and its values of discipline and excellence would continue to be a blessing and a curse. Instilled in me like a guiding rod, I used those tools to succeed academically: graduating in three years with honors and high distinction in the top 5 percent of my class; on the president's list (4.0 GPA for an academic year) and the dean's list; inducted into Phi Beta Kappa and Phi Beta Sigma junior year; and named Collegiate Scholar as one of the top twenty graduating seniors in the College of Liberal Arts. Mama attended my undergraduate graduation from Iowa. Papa did not come. It was as if he couldn't accept the fact that I had succeeded without him, not realizing that I had succeeded both because of him and in spite of him. I would have four more graduations in my academic career. Mama came to each one. Papa never came.

The cornfields of Iowa provided a place to learn goddess wisdom. In a December 19, 1985, journal entry after my first semester, I had written a few takeaways: *No lending money. Much more saving. More frank opinions. Find true friends and keep. More laid-back, less hyper. Go with the flow. Hit the books. Work on maintaining friendships. Keep perspective on life, but also on goals.* I was beginning to think about my goals, and one of the goals was to be a writer:

April 22, 1986
Told The Writer about writing. I want badly to be free, to learn religion, to learn the way things really should be and tell people, although I want to be alone. Also want to make people happy. Ultimately want to apply myself to the fullest of my potential. Exploit my potential to the fullest. To be free, to be peaceful. No worries at all. Try to see what the world should be. Understand humans. Read and teach but show the beauty of the natural world to others. Simple beauty.

Three years later in a 1989 entry to Love, I shared some ideas about what I wanted to write about:

Dear Love,

*So often I think I should write about my life, expe-
riences, loves, disappointments. So often I think I should
read not about other's lives, but about the wisdom they
have sucked and extracted out of life. So often, I, too, think
I should write about the truth that I have come to know.
I have stories to tell of the lives I've led. I have truth to
convey from quiet moments of meditation. I have humor
to help others laugh in moments of loneliness. Should I
not begin writing and telling these stories?*

*Love is what we all seek. We all desire to be loved,
fondled, touched, and romanced. The challenge of life is
to be calm and peaceful with oneself while searching for
companionship. Life, truly, is the art of balance, weighting,
tipping, and deciding. Feeling comfortable with our aloneness
while searching. We all have been given a set of obstacles,
barriers, and burdens. The challenge is to overcome them
with grace and dignity and without bitterness and anger.*

*We all have God within us—our soul, a light, a fire,
flame of undying brilliance, needs nurturing, babying,
love. Self-love, esteem, is keeping that fire alive. Being able
to call upon. The role of artists is to remove or amplify
(perhaps for a moment) the pains and reality of life. How
can I maintain and nourish my closeness to God? Music,
gospel, prayer, reflecting, praising, attending church once
a month, reading religious texts. Quiet, stillness, reflection
with humor.*

Approaching the end of being marooned in Iowa, I was
gaining clarity and confidence on my calling and purpose.
I was growing roots and building a reservoir of resilience,
strength, courage, and hope in the underworld of my soul.
Though I had not yet found Love, I was still determined to
find Her, and She was determined to find me.

Reflection Questions

1. What events influenced your understanding of your race, and how did it impact your life journey?
2. What events influenced your understanding of your gender and sexuality, and how did it impact your life journey?
3. Statistics suggest that a significant percent of women have experienced sexual assault, particularly in college. If you or a friend has experienced sexual assault, it may be helpful to journal about that experience and the concepts of victim, survivor, and warrior.

References

Pratt-Clarke, M. 2018. "A Critical Race Feminist Autoethnography: A Narrative about the Academy, a Father, a Daughter, and a Search for Love." *Journal of Colorism Studies* 3, no. 1.

THE FIFTH STAGE—Mothered

WHEN A SEED IS GERMINATING, it needs care and attention. Some combination of water, light, oxygen, and heat is essential for the vulnerable seed's survival as it starts to grow its roots in the dark soil-womb. Like a seed, our spirit requires mothering and sustenance in its underground germination journey. It is a time for nourishment and nurturing. It is time for the universe to show up and shower the spirit-seed with Her infinite compassion, regeneration, hope, and encouragement.

SCENE ONE: **Nourished**

After finishing my undergraduate degree, I decided to stay at the University of Iowa to get my master's degree, building on my honors project about William Faulkner and his depiction of Black characters in five novels. In graduate school, I focused on one novel, *Absalom, Absalom!*, wrestling with issues of White racism, the history of America, and the legacy of slavery and White supremacy. My last two years at Iowa would be a time for finding and falling in Love.

It began with Leonard. Leonard was a beautiful Black man with caramel-colored light skin; he was tall at 6'4", with a gentle, soft spirit. He was kindness personified. Nine years older than me, he was a soft-spoken, gentle giant, with piercing, curious eyes. We met in 1989 when I was getting my master's degree and he was getting his bachelor's degree in physics at the University of Iowa. We were both tutors in Upward Bound, a program for minority and low-income high school students. After the semester ended, he asked me if I had ever been to Chicago. I said that I had only been for tennis tournaments, but never really got to see the city. He unexpectedly invited me to visit Chicago to stay with him and his mother for the Memorial Day weekend. Excited for an adventure, I took the train to Chicago. He met me at the station, and we grabbed some ribs for dinner, and I met his mother. She was a wonderful, beautiful woman. She hugged me and told me I could call her Mama. The next day, Leonard and I went sightseeing, and our last visit was to Lincoln Park Zoo. When we left the zoo, Leonard grabbed my hand as we crossed the street, and I never wanted to let go. He didn't want to let go either.

When he took me back to the train station at the end of the weekend, I remember getting on the escalator and looking back at him. He was still looking at me. Our eyes locked, just like in the movies. We waved and waved. We talked almost every day once I got back to Iowa City. He was still in Chicago, but he was making my heart spin like a top, and I needed to write about it to process it:

June 11, 1989

Well, now I am at a very special stage in my life. I feel at a stage of true love. It seems now that I'm experiencing true love with Leonard. The feelings I feel for him, the emotions, seem to choke and stifle my heart— unspeakable. Today is just week two. Memorial Day weekend, we fell in love and talked to each other over the phone for a week. This past week has been truly wonderful. Sunday, he returned from Chicago, and we went to see the movie Hear No Evil, See No Evil *and then just walked around downtown feeling very awkward and uncomfortable. Finally, he asked me if I wanted to ask him to my house. We had an absolutely fabulous evening, made out to each other, kissed, and held each other. Monday, Tuesday, Wednesday, Thursday, Friday, Saturday—we spent each night together. He brought me lunch, came to see me. Talked of racism and sexism.*

It was absolutely blissful, stimulating me. I'm floating on a cloud. I feel I love him, yet I can't seem to say it. He says he knows I have a place for him and his heart.

We talked about birth control. Don't want to have an abortion so must carefully consider birth control. Hopefully, August will be the month of our first actual sexual intercourse, though we are moving quite quickly. He is my boyfriend, though I don't see him as such. I don't know how I see him. It's just different.

I had decided that I needed to be with a man for almost two months before having sex, an arbitrary time frame, to minimize the likelihood that I would be used for sex by men. Because of the intensity of our feelings and the depth of the attraction, we could not wait the arbitrary two months and quickly became intimate. We often wrote letters and little notes to each other. His letters were confessions of love, referencing *"such intense soul stirring and oftentimes emotionally overpowering feelings"*— the topsy-turvy feelings of love. Our hearts were beating faster together, as his letters to me attested:

July 20, 1989
   Him who loved you then loves you now, and loves you always.
—Leonard

July 21, 1989
   I miss you (U + I) - U = I. Every time that I'm not with you, I feel like I can't be in love and that I've fallen into a black hole. This all means but one and only one thing. That I LOVE YOU.

July 23, 1989, 2:30 pm
To Menah,
   In love with you thus far. We first began in Chicago. It's amazing what a few moments of isolated attention, one person giving and receiving to and from another.

Just think, the bonding is what got us both and is continuing through the ink on this page.

Beginning back at the first weekend of bonding in Chicago, I was both scared to death and excited beyond my wildest dreams. You had, have, and are my heart. So you go . . . so goes my heart. But what better place to build a house then on the rocks? In our case, the rocks of friendship, mutual respect, and admiration.

Because God has given us the opportunity to love (I am convinced that God has), I can't help but get a pit in my stomach/throat because you are in me. A large part of who I am and who I will become: you are in that special part of me, that special place in my heart. When I'm with you, all my hopes, aspirations, and dreams seem real. You help me to see infinity. You and I—we have become a new reference point of love, joy, happiness, and pain. But most of all, you are my love.

In summary: you have bonded to that special place in my heart which is built upon the rock of friendship, from which we both stand side by side looking out into our infinity of love.

September 22, 1989
I love, love, love, love, love, love, love, love, love, love, love, love You.
—*ALW*

Undated
Dear Ms. Menah,

I'll be back in a few. . . . I love you more and more and more. I am both excited and scared, happy and sad. But definitely, In LOVE, Leonard.

Our relationship created a space of safety and comfort. Feeling loved and affirmed, I wrote a letter to him with my self-affirmation:

December 15, 1989
Dear Leonard,

My self-affirmation may begin something like this. My name is Menah Adeola Eyaside Pratt. I've been told that it means a talented, beautiful gift from God. Although I must realize that even though God is the ultimate that is always within me and is, in fact, me, I must conduct my life in order to manifest the spirits' powers outwardly: to be kind, gentle, and forgiving of life and nature, to accept weakness in others. To be less critical and demanding from others. Patience and unconditional acceptance of others are virtues not easily acquired. Therefore, each day must be dedicated to increasing my tolerance. My life is truly a gift. I must be grateful for each day that is given to me and should live each day as if it were the last. Lived with fervor, excitement, enthusiasm, and passion. There must be balance for when my soul and spirit is weary. I must take time to find the center of peace, quiet, spirit within myself, and rest. As I begin my day (and in my day), let me always remember to be patient, understanding, gentle, kind, and thankful for another chance to live life and to remember that I am Menah Adeola Eyaside Pratt, a talented, beautiful gift from God. I must conduct my life as such.

We had fallen in love with each other. It was mutual and mutually intense. He made me feel beautiful, loved, and quint-essentially feminine. He was an intense flare of energy, setting my heart on fire. He made me breathless and giddy with joy. His nourishment would be complemented by the nurturing bosom of Mother Africa.

SCENE TWO: **Nurtured**

*I*n December 1989, Mama and I traveled to Freetown during the winter break. My father had decided that my mother and I should visit his family, including his mother and three stepsisters in Sierra Leone in West Africa. Mama and I spent three weeks in Freetown, meeting my father's stepsisters—Dorothea, Theodora, and Frederica—and their children for the first time. Papa did not travel with us but orchestrated our visit with his family. We stayed with my father's oldest sister—Aunt Dorothea. Her husband, Uncle Joe, was a minister of finance, and they were very well-off, with a driver, cooks, and maids.

The first morning after we arrived, Aunt Dorothea had her driver chauffeur us to visit Mama Pratt, as everyone called her. I wrote about my visit in a journal entry to Leonard:

December 18, 1989

We went to visit my grandmother and woke her up at 5:00 this morning. She was so happy. Really made my trip just to see the joy we brought her. But where she was living was incredible. A small room a little bigger than my closet with a bed and pots and junk. It is really sad at first but after talking I realized that she really is happy, content, healthy, vibrant, full of energy, and extraordinarily stubborn. Everything must be her way. No deviation, no discussion, or she will raise her voice and shout, and because she is old, she must be respected. But she took us to meet her brother's daughters (my father's cousins) Ola and Yamide, Yamide's husband George, and then to meet her sister and her sister's daughter, M'Beke and Auntie Janette.

I found out more about Eyaside and what it means. Eya means rebirth of a mother and ide means joy.

Everybody says I look so African and so beautiful and so much like Mama Horton, my great-grandmother.

Leonard, I feel so peaceful, so at Oneness. Life here is so laid-back, so calm, and you can see that people are survivors, endurers, and have so much inner strength. There is also so much belief in God and I can feel that it is not the White image. It is Spirit who looks out, is in charge, who gives strength and love. I'm really trying to recapture my comfortability with God that I once had.

We had gone to visit Mama Pratt early in the morning, because she wanted us to go to the cemetery to meet the ancestors and pour libation. During my visit, I learned a great deal about my father's culture and my grandmother. Growing up as a child around my father, I never heard him speak about his sisters or his childhood in Freetown. Although he enjoyed getting the food his mother sent twice a year, he generally seemed irritated with her long monthly aerogram letters that shared detailed updates about her never-ending construction project and always included requests for money. Usually, my father did not read the letters and gave them to my mother to read. My mother then shared the letter with my brother and me. Papa's only real interaction seemed to be ensuring that he sent money to her twice a year—for her birthday and for Christmas. In my journal I wrote a few notes about my growing understanding of my father and my grandmother:

December 20, 1989

You know that many Krio fathers are very strict. Actually, not just fathers, but parents. One cousin was punished for not being home enough by not having any presents on his 15th birthday. Another was punished for staying out too late and was told that he may have to go to boarding school. And oh, how they treat their daughter's boyfriends—openly insulting. "Who is this man? Who are his parents? He looks like a criminal. Don't ever want to see his face again. Never bring him to my house!" with their meeting and seeing the fellow for the first time. Ooh la la!

December 22, 1989

Last night, I began to feel sorry for Mom because she said she was a little bit lonely. So last night we talked a lot about Dad and Grandma and how my grandma may have abandoned him. How Dad has so many mixed feelings toward me. My mom feels Grandma is mean and cruel to her. Perhaps so. She does seem selfish and mean. And she does waste money. This trip is really showing me who God is and how important He is in our lives.

December 25, 1989

Today is Christmas Day. I am finding that I don't like my grandmother very much. She is too mean, too demanding, and says things often that aren't true. She talks so much, so much. Ah, so selfish.

Mama Pratt was a woman with ancient ancestral energy, a woman who spoke with the ancestors, a woman who lived between the living, the dead, and the dying. Her African Wild Woman spirit was complemented by another African Wild Woman—Aunt Dorothea. She was a tall and beautiful woman, with a powerful presence and a commanding voice. She was almost always immaculately dressed in African dresses, with matching headdress. Perhaps because she was an African Wild Woman, she was the only person that Mama Pratt trusted and could essentially get along with. Aunt Dorothea was an extraordinarily kind and generous spirit, but also fierce and forceful. As a deeply spiritual woman who was devoted to her

Christian faith, she woke up early to read her Bible, say her prayers, and sing her hymns.

She took me to watchnight service on December 31. The service was a transformational moment for me. During the altar call, I went forward to the pastor and "dedicated" my life to Christ. I'm not sure at the time I fully processed what I was doing. I was, however, moved by the service and felt a tug to focus on something greater than myself, something close to Love. Reflecting on the spiritual journey, I shared my experience in another entry addressed to Leonard:

January 2, 1990
Dear Leonard,

Today is Tuesday, January 2. So much has happened that I must write down. January 1, at the New Year's Eve Watch service, I dedicated my life to Christ. It made me feel so peaceful. I have felt that I was loving you too much. That I had made you the greatest thing in my life. Oh, I was missing you so much and was so worried about death, dying in the flight over the Atlantic Ocean. My heart was in anguish at the thought of not seeing you again that I felt I must make myself an alliance with something greater than mortal man. Ever since the Voices of Soul [gospel concert at Iowa], I have felt the need to know more about God, to be closer to God, and this trip I feel is my chance.

God has been so good to me. He has surrounded me with Christians and has given me opportunities to become closer to him. Today, I spoke with my cousin who is born-again, and she spoke to me about God, the Bible, and the Holy Spirit. She spoke of the power of the Holy Spirit and the gifts you can receive. How the Holy Spirit is gentle and kind, and how peaceful you feel when you have received the Holy Spirit, and how the Spirit can help you to be patient, more caring, gentle and understanding. My Aunt Dorothea, whom I'm staying with, is so good, has such a pure heart, and is very much a born-again. She gave a very moving testimonial that allowed me to see just how strong her faith in God is and how he is looking after her.

Leonard, she is so strong, tough, yet gentle, kind, loving. Oh, so loving. She has shown me my strengths and my weaknesses as well. She reminds me again and again of my similarities with my father—temper, impatience. Qualities I do not wish to have. I truly feel that if I can make God a more intimate part of my life, He will help me to mold into a better person.

The Color Purple was the book that first began my odyssey. It enabled me to come closer to a new perception of God. No longer did I see him as a White man, but a being who is strong, a kind spirit, a father, someone to go to with a need, and someone who would listen and be there. Oh, I really need, want to, learn more about God. I must go to the Black church every Sunday and try to go to some Bible study. Maybe you can help me with understanding the Bible. Religion is so strong here in Freetown. Christians, Muslims, etc. People here believe in God—a force other than themselves who is in charge of life. There is so much love in Freetown, so much concern for others. Men hold hands, women hold hands, without a second thought. I am beginning to feel much more calmer, peaceful about myself.

The experience at the watchnight service was powerful, and it lit a flame in my spirit. My mother, who was once deeply religious as a child and had obtained a master's degree in religion, was now agnostic. She did not go to the service. It was just my aunt and me. Though I was attending the Unitarian Universalist church in Iowa City, it was merely a job—a place I played piano

on Sunday to earn extra money for college. I didn't feel a deep
spiritual connection in church. But the watchnight experience
was different. I felt that I had experienced the Love of my journal, a kind and caring energy. I summed up my experiences in
Sierra Leone with the January 9, 1990, journal entry:

January 9, 1990

*Thoughts from Sierra Leone: Nigerian airport, ferry,
wash clothes, shortage of gas, survival ethic, belief in
God, New Year's Eve, Godparents, importance of dead,
pull na do [naming ceremony for a new baby] ritual,
snakebite, witchcraft protection, taxi rides, marketplace,
park, beach, quicksand, cookout ceremony, vultures,
dead, cola leaves, nut, generators, baths, lizards, snakes,
disco carnival, house party, wedding party, engagement
ritual, extramarital relationships, tailors, bargaining,
strictness of Creole fathers, college ritual fraternities,
sororities, secret society, devil dancers, caning, independence of school, studying, thieves, warning, Grandma
Pratt, witch, clock, strong, stubborn, bananas, love,
everybody holds hands, babies not cry—comfortable.*

The three weeks in Sierra Leone affirmed my Blackness
and womanness. For the first time in my life, I felt engulfed by
flames of family. In the United States, I rarely spent time with
my mother's siblings or her mother. No one visited us, and I
only remember rare visits to see family: once to Kansas City to
be a flower girl in a cousin's wedding when I was young and
once to meet my grandparents in Los Angeles. In Freetown,
I felt that for the first time in my life, I fit in. I was Krio
like my cousins, and I went where they went, did what they
did, and learned what they learned. I went to parties—house
parties, college parties, engagement parties, and weddings. I
felt embraced by all my aunts, who showered me with love. I

went to the tailor, who handmade new clothes that fit me in beautiful fabric. I bargained in the street for goods; I walked the streets with Mama Pratt; and I learned about the importance of honoring the dead in a cemetery libation ceremony. I learned about the cultural underworld of rituals, initiations, secret societies, witches, and devil dancers.

In Freetown, I connected with the Original Ancient Mother—Mother Africa. I saw love expressed powerfully through friendship and faith. The love between friends and family was tangible and demonstrable with a deep and genuine authenticity I hadn't experienced before. I was embraced by aunts, uncles, cousins, and family friends. Mother Africa was nourishing and feeding me love. It was as if She had been waiting for me all my life—to love me, to affirm me, to show me my value, and to embrace me with Her whole heart. Africa represented the energy of the divine feminine flame of unconditional motherly love, care, and compassion.

When I arrived back in Iowa City, Leonard shared with me the letters he wrote to me, missing me and loving me:

January 1, 1990
Dear most precious Menah,

Hello Menah, I hope that all is well for you. I want to thank you for everything that you have helped me to accomplish this semester. I have tried to contain how I feel but I am admitting that often I have cried, seemingly for no reason. I have so many feelings that they seem to overwhelm me. In your absence, I have missed you tremendously. I wanted to equate this missing you with love, but the two just don't equal. I love you. I simply do and that's it. I don't give all of myself to the relationship because I don't want to . . . ? Well enough for now.
Love,
Leonard.

January 3, 1990

Do I have you? My head says no! But I think for your touch, I cry for you, I miss you, and I love you. I can't help it . . . I do and always will. I am determined to love more and more and more and more . . . Do I want you? My head says no! But in your absence, I feel a void, a loss, like a piece of myself has been ripped out of me. And again, I cry . . . I am determined to love you more and more and more and more . . . Do I miss you? My head says no! Don't miss me till I'm gone. But I'm crazy waiting to see you, to touch you, and to get to know you. I am determined to love you more and more and more and more.

January 6, 1990

Hello Menah:

A moment of thanks is but a lifetime. A moment of love is eternity. A year of love is an eternity of lifetimes. And yet what I must ask myself, what is a moment, eternity, and a lifetime without love? I thank the gods that I shall never know a life without love, because love has somehow reached into that special part of me where in eternity dwells as it does in us all. Loving and being loved by you is both my eternity and my lifetime. A living dream, day by day, moment by moment. Each day, each moment, each lifetime with your love extends my eternity, from the future to the present. The now becomes my eternity. Your love and my love fuse time and space and consciousness into a single kiss or a single hug or a single moment, a moment of eternity, and eternity of moments. All fuse by love, not just my love and your love, but the love that has been passed down the generations, from great-grandparents to grandparents to parents to children who are great-grandparents, grandparents, parents, and children. All at the same time, if viewed from eternity. We have been called by the ages to protect and promote this love, the same love that kept our forefathers full of fervor for freedom, that keeps us loving, living, and learning and will keep our children chosen and chastised with their future, their past, and their present. Funny, I thought I just missed you, when in fact I was consumed in the process deemed my task by the gods. The task is simply to have been loved by you.

His letters reflect the anguish, angst, ambivalence, and all-consuming nature of love. Like Mother Africa, we were nourishment for each other, being sustenance and energy, helping each other experience the intoxicating energy of Love.

SCENE THREE: **Goddess Wisdom**

As Blackwildwoman in the season of germination, I learned important lessons about love. I learned the speechlessness of love when love takes our words and leaves us without. I experienced the out-of-breath sensation when the lungs and heart cannot keep up. I experienced the mutuality of love, simultaneously wanting and seeking each other. I knew what it meant to be desired. But I also learned the temporal nature of romantic love. I began to see love as an energy and a force that moves in the world, connecting disparate and dissimilar people in a special bond. I learned that, as an energy, it can be transformed, mutate, and shift. I learned that love is impacted by other dynamics and susceptible to environmental changes. Its form may or may not remain the same.

As Blackwildwoman I experienced Love in Mother Africa. It was a place, a community, and a culture that embodied

Love. Mother Africa embraced me in her bosom, allowing me to suckle and nurse from Her breast and feel the safety and security of Love. Mother Africa was an eternal flame, providing me with an inextinguishable feeling that I belonged, that I was accepted, and that I was special. I shared the wonderful friendship of cousins hanging out together, partying, laughing, and loving. And I was embraced by my aunts—African Wild Women. Mother Africa motivated me, as I wrote in my journal on June 20, 1990, to *"expand, grow, learn, explore new ideas, areas, and develop more holistically as an individual."* I was developing strong roots—roots that were grounding me and nourishing me for the next stage of my initiation: a metamorphosis.

Reflection Questions

1. What do you remember about your first love or the first time you "fell in love" or felt attracted to another person? What made that relationship special? Was it a flare and temporary or a flame and more permanent?

2. Have you had an experience that ignited a spark or fire in your life and caused you to see your life in a different and unique way? What was the experience, and how did it impact you?

3. Do you remember a trip to another city, state, or country that left an impression? Is there a place in the world you feel called to visit? What is it about that place that piques your interest? How could you create a plan to travel there?

THE SIXTH STAGE—Metamorphosis

AS A SPIRIT-SEED APPROACHES THE END of germination, it is changing. It is no longer a seed. It is no longer dormant. It has been watered and fed; it has roots that are being strengthened for the shoot to stand and rely on for its above-ground destiny. Like a caterpillar, it is undergoing metamorphosis, preparing to emerge from its chrysalis. It is time for the spirit-seed to shed its seed coat through destruction and reconstruction so that a new identity can emerge.

SCENE ONE: **Misconstruction**

My relationship with Leonard began to shift in the summer of 1990, perhaps due in part to our joint exploration of Islam and its differential impact on us. Arriving back from Sierra Leone to Iowa, I brought the memory of the presence of Christians and Muslims together. That memory empowered me to explore Islam, to read the Koran, and to look for connections and intersections between Christianity and Islam. I was drawn to the simplicity and practical lifestyle of Islam. I appreciated the meaning of submitting my will to the will of God. I understood, valued, and tried to practice the disciplined lifestyle of reading the Koran, praying, fasting, and tithing. The disciplined life resonated with my childhood. The tenets of Islam also resonated with Leonard.

In the early 1990s, African Americans interested in Islam often found their way to the Nation of Islam—an African American interpretation of Islam. Minister Louis Farrakhan, who was in his heyday, gave speeches across the country to packed halls. Leonard and I went together, the ushers separating us on entrance into the mosque with men on one side and women on the other. I didn't quite understand the sexism in some of the sermons, and the separation of genders was always a thorn with me. As Leonard became more invested in Islam, he decided that we had to abstain from sex and physical intimacy. And so we did. It was very challenging to me, but I sought to respect his boundary and to see abstinence as part of my spiritual practice. The abstinence, however, foreshadowed a shift in our relationship from an intoxicating infatuation to a distancing separation. My journal captured my feelings about our distancing:

June 26, 1990
Today is Tuesday, June 26, and I feel much better. Yesterday I felt so alone and isolated. It made me think about how affairs begin. If one person has time that they want to devote to the relationship and the partner doesn't, that time may get turned to other endeavors and could possibly lead to meeting another person, and voilà—affair. I felt really scared about talking to him. I think I may be getting too possessive. Tonight, we were to meet at 11 o'clock and we did but there was nothing to say or discuss. But with my girlfriend, it seems like we never run out of stuff to say. Leonard said he would try to make morning and evening time but maybe we should have topics and goals to make the time mutually meaningful. In sum, not a good summer. Not a good relationship.

Though I was reaching the conclusion that the relationship with Leonard was not in a good space, we continued to be together, waiting for the results of the Rhodes Scholar competition. That spring, I was a finalist for the Rhodes Scholar competition to attend Oxford University in England. During the interview for the scholarship, I was asked about my favorite book. I didn't say a profound and well-known classic. I said my favorite book was *Heidi*. *Heidi* was a classic children's novel about the experiences of a young Swiss girl who was sent into the mountains to live with her grandfather. I just resonated with the spirit of Heidi, a little girl like me with a complicated journey, seeking laughter and love. When I was notified that I wasn't accepted, I was a bit disappointed, feeling that I had met all the requirements, but perhaps I should have said a classic novel like *The Old Man and the Sea* instead of *Heidi*.

Since I wasn't going to England, Leonard and I followed through on our plan. We both graduated in August 1990, from the University of Iowa: Leonard graduated with his bachelor's degree in physics, and I graduated with my master's degree in literary studies. Always the steadfast affirmer of my achievement and success, Mama attended my graduation. Again, my father did not. After graduation, Leonard and I moved together to Nashville for him to pursue his master's degree in physics at Fisk while I pursued my law degree and doctorate in sociology at Vanderbilt. The joint law and sociology program at Vanderbilt was an exciting next step for me, as I wrote on June 23, 1990:

> *I'm getting really excited and also nervous about Vanderbilt. I'm so glad that this joint program seems as if it will work out. I think that the possibility of looking at both law and sociology side by side is fantastic. I will have diversity and intermingling of disciplines. I am really excited. Additionally, I will hopefully be creating many options and opportunities for further employment with a BA, MA, JD, and PhD.*

In August 1990, I started law school at Vanderbilt, and Leonard started his master's program at Fisk. For the next two years, we had an uncomfortable and awkward non-intimate relationship. Leonard and I lived in the same apartment building, in separate studio apartments. Because we could not have any sexual intimacy, there was not only a growing physical separation but also an emotional one. We both continued to explore Islam and began to inquire about the process to become an official member. Membership required that we write a letter to the headquarters in the handwriting of Elijah Muhammad, and we were provided a letter that they said was in the original handwriting of Elijah Muhammad. Our letter had to replicate that handwriting. Leonard and I both wrote our separate letters. His letter was accepted; mine wasn't. It was as if the universe was signaling that our relationship was over. Although we continued to discuss marriage from time to time, the flare that fueled our relationship was fading.

As I was struggling in my relationship, Mama was struggling in hers. On July 1, 1990, I wrote to Love and said, *"I went home yesterday and home is hell. Confusing."* My mother wrote me on July 11, 1990, echoing my emotions. Her *"dear daughter"* letter was short but clear: *"Menah, I am telling you this. Now, I am staying with your father to protect the family property and money for you and Dagin—otherwise, I'd retire and leave him. He seems to be getting more and more paranoid. But, I will stay. Hope all goes well with you dear. Love, Mom."*

I had visited my parents, and it was a tough visit. I didn't understand the criticism and anger from my father, but my mother's letter revealed that she, too, was struggling. Papa often appeared to be mentally ill, and it was clear that he was suffering from the trauma of racism. His anger, however, was unnecessarily directed at the one woman who would do almost anything for him. Her letters to me reveal her continued commitment to dance in between both of us. In her October 19, 1991, letter, written by her but signed *"We love you, Mom & Pop,"* she thanks me for sending a photograph of myself and says that she and my father *"both agreed that you are an African queen."*

A few months later, her letter shares more about her busy life of teaching, working on the Bloomington-Normal Black History Project, and working on the apartments. The Black History Project was her pride and joy. She was able to become a part of the local Black community and work with the historical society to archive her interviews of almost one hundred elderly African Americans to validate and affirm their lives.

On January 11, 1992, she wrote:

Dear daughter:

We are busy getting two vacant apartments ready to rent. The two girls whom we took to court moved out on Dec. 21st. I am also busy with the [Bloomington-Normal Black History] project and getting prepared to begin teaching on 1/13/92. It is difficult to get back in the "groove."

I know that you are as usual very busy, but at least send a card or short note to let us know how you are. When we returned home 1/6/92, Dagin had called and left a "Happy New Year," and "Thanks."

Menah, I will have the following schedule this semester:

Monday, 8:00–12:00; 309-438-8503
1:00–5:00 in class

Tuesday and Thursday: 8:00–9:00 same phone as above
9:35–11:00 class
12:35–2:00 class
2:00–3:00 Office hours (same phone as above)

Wednesday 8:00 am–3:00 pm at my office for the project, 30-9-438-2538

Friday 8:00 am to 3:00 pm 309-438-2538.

This will generally be my schedule, except if I am in meetings or out of town. I also have voicemail at each of the phones.

My dear, I wish things had been more pleasant for you when you were here. Perhaps, next time things will be better. I enjoyed you so much. You are my daughter as well as my best friend. I love you so much and am so proud of you. Take care and write when you can.
Love, Mom

I loved her too, and I loved getting letters from Mama. She knew what it meant to be me, a Black girl-woman trying to make it in the world, and she wanted me to always know that I was loved, even in the midst of a home environment that often failed to feel loving. The phone numbers and times she shared were her unwavering effort to create space for our relationship and conversation.

My relationship with her continued to be affirming, even as my relationship with Leonard was significantly changing, taking a turn I could not have anticipated. Over the July 4, 1992, weekend, Leonard went home to Chicago and met a woman who was a high school classmate. She told him she knew they were supposed to get married. Believing her, he called me on the phone from Chicago to tell me he was going to marry her. It was devastating. I had hoped that sacrificing intimacy would strengthen our relationship and prepare us for marriage. Instead, it had created a gulf between us. He tried to bridge the gulf when he returned to Nashville in late July. He said that he had a change of heart and that we should get married, but it needed to be right away. Excited, but also confused, we started to talk about when and how soon, and then we began to argue over who should get the marriage license. The conversation ended abruptly.

I had such anxiety about marrying him. I still loved him deeply but felt I couldn't trust his love that all of a sudden seemed so fickle and so easily shifted in the wind. While our conversation about marriage was on hold and my spirit felt like a ship tossing and turning in a tsunami of emotions, I decided to cling to the only tools I knew to help me survive: the tools of the Pratt Setup of excellence and discipline. Committed to my educational journey, in August 1992, I was starting the third year of the joint law school and doctoral degree program in sociology. I was also beginning the second year of teaching evening speech and grammar classes at the men's and women's prisons for American Baptist College, as an instructor of English. In addition, I was interning at two Nashville law firms. I was constructing my future, unsure of what was around the corner.

SCENE TWO: **Construction**

*I*n addition to my academic and professional life, I had recently found out that I was the owner of an old, dilapidated quadruplex apartment building at 1818 Jefferson Street. I had been a victim of a scheme by a Black Muslim man who orchestrated the sale to me for $74,000 when he had purchased it for $40,000. He acted as if we were partners and co-owners; I did not realize I was the sole owner. When I received the first mortgage bill of $700, which was twice my current rent for the small studio apartment, I realized I had to move into the building.

A friend helped me move and saw the terrible condition of the apartment building. She suggested I contact a man named Jerome. Jerome was working at the same frame shop where she worked. She told me he was from the Bahamas and was a hard worker. An entrepreneur with his own repair business, Exuma Enterprises, he could do carpentry, plumbing, painting, and roofing and could be a great resource to help fix the apartment. I called him, and he agreed to meet me on Saturday, August 1. He knocked at the back door. I had been painting the walls in the unit where I was staying and was covered with paint. When I opened the door, he gave me a very strange look and stared at me for a long time.

Finally, he spoke: "Hello, is Mrs. Pratt home?"

"Yes, I'm Menah."

"I'm looking for Mrs. Pratt. Is your parent home?"

"I'm Menah, Ms. Pratt."

"Oh. Okay. I'm Jerome. I understand you need some work done here."

Slightly insulted and irritated that he didn't think I was the owner, perhaps because I was petite and youthful looking, I became curt and short and said, "Yes."

I gave him a quick tour of the quadruplex. "I just need you to change the locks."

He said, "Are you sure that's all you need?"

"Yes, that's it."

"Okay, lady. When do you want me to do that?"

"As soon as possible."

"I can do it tomorrow."

"Tomorrow is Sunday."

"That's fine. I'll be here."

"9 a.m."

"9 a.m."

I remember feeling a bit uncomfortable with the conversation, perhaps because he had stared at me so long and because he didn't think I could own the building. I didn't know if he was trustworthy, but I was desperate for help and I really needed the locks changed so I could feel safer in the building. Since my friend had recommended him, I felt a bit more comfortable when he showed up the next day.

He came early the next day and said that we needed to go together to buy the locks. Annoyed, I told him he should have brought the locks with him. He said that he didn't know what I wanted and asked if I was willing to ride with him in his truck to get the locks. My instinct was to say no; I felt it was unprofessional to ride around with a workman to buy materials. Yet he persisted, saying the hardware store was just a short ride down the street in the Black neighborhood. Knowing the store was just a short distance away, I reluctantly acquiesced. I needed the locks changed, and he was my only option.

Because it was early on a Sunday morning, the hardware store was still closed when we arrived. He said he knew another one, also in the same community, just a little farther away. When we arrived there, it was also closed. He said he knew for sure that the Home Depot would be open. It was almost thirty minutes away. Sensing my frustration, irritation, and annoyance on the ride to Home Depot, he wanted to engage in small talk. I didn't really want to, but he was congenial and funny. At Home Depot, we debated a variety of different locks, settled on eight, then returned to the apartment. He proceeded to change all the locks, and I resumed my painting project from the day before.

We worked the entire day. At one point, we had a short conversation. He turned to me while I was painting and asked, "Where's your husband?" to which I replied, "Where's your wife?" He replied, "I don't think I have one anymore!" He thought he was divorced, but as I later discovered, he was only separated, not officially divorced. He had seen the paperwork but never followed through with filing it. He also had a young daughter who was eight months old.

At the end of the day, I asked how much I owed, and he said he wasn't going to charge me. He said, "I don't know if you know this or not, but, lady, this building is going to need a lot of work, and you are gonna need much more help than just changing locks." He said he would return the next day and detail the work that needed to be done. I was feeling more comfortable with him and was grateful, as I was having a rough time finding honest workmen to help with renovations.

I had found a roofer who asked for a significant down payment, which I had provided, and now was being unresponsive after having removed more than half of the roof. Jerome, on the other hand, seemed to be different, which I appreciated.

Since neither one of us had eaten all day, out of gratitude, I offered to take him to dinner that evening. He said, "Oh, goody, a date." I firmly told him it was not a date, especially since he did not appear to be of the caliber of man I was looking for. He was a workman, and I was still managing the chaotic relationship with Leonard. The idea of "dating" was not even on the radar of my mind. He said, "Okay," as if to pacify my thinking, but I could tell he was flirting with me. He was intriguing and charming in a unique, boyish way. He was about five years older than me, five foot eleven, with a beautiful, enchanting Bahamian accent and dark brown skin. I felt like he had a strong and powerful spirit. He lived just across the street and told me he would be back after showering and getting ready for our "date."

As he left to get ready, he walked down the stairs of the quadruplex where he had been working on the second floor. Barely halfway down the long set of stairs, the front doorbell rang. It was Leonard. Since the door wasn't locked, Leonard had opened the door and started to climb the stairs just as Jerome was descending. Their paths crossed as I was still at the top of the stairs. I awkwardly introduced them; Jerome left, and Leonard came in to talk.

Confirming my suspicions that the gulf could not be bridged, Leonard had come to tell me that he had decided not to marry me after all. Our relationship was over. In September, he married his high school classmate. I later told my girlfriend the crossing of the two men on the stairs felt like a changing of the guard. I realized then that I could cry over Leonard, or I could go on a "date" with the new workman.

And what a wonderful date it was—starting with dinner. At one point, I said to him, "What's your real name?"

He answered, "Jerome."

I said, "You don't look like a Jerome." I just had a feeling his name wasn't Jerome. His attitude, persona, and demeanor didn't seem to match with the name Jerome.

He laughed and said, "My friends call me O.B."

I said, "No, that's the name of a tampon. What's your real name?"

He said, "Obadiah." And since that day, I have always called him Obadiah or Ob (one syllable).

He told me he was named after a book and prophet in the Bible. Obadiah is the shortest book in the Bible. It is an Old Testament book, and in the book, Obadiah shares a vision and oracle of destruction for the nation of Edom and retribution for sins committed. It is a book full of judgment and condemnation, with verses that begin with "You should not have": "You should not have gloated"; "You should not have rejoiced"; "You should not have boasted"; and "You should not have looted." The prophet Obadiah, in addition to his admonition of Edom in the book of Obadiah, also appears in 1 Kings 18, hiding one hundred prophets to protect them. In the Bible, Obadiah is a faithful and loyal servant of God.

The Obadiah I met in Nashville was born in the small rural community of Forbes Hill, Exuma, Bahamas. He was raised by a single mother in poverty. His mother was harsh, demanding, and not loving or affectionate. In fact, once, when she decided to punish him for stealing money, she took a hammer and hit each and every one of his fingers. His mother had ten children, by five different men. She was never married, and in that small island culture, the children were known as "bastard children."

Like me, Obadiah had a rough childhood. There were parts of our experiences in life where we had common ground. Overcoming incredible odds, he had miraculously found his way to the United States to study mechanical engineering at Tennessee State University in Nashville. Overwhelmed when he realized mechanical engineering was much more than "fixing cars," he struggled to adjust to American culture and higher education. Dropping out of college, he found himself married, separated, and the father of a young girl. After a period of homelessness, he had recently moved into a small apartment across the street from the quadruplex. He was trying to get his life together by working at the frame shop and hoping to go back to school and finish his degree.

After dinner, he asked if I wanted to go to a movie. Since we'd had such a delightful time at dinner, I thought, *Why not?* So we chose *Boomerang* with Eddie Murphy, a romantic comedy. It was a lighthearted, fun, and funny movie. We both enjoyed it. After our "date," he took me back to my apartment. He came in with me to finalize plans for working on the quadruplex the next day. After we finalized the plans, he got ready to leave.

He had been carrying around a small blue duffel bag when I met him and even when we were out. As he prepared to leave, he almost forgot to take his bag. Curious, I asked him, "What's in that bag?" He slowly unzipped the bag, pulled out a bundle wrapped in a black cloth, and began to unwrap it. As he unwrapped the bundle, a small gun appeared. He handed it to me. Horrified, I instantly backed away. I had never seen a gun. "Why in the world are you carrying a gun around? Where are the bullets?"

He slowly dug around in the bag and pulled out four bullets. I had never seen bullets before either. He said, "There is a man I am looking for. He took my property; he stole my property from me. If I see him, I am going to kill him. But you can have my gun tonight. You are in an unsafe neighborhood, and this will protect you." I couldn't believe he wanted to protect me and leave his gun. It was paternalistically charming, but realistically disturbing. The gun unnerved me, as had his attitude and determination to commit murder.

I said, "Keep your gun. I will be so nervous that I will shoot myself instead of the intruder. Take your gun. I will call you if I need you." We laughed, and he wrapped his gun back in the bundle, put it back in his blue duffel bag. As he prepared to leave, I think he wanted to kiss me, but I was not ready for that, and he sensed it. He awkwardly hugged and said good-bye. He agreed to return the next day after he finished working at the frame shop.

After he left, I thought to myself, *An intriguing and strange dude.* It was like he was from another world, an ancient world of prophets and guns. His protective paternalism was endearing and irritating, all at the same time. I felt that I was independent and strong, and I knew how to take care of myself. At the same time, he had me wondering if perhaps I was naive about the dangerousness of the neighborhood. Knowing that he lived close gave me a bit of security, even though his possession of the gun was unnerving.

The next day, Monday, I went to work at the law firm where I was doing an internship. I sat down at my desk at 8:00 a.m., and I heard a Voice. The Voice said, "This is the man you are meant to marry."

I said, "What?" to no one and nothing in particular.

I don't even remember where the Voice was coming from. It was as if the Voice came out of thin air. I remember the Voice repeated itself like a mantra. "This is the man you are meant to marry." It was relentless.

I tried to argue. "What? This man? He thinks he's divorced, has a daughter, hasn't finished college after ten years of trying only to realize the difference between an automotive mechanic and a mechanical engineer. He is not what I am looking for, is not what I've been praying for, and is not what I want."

The Voice was insistent: "This is the man you are meant to marry."

"Him?"

"Yes, him."

This was the first time in my life I heard the Voice of Love. It was a clear, unequivocal message from the spirit world. A conversation a few days later with Obadiah provided confirmation. Obadiah explained that the reason for his intense staring when we first met was that he had a dream several months before. In that dream, a woman appeared. He told me that the woman looked like me. When he saw me, he said I was literally the woman of his dreams.

Obadiah was not the man of my dreams. He was as different and dissimilar from me as I could find; it was like a fairy tale. He was the carpenter, a man down on his luck. I was the homeowner, almost-lawyer, future-scholar sociologist. He was my workman, and I had hired him to work for me. How could he be the man I was meant to marry? He didn't fit the traditional polished and professional image I had formed in my mind for a partner. He was an old-time prophet returned to the world. He was interested in me, and he began to pursue me relentlessly.

He showed up every day the following week after his regular job to work on the quadruplex, doing plumbing, carpentry, painting, and even some electrical. He was fixing it up, making it safe for me and, perhaps, us. Toward the end of that week, the long-lost roofer appeared, asking for another deposit. Obadiah was working at the quadruplex and confronted him. He told the roofer not to "mess with his woman." I didn't even know I was his woman. His protective paternalism continued to rear its cultural head. Noticing that I was equivocating in our developing relationship, Obadiah asked me one day if I had heard the Bob Marley song with the refrain "waiting in vain for your love." I told him I had. He said, "Don't make me wait in vain for your love. I will not." It was clear that he would not wait for me in vain.

I needed to address my ambivalence about him, but we'd only known each other about a month. Still reeling from my heartache with Leonard, I wasn't ready for another relationship. Although Obadiah was in the midst of his separation and not-yet-finalized divorce and child visitation, he was impatient, almost like a dog eagerly wanting to play fetch. I was the catch, and he was not going to wait for me "to get myself together." I had to decide to either get on the fast-moving train of this relationship or stay at the station. The train was about to depart; its horn was bellowing and blowing, signaling its impending departure. Not wanting to be left behind and miss a potentially new and exciting journey, I jumped on board for the ride, not knowing the hills and valleys that were waiting around the bend.

We quickly became intimate and began to spend almost every day together. He was thirty years old and a mature, gentle lover. He was thoughtful and sensitive to my needs and desires. He was also affectionate and romantic, leaving love notes, holding my hand, snatching kisses, and giving hugs. He was sexy looking, smelled good, and was fun and funny to be around. But it was not all roses and red wine with him.

Obadiah was a complex and complicated spirit; he could not be categorized; and he didn't fit in a box. He was the antithesis of being defined. He was a bundle of confusing energy: hot one day, cold the next; fun and interesting one day, silent and brooding the next; calm and caring one day, selfish and self-centered the next; loving and gentle one day, harsh, blunt, angry, and impatient the next. Sometimes the mood swings were all in one day: he was one person in the morning, another in the afternoon, and a completely different energy in the evening, ranging from jovial and fun to irritable, agitated, and frustrated. I never knew which spirit was going to show up. Sometimes it was the angry, judgmental Obadiah of the Bible. Other times, the peaceful and protective Obadiah who hid prophets in a cave showed up. He was wrestling with his own demons and on his own initiation journey. He was like the king in the archetypical journey—a king on a spiritual journey.

Though he was wild, rugged, raggedy, and rough around the edges, there was a strong energy that drew me toward him. I was attracted to his ambition, his creativity, his persistence, and his determination to achieve. He was an extremely hard worker, working from sunup to sundown. I admired his commitment to his craft, to quality and perfectionism. He was a jack-of-all-trades with an arrogance that was charming and irritating all at the same time. He had a very powerful presence and a wonderful loving and kind spirit on many days. More importantly, he seemed to be developing a very deep love for me. I was also developing a deepening love for him, and it seemed that the universe had thrown us together on the train, even though we didn't know where we were going or how long the ride would be.

In October, we traveled to Champaign-Urbana, Illinois, with another couple to hear Awadagin perform at Krannert Performing Arts Center. Awadagin had won the Naumburg International Piano Competition in May. He was the first African American to win that piano competition. As part of that prize, he was touring around the country and world playing concerts. Winning the competition was the start of his professional career as a classical musician. It was almost validation of the Pratt Setup. It had worked for my brother. The benefits of the Pratt Setup enabled him to have a lifestyle of independence from the "system." My parents were at the concert in Champaign, and after the concert, they briefly met Obadiah with my other friends. It was their first introduction to him, and the meeting was short and cordial.

I reflected on that trip about the similarities between Obadiah and my father. He, like my father, was an immigrant from the African diaspora, and as Black immigrants, they shared some similarities: a fierce and fiery determination to succeed, a willingness to work extremely hard, and a commitment to be independent from the "system." They both had no-nonsense attitudes. Unfortunately, they had both been raised in poverty by single mothers who were often abusive and unloving; they also shared paternalistic and sexist ideas about women that were deep-seated and culturally embedded, and they would bubble up from time to time.

Still, a few short weeks later, Obadiah and I started talking about our future. He had an entrepreneurial spirit and was tired of working at the small frame shop down the street. He wanted his own frame shop and art gallery. He said he needed my help; he wasn't good with finances, budgets, and managing money. He asked if I would be willing to go into business with him. With apprehension about the time and financial pressure of helping to run a business, as I was still in law and graduate school and teaching at the prisons through American Baptist College, I, nevertheless, consented. He moved into the quadruplex with me and began to renovate one of the vacant units to be Exuma Frame Shop and Art Gallery. As co-owners, I was the business and financial manager, and he was technical and artistic manager. He cut mats and glass and made beautiful frames for prints. I was ordering supplies, writing a business plan for a small business loan to help finance the inventory, working on marketing materials, and reconciling transactions. It was a consuming lifestyle, but we were doing it together.

Marriage began to seem like the logical next step: we were living together in the quadruplex, and we had a business together. I hadn't yet had the falling-in-love feeling with Obadiah. I knew what that feeling was. I didn't have it, but I also knew that when I did have that feeling with Leonard, it didn't last anyway. What I did have was the Voice that told me that Obadiah was the man I was meant to marry.

There appeared to be no obstacles to our marriage because his divorce had been finalized. The divorce decree included child support obligations and a visitation schedule. His daughter had turned one year old in January of 1993. The visitation schedule was weekly on Wednesdays, every other weekend, and particular holidays. I was helping to raise and care for his daughter during her visits. She was a beautiful and sweet child who was well-mannered and fun to play with. The weekends with her, however, were exhausting. Obadiah was often busy with the frame shop, leaving much of the caregiving to me. I was also paying his child support, as the frame shop was not making enough money to cover the monthly support and the arrears. I just accepted these responsibilities as the cost of the bargain—a bargain that was about to become a marriage.

Consistent with his prophetic name, Obadiah was very embedded in the Christian religion and his cultural traditions, where the man needed to ask a woman's father for permission to marry her. I told him my parents did not have the authority to determine who I married. I was my own woman, and I had been independent from them financially for years. Given the complicated relationship with my father, I couldn't even envision how he would respond to being asked to give permission for me to get married. Obadiah, nonetheless, felt it was important to let them know. We decided, as a compromise, he could ask for a blessing.

SCENE THREE: **Destruction**

*O*badiah and I visited my parents for the July 4 weekend in 1993 and stayed at my parents' house. Summoning all the courage we had, Obadiah and I walked down the short hallway to my parents' bedroom, accompanied by my mother. My father was sitting at the desk. We gingerly knocked on the bedroom door to get his attention, and then Obadiah spoke:

"Dr. Pratt, I wanted to talk to you about your daughter."

"Yes?"

"My intention is to marry her, and I wanted to ask for your blessing."

Long pause.

"I am not the pope. I don't give blessings."

Dumbfounded, we just stood there for a minute. We didn't know what to do. He went back to his papers, and we left his room. We tried to process his response. We didn't know if it was good or bad. The next day, my parents, Obadiah, and I went to Lake of the Woods in Champaign-Urbana for the day. We all seemed to have a good time, boating, walking, talking, and eating. Later that evening, my father and I were speaking in the kitchen. He offhandedly asked me if there was anything I wanted to tell him about Obadiah. I wasn't sure what he was asking, but I hadn't told him that Obadiah was divorced and had a child. I thought in the spirit of being honest and transparent, I would share that information about his background.

I could not have anticipated his negative response. He became extremely angry. He aggressively confronted Obadiah about his marriage and divorce. Dissatisfied with the answers, in a rage, my father told us to leave his house that night. I don't know if he felt that Obadiah was dishonest in not sharing that information initially, or if he felt that I deserved more than someone who was divorced with a child. Regardless, at midnight, Obadiah and I drove back to Nashville.

The next day, my parents called me and invited me to meet them a few days later in Chicago to talk about the relationship and the issues that had been raised in the heated conversation. They occasionally took trips to Chicago to get away from the stress of the apartments, and they invited me to join them for this trip. Still ambivalent about the invitation, especially after my father's actions, I wrote them this letter on July 6, 1993:

July 6, 1993
Dear Mama and Papa (but especially Papa),

I am not exactly sure what to say. I know that I feel uncomfortable with the position that I feel that I have been placed in. So, I am just going to talk in writing since I communicate better in written words than spoken words. For me, spoken words lose their power in the heat of emotions. So, I will write and attempt to express some thoughts and feelings.

What am I doing, what do I want from life? I believe I must actualize potential through interdisciplinary mastery. Not only me, but everyone's challenge is to actualize potential. I feel most fulfilled by experiencing all of my possibilities. So, in life, I strive to do many things and to do them all well, though I do not feel compelled to be number one at all or any of those many things. I only strive to satisfy my expectations of my ability given the whole scope of my life I want to be a great role model and encourage and show and help others to reach their potential as well.

For me, there is much more to life than a career. Having a career is important to me, but so are other elements. I cannot imagine believing that I will have fulfilled my potential as a woman without having and raising children, which I believe is one of life's ultimate challenges. I don't want to be lonely and alone. I want to share my life with someone. And I am willing to sacrifice for that. But I will have my cake and eat it. How can I even begin to reach my potential if I already accept barriers and limits? Limits cause you to short-circuit your goals and potentials, and I will not do that. I will succeed and I will be successful in all that I do. I know that I will not fail, for there is no such thing to me as failure. There are obstacles, challenges, weaknesses, but I don't know failure and I don't believe in failure.

If Obadiah is truly not welcome in the house, I have no choice but to respect that. It is not my house, and in that house, I really have no rights and no say-so. I know that my actions are not without repercussions. I am not certain of the repercussions of this action, but I do intend to marry Obadiah after my clerkship, in two years. I hope that action and the present decision does not preclude me from having a meaningful relationship with you, Papa, but I have always tried to do the right thing. I believe telling you was the right thing and I believe that my decision to stay with Obadiah is the right thing, and I'm willing to accept those consequences. I can only hope that those consequences do not include exclusion from you.

Papa, I know that you will say, "Well, you have your mother," and "I have no daughter." But I am your daughter and will always be. You cannot do anything to sever that biological tie. Moreover, you cannot sever the emotional tie which creates so much tension between us. I want you to be in my life, and I want you to accept Obadiah as he is, with flaws, but strengths as well. But life is short and full of struggles, pain, loss, and death, and in the time that I am here, I must do what I believe in my heart is right, and that is continuing to pursue my relationship with Obadiah. I believe telling you about him, however awkward and with poor timing, was also right.

My heart is clean, and I am prepared to move on. I cannot be persuaded to leave Obadiah and I will not sever the ties and bonds that we are building. My conscience is clear. My decision is made. And I can move on, with clean hands, clean heart, and a clear conscience.
—Menah

This letter is reminiscent of the letter I wrote in 1984, almost ten years earlier. That letter was an attempt to assert my wildness and independence. Now, at age twenty-six, I was still trying to express myself and speak up for myself. I did visit my parents in Chicago, and during that visit, my father gave me a scientific marriage questionnaire of factors to consider before getting married: compatibility with family values, financial security, education, and baggage from prior relationships. The questionnaire encouraged reflection about the implications of divorce and whether the person would "go for the jugular." Though relevant with meaningful issues, it was irrelevant because I had heard the Voice.

In retrospect, I have thought about the questionnaire, the reference to baggage, and the implications of divorce. Obadiah did have baggage. His prior marriage was baggage, and I was paying his child support and attorneys' fees and helping him navigate his complex relationship with his ex-wife and her new boyfriend. In addition to the "past relationship baggage," Obadiah and I had different levels of education, and he had less financial security than I did, even though my own financial status had been compromised with the quadruplex mortgage, the frame shop loans, and supporting his child support. The differences in our financial and education status would have lasting impact on our marriage, but I never thought he would "go for the jugular." Another significant challenge with Obadiah was his tendency toward violent and reckless behavior, reflected initially by his blue duffel bag and gun. As a condition to marriage, I demanded that he sell the gun. I didn't want a gun in our marriage and relationship. Reluctantly, he agreed to get rid of the gun. A year later, when he was involved in a violent altercation, I would be grateful he no longer owned the gun.

We were on opposite ends of a spectrum, but fate had brought us together on the train. The engine and caboose had met in the middle, and our blended train was off and running.

I was the woman of his dreams, and he was the man of the Voice. Nothing and no one could derail our relationship. My mother, sensing my commitment to Obadiah, responded to my letter as she had my entire life with an affirming letter focused on my happiness:

July 12, 1993
My dear daughter:

I cannot write as eloquently as you can, but I can write passionately when it comes to you. It really pierced my heart to observe you in so much pain over the weekend. After much thought, I have decided that it is your life. You have done a fine job of bringing yourself this far in higher education. You've planned, organized your life, made sacrifices, worked hard, and if you believe Obadiah and you are meant to be together and you believe things will work out, then I say, "Follow your plan." I wish the best for you and believe you will both "be well." Know that I trust you and want desperately for you to be happy. I hope to see you in Chicago when Dagin performs and perhaps when he is here in Bloomington-Normal to perform in September. Be in touch to let us know your plans regarding Chicago and B/N performances. I look forward to coming to visit you this fall.

Do take care and say "hello" to Obadiah. He appears to be a hard worker, talented in many ways, and I think that after two years you'll be all set for marriage. I love you dear!

Note: I believe in time your father will come around—just don't worry.
Love, Mom

There was no way I couldn't worry. I was worried, but I also felt good about the direction of my life. I was making good progress in my joint degree program. I graduated with my master's degree in sociology in May 1993; Mama, of course, attended my graduation in May. Papa did not. Completing my third year of law school, I accepted a prestigious one-year federal court of appeals judiciary clerkship with Chief Judge Sam Ervin III in Morganton, North Carolina, beginning in September 1994. I was finishing coursework for my doctorate and starting to think about my dissertation. The frame shop was slowly growing and gaining customers. I was becoming a savvier businesswoman and entrepreneur. Obadiah had returned to school to finish his bachelor's degree. As he was never a strong student and not able to use a computer, I helped him with his written assignments, and he would be graduating soon. As a couple, we were doing well. We were ready to reconstruct our lives together.

SCENE FOUR: **Reconstruction**

*O*badiah and I got married two months later without the knowledge or blessing of my family on September 18, 1993. Since Obadiah was not close to his mother or family at the time, the wedding was just about us, our love, and commitment to each other. We didn't plan the wedding day well, so it didn't feel as special and sacred as it could have. Spontaneously, we chose a Saturday when the pastor and his wife were available, the church was available, and Obadiah's eighteen-month-old daughter was available for her weekend visitation. Each of us asked a friend to be present as witnesses. We only had a week to plan the event.

On our wedding day, there were several ill-fitting puzzle

pieces. I was wearing a beautiful kente cloth dress that Aunt Dorothea had made for me in Freetown. I had wanted to honor my African heritage, but it wasn't an African wedding dress; it was just an African dress. Though Obadiah also wore an African outfit, it was borrowed from the best man and not a wedding suit. Not only were we not in matching outfits, but we were also in mismatched outfits. Our witnesses also looked mismatched in colors that were not coordinated at all. We were a ragged-looking, half-put-together wedding party.

Another misfit was our vows. I had spent time writing our vows because I wanted us to say our own vows and not the traditional "obey" vows. That was a point of contention for us. Obadiah wanted the traditional vows, given his conservative Christian upbringing. Even though we were able to say the vows I wrote for us and that we had discussed, the conservative pastor incorporated many traditional vows into the ceremony.

The final misfit was the lack of community and support. I remember standing outside the church—alone—waiting to walk up the aisle of an empty church, alone. I reminded myself standing outside alone that the Voice was with me and would honor my obedience. It was a lonely and isolating feeling, though, standing outside by myself, then walking up the aisle of a completely empty church to "Here Comes the Bride," played by the pastor's wife on the piano. I walked up the aisle to Obadiah, who was standing there with his daughter.

After the short ceremony, everyone went back to business as normal. Our friends went back to their lives, and Obadiah and I went back to the apartment, changed our clothes, and went back to work. There was no honeymoon, no reception, no dinner, and no celebration. We settled into our married life: running the frame shop and having weekend and weekday visitation with his young daughter. I was still going to school, working on my PhD, and teaching at the prison. We were living our secret married life—a marriage destined by the universe and seemingly destined for eternity.

The tools of the Pratt Setup—excellence and discipline—were still guiding my life. In December 1993, I finished law school, and I took the bar exam in February 1994. As a graduation gift to myself for completing law school, I decided to visit Sierra Leone in March 1994 for a few weeks. My father was not supportive: he was worried about the impending civil war since Mama Pratt's letters often referenced rebel fighting. Yet Mother Africa was a flame in my heart that could not be extinguished. Against his wishes, I went to Freetown.

While in Sierra Leone, in the womb of Mother Africa, I was again fed and nurtured by the African Wild Women spirits of Mama Pratt and Aunt Dorothea, as well as my other aunts and cousins. I helped plan Mama Pratt's eightieth birthday party and felt more connected to the ancestors on our ritual cemetery visit. During my visit, I wrote a letter to Obadiah in my journal sharing my thoughts about being initiated as a woman, mother, and wife and contemplating the idea of having my own children:

March 1994
Obadiah,

I can feel God transforming me into a woman. I'm going to be an amazing woman, mother, and wife. I can feel it. I just need to stay conscious of God's will for me and follow it. I have been trying to think about what I have gained from this trip. I think it is just a renewed perspective of where I am now in my life and where I want to be, and where I want us to be. I can feel myself changing into a woman. I need to work on being more assertive, aggressive; but also looking more mature, womanly. I realize appearance, though often superficial, is also important, and if I want to become a particular person, I need to act that way. So, no more young-child looking or acting. I'm a woman now! This is part of the initiation I must experience in preparation for motherhood.

This is consistent with the initiation journey where the woman assumes a new role and responsibility. In the archetypal experience, as part of a marriage, there is a shift of identity, and a woman often receives a different level of knowing and sensing. As part of my doctoral work in sociology, I was learning about Black feminism and exploring issues of race, class, and gender. My journal entries to Love and God reflect this growing awareness of my emerging new identity:

April 26, 1994
Love,

As I read Black Feminist Thought *and feel myself connected to Black female intellectual circles, I am forced to confront my own ideas about motherhood,*

Black women, loneliness, and isolation. Why I am so driven? Upbringing, competition, striving for excellence, and perfection. What am I driven toward? God. Why am I driven toward that thing? Angel. I am driven to fulfillment of Self and all my possibilities.

May 9, 1994
Dear God,

Yet another day to praise you and try to come closer to you and the power you represent and epitomize so that it may actualize and manifest itself in me. I am trying to keep you at the center of my life so that you can govern and control and lead me. I feel myself on the brink of greatness, of actualizing an almost discovered part of me. This dissertation is so challenging, intellectually,

*spiritually, psychologically, and emotionally. I feel I'm
at the height of my capacities as Menah and it's almost
frightening. I feel simultaneously pushed and pulled both
toward and away from my goal. Oh, my goodness, it's
exhilarating and breathtaking all at once.*

*I know that I must continue to walk side by side with
you because you will give me the focus, the discipline,
and the perseverance to understand, rise, interpret, and
analyze, and you will explain a new way of seeing and
understanding the complexity of my existence and of
yours within me.*

*I feel so challenged to stay the course, to actualize, to
be a mother, to practice law, to feel out and fill out myself
with your energy in me. Oh, my goodness, I could almost
burst. As I thank you, praise you, I must also pray for
my father. I ask that you soften his heart and lessen the
sinews, make them pliable with love and understanding,
allowing your love to embrace all of us. God, it's 9:00
p.m. and I'm in church feeling and searching for that connection, strength, guidance that I need to succeed. I sorely
need a connection to young Black female intellectuals.*

Beginning to work on my dissertation, I was committed to
an interdisciplinary dissertation that combined issues of law and
sociology and addressed issues of race and gender. The universe
sent an ideal subject for analysis and exploration. As part of the
debate in the early 1990s about the Black male crisis, Black men
were referred to as an endangered species, given the increase in
homicides, dropout rates, imprisonment, and unemployment.
While I was sympathetic to the Black male crisis, I noticed a
disturbing pattern in some of the discourse that seemed to blame
Black mothers and Black girls for the Black male crisis.

There was one particular legal case that caught my attention. The Detroit School Board had decided to create three

all-male single-sex elementary schools to address the Black male crisis. The justification for these schools included language that implicated women as mothers and teachers, and girls as classmates. A Black mother, Shawn Garrett, and her daughter Crystal filed a lawsuit—with the assistance of the National Organization for Women Legal Defense Fund and the American Civil Liberties Union—against the Detroit School Board, alleging that the schools discriminated on the basis of sex. An eventual legal settlement allocated 136 seats for girls, out of the total of 560 seats. Only 36 girls enrolled after weeks of protests by the Black community that encouraged Black girls to not attend the schools and to "stay at home."

In my research, I wanted to answer the question "Where are the Black girls?" to understand the dynamics influencing the marginalization and minimization of Black women and girls in the Detroit Male Academy debate. My research involved reviewing legal documents, Detroit School Board memos, American Civil Liberties Union memos, and National Organization of Women memos addressing the issue of whether little Black girls should be able to attend schools that had been created as single-sex schools for Black boys. I was exploring issues of race, class, sexism, Black nationalism, and Black male sexism. I wanted to help little Black girls have a place and space in the world; I didn't want Black girls to have to "stay at home," as some of the placards read at the marches in support of the all-male academy in Detroit. I wanted Black girls to be able to live an above-surface life and not a below-ground existence.

I was writing not only for the little Black girls of Detroit but for my own little Blackwildgirl. As I began to write about the story of the Black girls and women in Detroit, I experienced a crowning, ascending to a new role as a wife, stepmother, scholar, and evolving Black feminist. My crowning was symbolized by a visit to the White House and meeting President and Mrs. Clinton on June 12, 1994. Awadagin had been invited to perform a piano recital for President and Mrs. Clinton. My father decided that my mother and I should go, and so we tagged along as my brother's guests. I got autographs from President and Mrs. Clinton, Whoopi Goldberg, Vernon Jordan, Colin Powell, Marian Wright Edelman, and Hillary's mother. I also saw the Blue Room, Green Room, and Red Room and a silver vase for John Adams.

This visit to the White House was the first of three. My brother performed twice for President and Mrs. Obama. Each time my mother and I went as my brother's guests. Each time was thrilling and fun. I always felt how special it was for my mother to have come from such a humble background and using outhouses to being a guest of the president of the United States at the White House. At the same time, as her daughter I was emerging as a Black woman into new places and onto new stages, meeting powerful leaders and people. My roots were propelling me above the surface.

I was on the path toward fulfilling a childhood dream to be just like Mary McLeod Bethune. In the personal statement I wrote for the American Association of University Women dissertation fellowship application, I share my admiration of her and my goals to be a role model like her:

> When I was about seven years old, I read the "Biography of Mary McLeod Bethune," and decided I wanted to be just like her . . . an educator. . . . As I began working on my dissertation, I read Black Feminist Thought by Patricia Hill Collins and felt as if I had entered a whole new world. Reading Deborah King, bell hooks, Angela Davis, Pauli Murray, Paula Giddings, and many others, has been an emotional roller-coaster, yet wonderfully thrilling and inspirational. It has forced me to examine my own experiences and to critique my responses to those experiences as a black woman, not just from a

racial perspective, but from a gender perspective as well. Working on my dissertation has confirmed my desire to be an educator, to be able to share with others the wonders, the knowledge, and the joy that I have experienced in my academic career. . . . Having occupied the role of lawyer, judicial clerk, and professor, . . . I know that I must continue to be a role model for other women as an educator in the tradition of Ms. Bethune, nurturing a desire for knowledge. This dissertation, then, represents my commitment to education and knowledge as tools to address racial, gender, and class inequality.

SCENE FIVE: **Goddess Wisdom**

*T*he Blackwildgirl initiation journey is about the recovery of one's power as a woman and our original instinct. It is about recovering the crown that was removed, symbolizing the part of ourselves and ways of being that were taken from us in the bargain without our consent. This process requires an initiation journey in the underworld of our psyche, exhuming our buried and sacred self. Shortly before I got married in September 1993, I began to find the part of myself compromised in the bargain: Blackwildgirl. She emerged unexpectedly in a letter I wrote to Obadiah where I introduced him, and perhaps myself, to Blackwildgirl. I wrote the letter after the July visits with my parents and before we got married in September. I wanted him to know that I was still committed to him, to the relationship, and to getting married. I also wanted him to know about my needs and wants. In this letter, I refer to my Blackwildgirl spirit by my middle name, Eyaside:

Obadiah,

I want to be with you and I hope you want to be with me as I am, the good and bad. There are two Menahs: One is a tough, hard, rough, intolerable, unbending, hard-nosed disciplinarian, and a perfectionist, and the other is a soft, sensitive, emotionally vulnerable, gullible, and naïve girl. So, these two intermingle and exchange themselves and appear as me at different times. So, know that the soft, delicate, incredibly fragile part desperately needs you, needs you to love, care, and nurture me. I need your physical contact, your hugs, kisses, caresses, letters. The soft part of me is also spiritual and it is through her that God appears and when I become an instrument and His angel. The soft part of me—Eyaside—is mostly me, pretty weak, dependent. To overcome that, I got Menah Adeola together—"the tough sister"—standing out, tough, strong, hard, insensitive, defensive, protective.

So, there are two me's and I'm trying to reconcile them and through God's grace, I will. So often I feel so much pressure, responsibility, and burden, like I'm holding up mountains and pushing mountains toward God. So, I have to be tough. I can't afford to break. Too much is literally riding on me. The spirit at times gets weak and tired, but I forge on to God. So, Obadiah, that's all for now.

I love you very much. Menah

I was introducing Obadiah to Menah Adeola Eyaside Pratt, Blackwildwoman and Blackwildgirl. I was reminding myself and him of my identity and of my needs: my need for love, physical contact, hugs, kisses, caresses, and letters and my need for Love, unconditional acceptance, and affirmation. The spirit had pushed up through the womb-like darkness to birth itself into the world. Piercing the heavy soil of life required shedding what was no longer helpful or needed. The Voice had sent me Obadiah, but I wanted to make sure that Obadiah knew that I was committed to him and that I hoped he was committed to all of me, including the me that was the little Black girl of the Pratt Setup, who still needed to be loved.

In looking for the love from my father that was not given, I was searching for that same "fatherly love" in other relationships. Unwittingly and unconsciously, I married a man in Obadiah who was much like my father. In addition to their similar cultural and religious background and upbringing, they shared a moody and brooding spirit, and dependence on alcohol to numb the areas of frustration and disappointment in their lives.

Over the many years that Obadiah and I were together, I not only realized how similar to my father he was but also how much he exemplified the qualities of the biblical prophet Obadiah. Like the biblical prophet, he was loyal and protective, but also judgmental and condemning. These qualities appeared through the many tests and trials that were part of my continuing initiation journey with him as my husband. As his wife, I became part of another bargain, for marriages are bargains, bargains that we will give love and we will also receive it, never knowing the duration, reality, or cost of the bargain when we jump on the whistling, speeding train. I was about to start experiencing the costs of the bargain.

One cost of the bargain I had not anticipated related to Obadiah's blue duffel bag—the duffel bag of the gun. Though he had gotten rid of the bag and the gun, he had not gotten rid of his intentions and passions with those who had "done him wrong." In his mind, if someone "did him wrong," there needed to be judgment, punishment, and retribution. Unfortunately, that mindset led to traumatizing engagements with the criminal justice system.

On the morning of my law school graduation on May 13, 1994, my always-present-at-graduation mama came to the house for us to leave together. My father, as usual, did not attend. While Mama and I were finalizing our plans for the day, Obadiah mysteriously said that he had an errand to run and would be "right back." While he was gone, the police showed up at the house asking for him. I told them he was not home. The police did not explain the reason for their visit, only asking that he follow up with them when he returned. I was thankful that Mama didn't know that the police had shown up and she was still upstairs in the apartment. I just told her it was customers. Feeling anxious about the police and Obadiah's long absence of almost an hour, I could only hope he would come home in time for the graduation. Mama continued to ask where he was, and I couldn't answer her question. We were both almost at our wits' end when he finally appeared only minutes before Mama and I were leaving the house. Frustrated and irritated, I asked him where he had been. He said that he had to "take care of some business." He did not want to elaborate, even after I shared that the police had come to the house.

A year later, there was a warrant for his arrest, and I learned that Obadiah was charged with aggravated assault and shooting a BB gun at a man's throat. Obadiah had loaned the man some money and hadn't been paid back. Upset, he went to the man's house and shot him in the neck with the BB gun "to scare him." This man was the best man at our wedding, the witness that Obadiah invited, and the man who lent him the African outfit for the wedding. I was speechless and horrified.

This was the first of a number of run-ins with the law and the criminal justice system, including warrants, allegations, and arrests relating to drugs and violence. Although most of the charges were eventually dismissed and expunged, there was a significant financial cost for lawyers and many days of heartache and headaches for me in our marriage. The roots of resilience, grit, and endurance that I had developed would be tested by the weeds of life's trials and tribulations. There were mountains to climb and valleys to descend, even as Eyaside, my Blackwildgirl spirit, earnestly and sincerely sought to become a force in the world. But first, she had to withstand the vines that would seek to strangle her budding spirit.

Photographs and Images

Photographs tell their own story. These photos capture some of the salient moments in Act II. They include photos and images from my time in Nashville, excerpts from poems I wrote in Iowa City, and communication from my parents and Aunt Dorothea.

I hate it

Me
a woman
African descent
in
America

I hate it.

Excerpt from a poem I wrote in fall of 1985 during my freshman year at the University of Iowa about being a Black woman.
Photo credit: Menah Pratt

So,
    It's either suffer in silence
growing bitter
    always wondering
    Is it me, my skin, or them?
or

    It's speaking out
growing stronger
Knowing it's not you
but your skin and them.

                    Menah.

Excerpt from a poem I wrote in 1986 during my freshman year
at the University of Iowa about being Black. Photo credit: Menah Pratt

Menah Pratt, photo in 1991, that my parents referenced as
an African queen. Photo credit: Unknown

10/19/91

Our dear daughter:

We were so very delighted to receive that glamorous Photograph of you. We both agreed that you are an African queen — and a fine young woman whom we are pleased to have as our daughter. Thanks, and continue being the fine young woman whom we know as Menah. We agreed that I should hang the Photo in my office, which I shall do on Monday.

We are both well, and looking forward to Christmas when we shall all be together, the first time for quite a few years. I'll prepare all of the special dishes for you an Dogin for the "free for all".

I received a nice long letter from your aunt Theodora. I must write to her.

I don't know if I told you before, but Butch, your aunt Cross son is now at Iowa State University where he is in charge of the T.V. Program there.

Well dear, take care and —

We love you,
Mom & Pop.

A letter written to me from my mother, referencing me as an African queen. Photo credit: Menah Pratt

Exuma Frame Shop, 1818 Jefferson Street in
Nashville, Tennessee, at the quadruplex I bought as a
first-year law student in 1992. Photo credit: Menah Pratt

PARTY A'S PROBABLE DEMANDS
3a.

  b.

  c.

WHO MAY WANT OUT OF THE MARRIAGE/RELATIONSHIP

	PARTY A YES | NO	PARTY B YES | NO
1. The marriage or relationship is boring		
2. The marriage or relationship is restrictive		
3. The marriage or relationship turns out to be a disappointment		
4. Does other party's values clash with other pre-existing (say family) values ?		
5. Is approval by family or pre-existing relationship needed?		
6. Is rubberstamping by the pre-existing relationship expected?		
7. Too much outside (family) interference.		

CONSEQUENCES OF THE DISSOLUTION OF THE MARRIAGE/RELATIONSHIP

	PARTY A YES | NO	PARTY B YES | NO
1. Would likely be hurt (extremely or otherwise)		
2. Would seek retaliation (legal or otherwise)		
3. Would go for the jogular in an all out fight		
4. Likely to use past experience of a DIVORCE SITUATION		

PROTECTION FROM ABUSE IN DISSOLUTION

EITHER PARTY

1. PRENUPTIAL AGREEMENT (needed, not needed)

2. INJUNCTIONS (etc---- all legal--rule to show cause--etc, complications

Excerpt from Papa's three-page premarital questionnaire that he sent for me to take prior to marriage, circa 1993. Photo credit: Menah Pratt

Freetown
6th 7 Feb. 1994

My darling Menah, Praise The Lord!
God is so good. I was extremly happy
to hear about your success in your
exams, Congratulations to you my dear.
Anyway its only the time factor, but I
was not at all supprise to hear about your
success because you are very hard working
once more I say well-done to you and also
will wish brighter years ahead of you.

I will be very happy to see you
once more in Sierra Leone, So many
students all over the world come for
Christmas and they all enjoyed their
stay very much. Sierra Leone is a
small and peaceful country, You are
most welcome.

Donot strain yourself to get me
anything. All I want from America is
your self. Hope to see you soon.
My regards to your Mumm and Dad and
May God richly bless you all,
Love
Auntie Doro.

Letter to me from Aunt Dorothea, February 6, 1994.
Photo credit: Menah Pratt

Reflection Questions

1. How did your relationship with your parents change as you grew older and more independent?
2. Reflecting on your partners in life, have they had traits and qualities similar to your parents? What were those qualities? Do you think this was a conscious or unconscious decision?
3. Do the photos generate any emotions in you? What are they and why? What photos are important in your own young adulthood experience?

References

Collins, P. H. 2009. *Black Feminist Thought: Knowledge, Consciousness, and the Politics of Empowerment*. Routledge.

Act III: Weeds

Entangled.

Intertwined.

Struggling.

THE SEVENTH STAGE—Spiritual Trials

THE SEASON OF GERMINATION, EXPLORATION, and discovery underground has strengthened the spirit-seed. Slowly shedding its seed coat of protection, it has nevertheless entered a time of vulnerability. The spirit-seed has roots, yet those very roots can compromise its survival. They are still delicate and tender and not deeply embedded. Exposed, they will inevitably become entangled and intertwined with the weeds of life's tribulations. It is a time for the spirit-seed to demonstrate its ability to withstand the tests and trials that, like grit in an oyster, will create friction in the cultivation of a pearl.

SCENE ONE: **Fatherhood Trials**

*I*t was the summer of 1994. Obadiah and I had been living our secret married life for almost nine months. Because of the lack of support from my parents, we felt it was important to start our marriage with only positive energy and to create a solid foundation for our new life together. This decision, however, caused our marriage to exist under an uneasy cloud of deceit. I felt guilty and hypocritical for not telling my parents, and I knew I needed to conquer the fear of their judgment and disappointment. I began to think about an ideal moment to shed the veil of secrecy. Since I was going to be moving to North Carolina in August to start the federal clerkship, and Obadiah would be remaining in Nashville, we decided that we should tell my parents.

So, one random day in July 1994, I called my parents and told them that Obadiah and I were married. I was nervous, and though I knew what they thought shouldn't matter, I still didn't want to experience their disappointment or anger. Though I don't remember the discussion or conversation when I told them we were married, I do have the letter my father sent me a few days later on July 27, 1994: *"This is your biological father telling you to come pick up your things from 1405 West Hovey and never return to 1405 West Hovey again."* On one hand, I was shocked, offended, and hurt. On the other hand, the letter was almost irrelevant; I didn't have anything at 1405. I was quietly rejoicing, feeling validated by my decision to get married without waiting for his never-coming permission. Less concerned about him, I was more concerned about the relationship with Mama. True to form and pattern, Mama sent me a series of letters soon after I received my father's:

July 30, 1994
Dear Daughter:

Oh yes, I said to your father, "You mean if I should become ill Menah could not come in this house?" and he said, "Oh, you know there are exceptions." Interesting!

You will be fine. I'll call you soon. You just call me here at home anytime you wish to talk to me. If your father is here, we will just be careful what we say.

Take care. I love you lots, Mom

September 1, 1994
My dear daughter:

I drove up to the O'Hare airport yesterday and picked up your father. Well, he informed me that he had been thinking and had decided on a socioeconomic plan. He said he'd decided to pay off the small remaining mortgage on 1405 West Hovey and 606 East Taylor. He'd take 606, 4 Larry Court, and 104 Shelbourne, and give me 1405 West Hovey mortgage-free. I could take my retirement monthly payment and my social security check, and we'd divorce. This was his proposal as a reaction to his displeasure with your marriage to Oba-diah. He said that then I could be free to travel as I like and have anyone in the house I wish. He said he could then "have his own life," live in one of the apartments, and when he spends all of his money, he would will the property to various colleges and then just die. He said he does not want you in the house or calling here when you want. I listened and decided that divorce does not make sense at our age, even though it would give me a great deal of freedom.

Menah, I've decided that we will communicate by writing. I will call you from pay phones at least once a week. When I am on trips, I'll call you, and we will see each other at some of Dagin's performances. We can plan when we'll both see him perform. Further, your father plans to go to Sierra Leone, perhaps December or early in the new year, and you can come home. At this point, I've decided that we can have contact and communication without disturbing him. I cannot call you from home because Sprint charges a few cents and it shows up on our telephone bill.

I think you understand. You have established a fine life for yourself. I'm proud of you. You have a husband who seems to love and care for you, as well as supports you in your career goals and activities.

I never thought this would happen, but your father is just very rigid, based on his own childhood experiences. Do not call home unless there are some problems, because I'll just call you once a week from a pay phone.

I am fine, and can live with this messy situation. If it gets too unbearable, I will consider the option he offers. I think it is worth the adjustment to preserve what we all worked so hard for (the property).
Love you dear, Mom.

Mama's commitment to me remained steadfast. We had communicated secretly for years: she regularly sent me letters; she called from pay phones; and we talked during her office hours. We nourished our relationship without my father's knowledge. Yet Mama navigated the "messy situation" because she had compassion and love for my father. She knew he had an unloving childhood with Mama Pratt and his father, who disowned and disgraced him. Repeating the generational trauma, Papa had abused, disowned, and disgraced me. Like a tightrope walker, Mama balanced her joint responsibilities to me and to my father, as a mother and wife.

Four months after his July letter to me, Papa suffered a significant stroke that paralyzed the entire left side of his body in November 1994. During his four-week hospitalization, my mother drove forty-five minutes each way between home and the hospital every day, and sometimes twice a day. While he was there, she wrote "An ode to my husband":

Since you have been in the hospital, I think of all our years together—the smiles, laughter, pains, hurt, good times, [and] joy. [The] goose bumps and joyful tears remind [me] that the smiles, laughter, good times, and joy have been in much greater supply than the pains and hurt. As I reflect, I have not been a perfect wife, but I have tried and have loved and cared for you—and I still do and will continue doing so till death do us part. Today, I sorely miss your "Mildred," as you call me in your own way. And, most of all, I miss your hearty laughter, which from the first day I met you was for me your trademark. As I close this ode, I want you to know that I will not make the decision as to where you will or should go when you are released from the hospital. That is your decision to make. I just want you to know that wherever you are, I will care for you as best I can and with love. I love you.

Mama cared for him as best she could, and my father was grateful for Mama and her love, even though he rarely showed or expressed it. On the day of his release from the hospital, still

wheelchair-bound, he asked my mother to drive him to a jewelry store. At the store, he directed her to the jewelry case and
asked her which bracelet she liked. As she wrote in *A Tribute
to Love*, her book on love and marriage, "Tears welled up in
my eyes as I selected one. He insisted I take two. Always the
subtle romantic, he had done just what he did five years prior
when he wanted me to have the diamond ring I never had"
(Pratt-Clarke 2018, 233). Papa bought Mama two diamond
tennis bracelets.

Not only did Mama care for my father, but she also cared
for me, as best she could and with love. I needed her help.
Obadiah and I had been living in the quadruplex in one of the
upstairs units. The frame shop was in another unit, and the
other two units had tenants. With the frame shop growing, we
needed to find another place to live as our home. While I was
working in North Carolina, Obadiah found a house for us to
buy at 1601 Dr. D. B. Todd Jr. Boulevard in Nashville. It was in
a perfect location, just down the street from the frame shop on
Jefferson Street. It was a three-bedroom red brick house, built
in the 1930s. It had three full floors, including a full basement
and a full attic. To buy the house, we needed a down payment.
I called my mother and asked for help. She discussed it with my
father, and surprisingly, they both agreed to give us a loan for
$5,000. I was to pay the loan back monthly based on a loan
agreement I wrote up that was signed by both my parents and
me on January 16, 1995.

In the fall of 1995, having finished my one-year clerkship, I returned to Nashville, the new house, and the frame
shop. I started working at a large law firm in Nashville as a
commercial lending, real estate, and public finance lawyer.
I was the only Black attorney at the firm and the first Black
woman attorney. It was a challenging job, learning the Southern corporate law firm culture. The Whiteness of the lawyers
was accented by lunches and dinners with Black servers with

gloves in penthouse hotel floors and mansions. My office was on the twenty-sixth floor, but I enjoyed going down to the twenty-fifth floor to see and chat with the Black people in the mailroom. But mentors quietly told me that the twenty-fifth floor was not my floor. I was not supposed to be seen socializing with "them." I was to be on the twenty-sixth floor, in my office, learning the ins and outs of the red marks on loan lending documents, with edits from my mentor revealing the inadequacy of my legal training and preparation. Practicing law reminded me of my father's amateur legal practice with the apartment buildings. Perhaps my desire to be a lawyer was unconsciously fueled by his life.

I sent my father a card for his birthday on September 19, in which I reflected on his influence on me. I always sent birthday and Christmas cards, and he never responded. Unexpectedly, I received a thank-you card from him on September 23, 1995. In the thank-you card, he wrote: *"Some people say that young women are beautiful people . . . innocent. Strange that I could have used the word [innocent] in the 60's, but those children who were born in the 60's have been found to be sassy in the 90's."* He signed the card *"your father, Ted."* So, in his eyes, I was both innocent and sassy—womanish, in the Alice Walker way. He accurately defined my essence. He knew and saw the Queen of Sheba—the queen he wasn't able or prepared to nurture.

Four months later, he sent the January 6, 1996, letter referencing the Pratt Setup and signed *"your biological father."* My monthly payment on the loan arrived late, and his letter, in part, was influenced by that late payment. The letter also mentions my marriage and my letter to my parents about my marriage in 1993. Still recovering from the stroke, he typed his letter with this confusing combination of capital and lowercase letters:

Dear MENAH,
I got your check dated 12-31-95 apparently as one
Installment payment which might be either for DEC.
95 OR jAN 96.
THIS TYPE OF CONFUSION IS NOT TOTALLY
UNEXPECTED *since I already believed that* YOU ARE
LIVING BEYOND YOUR MEANS.
LIVING BEYOND YOUR MEANS IS ONE OF THE
WORST THINGS YOU COULD DO ESPECIALLY
IF YOU HAVE LEGAL TRAINING.
You might as well recall or realize that the LOAN MADE
TO YOU WOULD NOT HAVE BEEN MADE HAD I
BEEN IN PROPER HEALTH—*so you really benefited*
from my illness—LUCKY.
YOUR ACTIONS *since 1994,* HAD BEEN IMMATURE
AND MYOPIC—*under the guise that "I am grown-up*
and can do anything at my age."
You may recall my letter to you in JULY 94. I STAND
BY IT ESPECIALLY THAT I KNOW THAT YOU
FEEL THAT YOU ARE ALRIGHT NOT KNOWING
OR BOTHERING THAT YOU ARE HEADING IN
THE WRONG DIRECTION.
WHEN YOU WENT AND GOT MARRIED WITHOUT
MY KNOWLEDGE AND PERMISSION,
your action could only be considered as a "PROTEST."
WHY AND WHAT ARE/IS BEING PROTESTED?
YOU TALK ABOUT SACRIFICES! *Shame but* PITY.
CAN YOU EXPLAIN SACRIFICES OR DO YOU,
even as an ENGLISH MAJOR, *know what it means?*
You do not know what PREOCCUPATION WITH
SUCCESS FOR YOUR BLACK CHILDREN *in this*
country means. It was a 24*hrs job* NO SLEEP—
LYING IN BED OR NOT.

THE FACT IS THESE WERE/ARE CHILDREN OF PARENTAGE, highly EDUCATED IN THE UNI-VERSITIES and on the streets but with inadequate FINANCIAL MEANS desirous of MAKING AN EASY and COMFORTABLE LIFE for everyone in the FAMILY. PARENTS WHO DID NOT HAVE ANY INHERITANCE OR initial financial family lift.

I AM NOT UNFAMILIAR WITH YOUR WEAK-NESSES OR STRENGTHS FOR A RATHER LONG/SHORT PERIOD OF TIME.

YOU MAY CONSIDER THIS AS A TIMELY REPLY TO YOUR JULY 6, 1993 LETTER.

I DO NOT HATE YOU BUT I FEEL DEEPLY BETRAYED—maybe I had been living a LIE (WITH ALL THIS HARD WORK AND PREMATURE GREY) about FAMILY and FAMILY MATTERS within the PRATT–SET-UP.

PLEASE REPAY THE balance of the LOAN immediately at least in keeping with the terms of your CONTRACT. THERE ARE NONE OF THOSE NICETIES as I love you.

THE FACT IS—YOUR BIOLOGICAL FATHER."
"TAECP."

"The fact is—your biological father." He was my biological father. He was also the father of the bargain, who did not hate me but could not say, "I love you." He was the father who was not the pope and couldn't give blessings. He was the father who disowned and then loaned. He was the father who was Ted and TAECP. He was the father who was the source of my success and who had given me discipline and excellence. He was also the father who was the source of my sorrow and sadness. He was the father of Awadagin, the first African American to win the Naumburg International piano competition. He was the father

of a world-renowned and world-class musician who had been invited to the White House three times to play for presidents. He was the father of a daughter who was finishing her doctorate while working as a lawyer. He was the father who would invite my mother to a Valentine's Day dance at a local hotel where they would take a beautiful picture together. He was also the father who would be diagnosed with pancreatic cancer in August and be given just a few months to live, as I wrote in my journal:

September 29, 1996, 10:00 p.m.
God,

Papa is sick—cirrhosis of the liver, cancer, diabetes, high blood pressure, distended heart. We are planning a surprise party for his 60th and Mama's 68th birthdays. I need to get good at just giving it all to you. I will. Thanks for being there.
—Menah

Years of drinking the stashed-away bottles under the kitchen sink and cans and cans of beer had taken its toll. Aware of his quickly severing strand to life, we decided to have a surprise belated birthday party for him on October 13, at a local hotel. His birthday was September 18. My father, miraculously, allowed Obadiah and me to stay at 1405 during that short weekend visit. Papa was shell and bones, emaciated and confined to a wheelchair. Because he was so weak, he didn't want to leave the house that morning. We had to spoil the surprise to get him to leave the house. Aunt Dorothea was visiting family in New York, but once she learned that Papa was ill, she immediately came to visit for several weeks. During her visit, she read scripture to my father and prayed with him. Mama said that Papa really seemed to appreciate her presence. Aunt Dorothea created a church in 1405. Papa trusted her, and she was able to help persuade him to come to the celebration.

Papa and I had a moment of reconciliation at the party. Obadiah had stepped away for a moment, and Papa said to me that it seemed that Obadiah cared for me and would be a good husband. And so, Papa became the father who disowned and then owned. Although Mama thought the party was for my father, we surprised her and celebrated her October 15 birthday early. We had matching memory albums with pictures and letters from friends for both of them. At the party, Mama had asked a friend to sing "Wind Beneath My Wings," as a tribute to Papa. In reality, they were both the wind beneath our wings as our parents. My brother and I were who we were because of the Pratt Setup, the *"hard work and premature grey"*; the *"preoccupation with success for your Black children"*; the *"no sleep"*; and *"none of those niceties as I love you."*

About two weeks after the party, I visited my father again, staying at the house for a short weekend visit. During that visit, he couldn't speak. He was too weak. He was lying in a hospital bed in my brother's room. My mother was caring for him so tenderly and lovingly, just as she had promised in her ode when he was in the hospital recovering from the stroke. His final hours were approaching, and death would be knocking on the door.

As my weekend visit ended, I walked into his room early Monday morning to say goodbye. He was lying in the bed with his eyes closed. I stared at him a long time, trying to decide what to say. He briefly opened his eyes. I reached for his hand and said the Lord's Prayer to him:

Our Father who art in heaven, hallowed be thy name. Thy kingdom come, thy will be done, on earth as it is in heaven. Give us this day our daily bread and forgive us our trespasses as we forgive those who trespass against us. Lead us not into temptation but deliver us from evil. For thine is the kingdom, the power, and the glory forever. Amen.

I'm not sure why I chose that scripture, but when Mama told me that Aunt Dorothea was reading scriptures to him and praying with him, I thought the Lord's Prayer would be comforting and familiar to him. After saying it, I suffocated and swallowed my tears, as I had learned to do all my life as a little girl. He hated seeing tears and saw them as a sign of weakness; we were not allowed to be weak. Letting go of his almost lifeless hand, I slowly walked toward the door. Turning to give him one last look, I said, "I love you." I don't know if he heard me or not. I felt I had to say it because I didn't want to regret not saying it. To me, "I love you" wasn't a nicety; it was a necessity.

I drove back to Nashville and was back at work on Tuesday. Late that night, my mother called me and told me to come back to 1405. Hospice had told her the transition was close. As I drove the six hours back home into the darkness of the night and toward the darkness of my father's dimming light, my mind raced, thoughts passing furiously like the dotted lines along the highway. Mama met me at the door, and the beautiful hospice lady, Judy, encouraged me to sit down. We all sat down on the long plaid-green couch, and they calmly told me that Papa had peacefully passed away at 1:00 a.m., about thirty minutes before I arrived. His body was still in the house. My mother told me I could go into the room if I wanted. I decided to say goodbye.

I remember getting up from the childhood couch of shame, with pieces and parts of Papa's African-accented lectures bubbling to mind. As I walked down the short hallway to my brother's converted hospital bedroom, memories of my life as a child and my relationship with my father flashing from incomprehensible scene to incomprehensible scene accompanied me into the room. I could feel the brownness of my brother's wood panels closing in on the room, like the darkness of death itself. There he was. Papa. My mind was filled with quick questions and thoughts: "What do I say to this man? Will he hear me? Where is he? Is his spirit in this room, still?"

He was Papa, once all powerful, almighty, and almost omnipotent; Papa, the physicist with a dream denied, whose livelihood and career were snatched and stolen; Papa, the strict and unyielding disciplinarian; Papa, who loved my mother but rarely showed it; Papa, who could not say "I love you" to me; Papa, the genesis who sent me on a search for Love; and Papa, who lay still and dead, with his eyes closed and a blanket covering all but his face. America's racism had killed him at age sixty.

Obadiah had told me that Bahamian custom encourages asking the deceased's spirit to carry any challenges, problems, or burdens to the spirit world with them. I decided to ask the man who had created so much fear in my life to take my fear. I don't know what I was afraid of. I think I was still afraid of him. Trying to summon my courage, I stared at him for several minutes, with countless and wordless thoughts rushing through my mind, almost rendering me speechless: "Papa, please take my fear with you on your journey. Thank you. I love you." A bit relieved, I took one last look at Papa and walked out of the room.

After my father died, my mother wrote a letter to Mama Pratt about Papa's death. Aunt Dorothea, who was still visiting in the United States, agreed to hand-deliver it to Mama Pratt when she returned to Freetown. One Wild Woman would share the death with another Wild Woman. The letter said:

Dear Mama Pratt:

Your dear son never thought that death would come so soon. At the time when we began planning the surprise birthday party in June this year, we had no idea of his impending death. When Dorothea called to inform us that she was in New York, we were so happy that

we immediately invited her down to spend some time
with us. She was sad, as we all were, to see your dear
son's health deteriorate so fast—but that is the way with
late-diagnosed cancer. Each morning that Dorothea was
here with us, she sat on the couch with her brother, read
the Bible to him, and prayed. He looked forward to
these inspirational sessions and believed in them. While
they helped his spirit, it's clear that God was ready for
him to be relieved of his pain. The children join me in
thanking you for your son. We're always keenly aware
that he sacrificed life in his own country with you and
his other relatives and friends for us. We shall always
remember that. Our love for and gratitude to him is
enduring. On his deathbed, I assured him that I would
do my best to assure that you were cared for—though
at that time he was too weak to speak, his eyes told me
that he understood and trusted me to do so.
We love you,
Mildred, Awadagin, and Menah (Pratt-Clarke 2018, 234)

Though my father had transitioned from the earthly world,
his indomitable spirit would continue to live. His flame could
not be snuffed out. My father had left a little sticky note on
his dresser mirror before his death. It said, *"No funeral, no*
obituary, no memorial." When he died, we tried to honor his
request. A few close family friends—including Pam, Patsy, and
Darlene and their husbands, Jack, Jack, and Marc—came to
the house and started to think about how to honor his life. A
vision emerged of a foundation that would provide free music
lessons to elementary, middle, and high school students with
talent and need through a partnership with Illinois Wesleyan
University. My father would continue to live on in some way
through the Pratt Music Foundation, and Mama would carry
this mantle to ensure his legacy.

SCENE TWO: **Motherhood Trials**

*T*he summer of 1996 was a season of navigating life and death. Obadiah and I had been trying to have children but had been unsuccessful for almost two years due to my irregular periods, perhaps as a consequence of years of birth control pills. I started taking fertility drugs, and in the summer of 1996, I became pregnant. I was excited, ecstatic, and proudly displaying my three-month little round bump. Unfortunately, Labor Day weekend would, ironically, be my labor day.

I was alone in our house on D. B. Todd. I don't remember where Obadiah was that day. I began feeling intense stomach cramps, tumultuous pulling and contracting. With the intensity increasing, I decided to take a warm bath. I turned on the water and slowly took off my clothes. Sitting naked on the edge of the tub waiting for it to fill up, I suddenly felt like I needed to use the toilet. I gingerly got up from the tub, took a step, and sat on the toilet. Suddenly and startlingly, I felt a strange, inexplicable sensation. Something had come out of me. Shocked and horrified, I realized what it was. It had come out, attached but not attached. I never looked at It. I couldn't. I knew what It was. With It dangling between my legs, I ran to the phone and called 911. I unlocked the front door and lay on the floor, crying, screaming, shaking, waiting, with Morning Glory, as we later named It, precariously tethered to me. I was naked, bleeding, and hysterical when the emergency rescue team of men came in. They placed me on a stretcher, covered me and It with sheets. This was before the era of widespread cell phone use, so they left a note for Obadiah that I was being taken to Vanderbilt Hospital.

At the hospital, I don't even remember what happened. I never looked at It, but the doctors removed It from its tether. They gave me a little folder with Morning Glory's ashes and

footprints, small and tiny but evidence of a life. My obstetrician—
an amazing African American woman—immediately diagnosed
me with an incompetent cervix. She said my cervix was too
weak to carry a child. In the future, when I got pregnant, I
would need a cerclage—stitches in the opening of the cervix—to
hold the baby in.

Two months after my father's death, in December of 1996,
I became pregnant again. Perhaps Papa's spirit paved the way
for new life to come forth from the universe. The year 1997
would be a season of milestones: moving Mama to Nashville,
since she no longer felt safe in the house without my father;
celebrating my thirtieth birthday; defending my dissertation;
and giving birth to my son, Emmanuel. Infrequent journal
entries bear witness to these moments:

April 10, 1997
God,

*Today is April 10, 1997. So much has happened.
Papa died on October 30, 1996, at 1:00 a.m. I still can't
believe that he is gone. I moved Mama to Nashville in
December, and she really seems to be doing well: traveling places, taking care of herself, health, meeting people.
She sounds good when I talk to her. I am happy about
that. Since I hadn't written for a while, here I am.*

*What else is happening? I am pregnant. Thirteen-
and-a-half weeks. I trust God will let me keep this one.
I defended my dissertation on March 24, 1997. Yes, you
can call me doctor. I am going to look for another job
after I have the baby in October.*

April 17, 1997

I have just finished reading Susan Taylor's In the
Spirit, *an incredibly inspirational book. I am at a
crossroads in my life. Trying to grow in my spiritual*

*relationship with God, trying to understand my purpose,
trying to set new goals, being pregnant, being the sole
breadwinner. Some options aren't there. What to do?
How to most effectively use my skills and talents? How
to contribute?*

April 24, 1997

*God, so many thoughts. I need to set some new goals.
I'm starting to really feel excited about the baby. I think
it's going to be a boy. If so, we will call it Emmanuel
Obadiah Awadagin Clarke. Emmanuel, of course, was
one of Papa's middle names and means God is with us.*

*It's so hard to keep track of life, people, contacts,
friends, daily stuff, bills, and work. This life is such an
awesome responsibility. Mama and I have been having a
wonderful time lately, planning for my party—my graduation and thirtieth birthday party.*

*Obadiah and I have had some wonderful loving
moments together. He is truly a blessing in my life—
one that I am eternally grateful and must never take for
granted.*

October 21, 1997

Dear God,

*Today is October 21, 1997. It is 5:00 a.m. Little
Emmanuel [born September 28, 1997] is sleeping and
so should I. For some reason, Obadiah's spirit is off, and
so is mine. One challenge of marriage is dealing with
your spouse's emotions. It is so hard not to let them
become yours.*

*There is also a part of me that feels I should be get-
ting my life all sorted through so when I die, nothing is
messy or unorganized for someone else to deal with. It is
very strange living to live and living to die. I'm 30 now,*

young, yet not. I have so many gifts and I'm not using
any. I'm wondering how to balance being a mother and
giving to the world.

I've applied for an in-house position at Vanderbilt
doing what I do now. It will give me more time to live
life. If it is for me, I know it's mine. If not, I know you'll
provide other opportunities.

I was given a four-month maternity leave from the law
firm, and I used that time to apply for other jobs, knowing
that the corporate law firm life was not conducive to being a
mother: all the male attorneys had stay-at-home wives, and
all the female attorneys had live-in nannies. I would have neither, and I was committed to raising my child. In the spring of
1998, I was blessed to get hired at my alma mater, Vanderbilt,
working as an attorney with the board of trust and the legal
office. My Mother's Day entry reveals the ongoing challenge
of juggling all the roles of mother, daughter, wife, sister, friend,
and lawyer:

May 10, 1998
Today is Mother's Day—my first, actually. It was an
okay day. I think it helps not to have expectations—then
you are never disappointed. Obadiah gave me a negligee,
but I still had to watch Emmanuel, fold clothes, wash
dishes, and didn't get to go see a movie. I guess just
another day. Church was good, too. Talked about the
greatest commandment—love one another. God, some-
times I feel so close to you and to Obadiah. Other times
distant. It's all work and attitude and effort.

Mama's and my relationship isn't great, now. I don't
think she'll ever quite accept Obadiah. I feel like I have
all these roles: mother, daughter, wife, sister, friend,
lawyer—none easy. I am working at Vanderbilt and it

is a good job and exciting. My official title is Assistant
Secretary to the University and Staff Attorney. Thank
you for loving me, Lord.
—Menah

Because Mama tried to be so supportive of me and my decisions, including the marriage, I didn't want to acknowledge that she really wasn't fond of Obadiah. His spirit just didn't align well with hers. They were on opposite ends of a spectrum. She was proper to the nth degree, and he was uncouth to the nth degree. She was about china plates and proper place settings; he was about paper plates and plastic sporks. He was a bone-sucking fish head and eyeballs eater, and she was a boneless salmon cooked in white parchment cloth connoisseur. He was brusque and abrupt; she was deliberate and purposeful. She was very educated; he had barely graduated from college after ten years. Mama wasn't comfortable around him and so would rarely come to our house. I often had to drive to her apartment, which didn't happen as often as I had hoped. But Mama wasn't the only one uncomfortable with Obadiah. I was becoming increasingly irritated, frustrated, and annoyed with him. Our marriage began to face some critical trials.

SCENE THREE: **Marriage Trials**

Someone—perhaps an unhappy, non-rent-paying, about-to-be-evicted tenant—had called the city building inspector to the quadruplex. A surprise inspection generated a ten-page letter of violations, from electrical to plumbing to structural. The building was condemned and deemed uninhabitable. We had ninety days to repair the building. We tried and tried with all our might, but we could not find the funds or make all the repairs. Unable to make the deadline, the city demolished the quadruplex and our beloved frame shop. The demolition caused a lien to be placed on the land for $40,000. This was in addition to the first mortgage of $74,000, plus a second mortgage of $20,000. We were in significant debt, with only one source of reliable and dependable income.

The loss of Obadiah's livelihood with the frame shop was devastating. It would be several months before I would fully realize its impact on him and our marriage. He would become addicted to crack cocaine, and for many months, I would be unknowingly living with an addict. I was also pregnant with our second child. My journal entries, often written as letters to God, document my frustration, confusion, and growing awareness of the impact of his addiction:

October 3, 1998
Dear God,

I am at a conference in Tempe, AZ. This has been a small chance for me to spend some time with myself— relaxing, thinking about myself, my marriage. I have felt very challenged lately. Obadiah, I have felt, has not been truthful with me about financial affairs. He has stolen money from me, written checks on my account without telling me, used my ATM card without my knowledge, written checks on a closed account, given his sister a check for $500 without consulting me, telling lies on me to his sister, lying to me, and not talking to me about money.

I have felt betrayed, and that I can't trust him. I need to find a way to get past my anger, hurt, betrayal, and disappointment in Obadiah. I am planning on going to a counselor on a fairly regular basis for at least six months to a year to deal with some lingering childhood emotions, feelings about Papa, and anger management. I think it would be very good for me, personally.

God, I would like you to help me be a better, more loving, and supportive wife and mother. I love Obadiah and Emmanuel dearly and I'm getting ready to have another baby, probably Eyaside Rebecca Emmalee or Inez or something.

I need to work on growing in my faith and my spirituality. I need to find time on a daily basis to focus on you and growing in your spirit. Please help me to be less judgmental of Obadiah and more patient.

We just had a birthday party for Emmanuel. He turned one year old. I just love him and thank you for him.

December 27, 1998

Obadiah and I are going to a marriage counselor and he is going to A. A. [Alcoholics Anonymous]. He says he is an alcoholic and drug addict and has been stealing from me to finance his habit. Part of me (most of me) is still in shock, despite having very strong suspicions.

Anyway, tonight we prayed to you, as Obadiah knew you as a child and you heard our prayer. You gave us a clean slate for our marriage and let us consecrate it and make it holy again! Our daughter shall be called Raebekkah and it shall mean Mother of Love as you have spoken to Obadiah. God, be with us as we try to grow in your spirit!

In January 1999, our daughter, Raebekkah Eyaside Emmalee Pratt-Clarke, was born. Obadiah was still addicted, spending inordinate time in the attic of our old house, getting high, smoking crack, and drinking alcohol. He often locked the door leading up to the attic, distancing and separating himself, locking himself in his own mind of defeat. Ignored, unloved, and unwanted, I started spending time with a beautiful Black woman with dark chocolate skin and a personality so full of light I called her Sunshine. She called me Moonlight. She would be a source of solace. She would counsel and console; she would also kiss and caress. I would melt into her softness and gentleness, and I would feel Loved. She would metaphorically nurture me with her breasts of compassion and kindness, laughter and joy. Her eyes would hold mine with concern, conveying a commitment to care and tenderness, even and especially in the madness of marriage. We were each other's essence, essential for many suns and moons.

Obadiah encouraged the friendship because it absolved him of any responsibility to me. Crack was his wife and lover. I was just the mother of his children, the payer of his child support, the provider of the shelter, the preparer of food, and the chaperone for the children to and from daycare. The world was continuing to revolve with him on the periphery, upstairs, in the dark attic, ruminating on thoughts without end, comforted and consoled by the snorting of crack cocaine.

On June 14, 1999, I received a phone call in the wee hours of the morning, just after midnight: "Collect call from an inmate. Will you accept?"

Confused, and thinking perhaps it was one of the students that I had taught when I was teaching at the prison through American Baptist College, I said, "Yes."

I was shocked to hear my husband's voice saying, "It's me, Ob." There was silence. He filled it in: "I've been arrested."

"For what?"

"Kidnapping."

"What?"

"Kidnapping. I'll tell you more later. See if you can visit and bring my Bible."

That conversation was the start of legal hell. I asked my girlfriend to stay with my children, and I went, barely dressed, in the early morning hours to the bail bondsman. I discovered the bond was $10,000, and I didn't have enough money.

Me, the lawyer, the professor who had taught inmates, now had her own inmate behind bars. I called Mama to tell her that Obadiah had been arrested and asked her for help. She said, "No, let him stay there." I was hurt but not surprised because I knew she had never really accepted him. While I was exploring options for getting the bail money, I was able to visit Obadiah in jail. I saw him behind bars, in an orange jumpsuit. A range of emotions flooded my being. I was embarrassed for him that he had created such a mess for himself. I was embarrassed having to visit him in a humiliating environment. I was angry that he seemingly couldn't control his emotions and had put me in this position of having to get him out of jail, deal with bail bondsmen, and try to find lawyers. I was also thankful that he didn't have the gun of the blue duffel bag. I brought his Bible and put a note in the Obadiah chapter. While he prayed and read his Bible in jail, I tried to think of solutions to get him out. I was not going to "let him stay there."

I called a friend of mine, a lawyer at the firm where I used to work. She loaned me $5,000, and I got him out of jail with a $5,000 loan shark loan. When he was released, I learn more about the arrest and the charge of aggravated kidnapping. It was an accusation involving Obadiah, another man, and a machete. Apparently, some argument led to Obadiah getting his machete from his truck. It was a long machete, with a red handle, that he used for tending the garden at our house. That evening, however, upset at the man, he put the machete to the man's neck and was holding it there when the police arrived. The charge was eventually dismissed, but while it was active, I was part of the criminal justice world. It was a world of hearings, lawyers, petitions, and documents, a world I had studied but had never known so intimately. I also learned that Obadiah had two prior misdemeanor charges of drug possession from March of 1998. Five days after his arrest for aggravated kidnapping, he was charged with another drug possession misdemeanor.

As he wrote in one of my journals a few years into our marriage, he was struggling with his faith, his demons, and his gift:

Sometimes I lie! Not Good! Sometimes I get mad—Not good! Sometimes I want to do evil. Most time, I find myself praying, asking God for strength, then difficulty comes my way! I pray for courage but sadness would overshadow me. I pray for wisdom only to be confronted by evil! I thank you dear God for 1992, the year you sent your earthly angel to take care of me, your prophet, Obadiah. Her name as you already know is Menah P. My special love you sent me. I thank you for the guidance you sent through Menah. I thank you for the partnership you gave to me through MenahP. God, I have mistreated your gift. I have lied and misused MenahP. That's how I feel—because she is love. She sees no evil. She hates nobody or persons. I am sorry God for all the way I had mistreated your gift, lied, and misused your gift.

The note was validating. I knew Obadiah was struggling, and I knew he cared for his MenahP, as he affectionately called me. While he professed to love me, because he did not love himself, he would inevitably continue to mistreat and misuse me. Because I was committed to him and to our marriage, I always tried to see the best in him. I could not, however, have anticipated the depth of the gut-wrenching pain that I would experience at his hands over the next few years.

SCENE FOUR: **Goddess Wisdom**

As 1999 ended and 2000 approached, my world would be significantly changing. A few months after Obadiah's arrest, my mother decided to leave Nashville and go back to her community in Bloomington-Normal and her friends: Pam and Jack, Patsy and Jack, and Darlene and Marc. She wanted to work on the Pratt Music Foundation full-time. I was disappointed that she would not be in Nashville with me, but I understood the depth of her commitment to my father's legacy. It was her number one priority. I would be left to manage my marriage and motherhood alone. My mother and her sister, Mozelle, celebrated Christmas with us in Nashville, and at the end of 1999, I started to think about what would be next for me:

December 26, 1999

I am all of a sudden so full of thoughts—don't know how many I can express. I had one of the best, if not the best, Christmas ever. Mama and Aunt Mozelle came to Nashville. It was nice. I was just a little disappointed in Ob's gift. But the children are/were very happy. I have a week off from work and I feel reflective on the past year and future year. What's important, what do I want to change, what routines do I want to have? What goals do I want to achieve? I want to be a great wife and mother. I want to write in journals—my journals and the children's—to keep track of changes, years passing, them maturing, getting bigger, wiser.

I want to be in sync with the Spirit of Life, to dance in harmony with it. Not necessarily in unison, but still make beautiful music in my everyday existence.

What does it mean to be a great wife? Supportive, helpful, loving, understanding, slow to judge, patient, caring, nurturing, life/energy/strength-giving, sustaining. I want to be good to myself. I want to take care of my health and asthma. I want to eat right, exercise, lose weight. I want to put music into my life in a daily way with piano or violin.

I want to take more baths in the evening. I want to read the whole Bible in one year. I want a new, sexy look for the new year: shorter hair, nice pants, a few skirts, nice jackets, new shoes. I'll write more tomorrow!

As one year ended and the new year of 2000 approached, my hopeful optimism belied a harsh reality. While our children were a source of such joy, I was in the midst of a marriage on life support, barely breathing, sustained often by my own fierce determination and commitment to the marriage, even at the cost of my own needs. Our financial condition was as precarious as the marriage. Unable to pay the lien, the mortgage, the credit card debt from financing the frame shop, or the initial repairs to the quadruplex, we had to file for bankruptcy. I remember sitting in the bankruptcy courtroom listening to everyone's financial pain and humiliation and feeling so disappointed in myself knowing that I was one of "them." I had always thought I was "too good" to be one of "them." I was not supposed to be one of "them."

I was a Pratt, as Mama's first letter to me affirmed: *"You are special—you are a Pratt. You are African—part of one of the oldest cultures in the world. Remember that and never take a backseat to anyone."* Yet, on that day, sitting in the back of the bankruptcy courtroom with other debtors, I was not special. I was one of many other people who couldn't pay their bills, feeling the invisible scorn and judgment of the world as my financial circumstances were publicly described for all those ears to hear. It was as if my father's pronouncement in his Pratt Setup letter had come true; I was heading in the wrong direction and living beyond my means.

Humbled by the bail bond office, the jail visit, and the bankruptcy court hearing, my self-concept and self-esteem were at rock bottom. Once the owner of two homes, I was now approaching homelessness and would be unable to buy a home for years. Obadiah and I had nothing except our furniture and clothes and had barely managed to find a place to rent before the bankruptcy was finalized. We had lost so much, including our hopes and aspirations for our future. And soon, we wouldn't even have each other.

In April 2001, Obadiah announced that he would be moving back to his childhood home in Exuma, Bahamas. Still addicted to crack, he felt it was the only option for his sanity, his mind, and his life. He would use the ocean and his homeland to detox and get off drugs. In addition, my girlfriend of the kisses, hugs, and caresses was moving, and our special and beautiful time together would be ending. Her final gift to me at Christmas on December 25, 2001, was a journal. On the inside, in her beautiful cursive handwriting, she wrote: "For those moments when you feel that you cannot share your thoughts with anyone . . . Love Always." In gratitude for the three years we spent in almost constant friendship and support, I sent Sunshine a poem on January 8, 2002:

You cannot be replaced
The empty space is not filled
My blessing is that it no longer causes tears or pain
The silence created by your absence is now filled with
other sounds
However, the space remains open
It is no longer an open wound
It has been covered by God's grace and mercy
The need that was filled
The desire that was satisfied
Remain unfilled and unsatisfied

*I continually pray and trust that one day the Spirit will
see that
Those needs and desires are filled and satisfied
The Awesome Spirit of the Universe knows what I
need and desire
And I have Patience, Faith, and give thanks that She
will bless me
With Blessings surpassing my conception and
imagination
Your name is continually on my lips
Your spirit is continually on my heart
Your memory is continually on my mind
You are in my prayers daily as I pray for the Spirit to
bless you
With Blessings surpassing your conception and
imagination, as well.*

*Your friend,
Menah*

I would move forward on my journey, still trying to birth
myself and push the delicate stem and leaves of my spirit
through the soil of life. The garden of my life had been weeded,
and I was ragged. I had been stripped to the bone. With barely
any money or pride in my pocket, I was off to the next stage
of the initiation.

Reflection Questions

1. Have you had "harrowing of the soul" experiences, a period of trials that tested your courage and self-confidence? What were those experiences? What lessons did you learn from them? How are you applying these lessons in your life?
2. Have you experienced the death of a close family member or friend? What do you remember most about the death and dying experience? What lessons did you learn about life and living from that experience?
3. Have you ever experienced financial challenges? What led to those challenges, and have you been successful in trying to recover from them?

References

Pratt-Clarke, M. 2018. *A Black Woman's Journey from Cotton Picking to College Professor: Lessons about Race, Class, and Gender in America*. Peter Lang.

THE EIGHTH STAGE—
Spiritual Questing

A SPIRIT-SEEDLING WITH ITS GROWING roots will continue to encounter weeds that will compete for nutrients, potentially stifling and suffocating the seedling's growth and compromising its health and viability. The spirit-seedling will need to push against dark and terrifying forces and find alternative sources of energy. This season is a time of searching for meaning and understanding and for direction and discernment.

SCENE ONE: **Direction**

*B*eginning in 2002, as Blackwildwoman, I was experiencing an intense yearning for direction in the midst of the underground darkness. Alone with our two young children and with Obadiah away in the Bahamas, my spirit was restless, hungering for the Love that I had so desperately been seeking. I needed to find my inner compass to guide and direct me in my search. The journals bear witness with frequent references to questing—an arduous and tedious journey. It was a spiritual fight for my own self-worth and value:

June 1, 2002

The layers of my life. Spiritually questing: seeking; searching; understanding the dynamics and circumstances of life; desiring to respond appropriately; consciously shaping my soul to be in harmony with Spirit.

July 5, 2002

I am always struggling with the same issues: purpose; peace; spiritual fight amidst daily existence; connections; harmony; the aloneness of it all; the unanswerables; my insignificance in the scheme of the masses of humanity. Less than a grain of sand, less than a drop of water into an ocean, less than a breath. Yet, God placed me on this earth; I am still here. Why? He has use for me still . . .

So, I must continue to fight the daily battle of life's little petty challenges. I must continue to take up the armor for others. I must continue to share my gifts. I must continue to struggle to live a disciplined life. I must, I must, I must keep going for the little people, and if no one else, Emmanuel and Raebekkah.

September 17, 2002
Precious Lord and Savior Jesus Christ,

Sometimes I just want to be with you in your bosom, in your embrace, in your love, compassion, kindness, protection. Lord . . . I need you. . . . I need you. . . . I need you. . . . The voids in my life can only be filled by you. Human beings are so unreliable, self-centered, self-absorbed, and selfish. God, just be with me. Guide me.

October 29, 2002
Thoughts: Life doesn't have to be hard. Monitor my thoughts, words, and expectations. God is in me which means power, energy, strength, and joy are in me—if I access them through prayer and meditation. Each of us comes into life with a promise, a gift, a passion, and a deep heartfelt desire. What do I want my legacy to be? My testimony. The story I leave behind.

November 15, 2002
God,

Questing for your peace and joy and love at all times, in all situations, in all circumstances.

"I need you." That was my call to the universe to show up and support me. And She responded. She sent me a sister-friend who was grieving the sudden, inexplicable loss of her twenty-four-year-old amazing and incredible daughter. We began traveling together to places where perhaps we both had ancestral pullings and longings. We started in San Francisco, walking in Muir Woods and talking about the spirit world and spiritual things. She was from the Caribbean and shared her knowledge about Yoruba religion, Spiritual Baptists, and the blending of Christianity and African religious thought. During our time together, I was wrestling with core Christian concepts:

December 5, 2002
God,

Here I am in San Francisco. Learning about you from my friend. Learning about moaning, spirits traveling, communicating in other language with other spirits. Spiritual Mother interprets dreams and assists with spiritual development.

Concepts that I am struggling with: God as masculine. Jesus Savior as masculine. God as God of judgment. The relationship between judgment and love. Unconditional love. Consequences of actions. Challenges of language to use to speak with God to pray. What it means to make sacrifices.

My thoughts: God as both mother and father, masculine and feminine. The embodiment of good and evil of all opposites. Using the Bible as a source of the familiar and accepted as a starting point for ministry to build in a broader, more inclusive focus. Learning scripture to be able to share with others as encouragement.

Again, what is my specific role? Tension between God's perfection and man's imperfection? Is man imperfect though? If yes, is there a route to perfection? If so, what is it? Belief alone? Action? Intention? What is forgiveness? By God? How does that concept work? Again . . . what is my role?

The questions about the nature of God, the purpose of religion and scripture, and my role in the world would become more intense in 2003. I would be completely alone, without the children. The island, with its ocean of compassion, had offered Obadiah healing. Conquering his addiction, Obadiah became a high school teacher in Exuma, Bahamas, teaching auto mechanics and drafting—trades he had learned in the Bahamas before coming to the United States. Feeling secure and living in the house where he grew up as a child, he asked for the children to live with him in the Bahamas. Reluctantly, I acquiesced, believing that it might be good for him and them, even though I knew that I would miss them with a gut-wrenching intensity. Since my brother and I had lived in Brazil as children, I knew that exposure to different cultures for children was very powerful, important, and perhaps transformational. In the early spring, I packed their clothes and cherished toys and sent Emmanuel and Raebekkah to live with him. They were six and seven years old. We didn't discuss a return date.

In my aloneness, I started voraciously reading, devouring books and spiritual texts: *Jonathan Livingston Seagull* (Bach 2006), *The Greatest Miracle in the World* by Og Mandino (1977), Norman Vincent Peale's *The Power of Positive Thinking* (2003), Iyanla Vanzant's *One Day My Soul Just Opened Up* (1998), and *Of Water and the Spirit* by Malidome Patrice Somé (1995). I was also reading about different religions—Islam, Sufism, Christianity, and Orisha. In my journal, I wrote about the spiritual search for meaning, feeling that I was part of an initiation:

May 5, 2003
Precious Savior,
   Searching, Lord, for direction and purpose. For my passions to match my professions. For my life to fulfill the purpose for which I exist. To reflect your love, Spirit, essence, joy in all. To garner knowledge and wisdom for

dissemination. To influence the world appropriately. To leave an impression on this world. To be you. To stand in the intersection of life and death. To live in all of it at the same time. To understand as much as my spirit can handle. To understand the spiritual world. Feel that tension and pull, attraction and repulsion, fear, power, powerlessness. How close can I get to God and still be human? What gifts do I have to share?

Love—need to love, be loved, feel love, share love, God's love, spiritual love, emotional love, friendship love, romantic love, share intimacies. Do I need to understand life . . . or just God? What's up with sadness, sorrow, grief? It severely disturbs me to see others in pain . . . yet that triggers in me that ability to serve, share love, reflect the Holy Spirit, and provide healing, comfort, soothing, and peace.

Who am I? Who are my ancestors? What do I reflect and embody about them? What do my children reflect, embody from them? What are their destinies? What is the exile, loneliness, outsider perspective, differentness? Is the path of those who earnestly seek God . . . solace, connectedness?

I am being led into an initiation by an ancestor spirit that is directing my path of knowledge.

June 22, 2003

The goal of life is to seek to return to Oneness with God. Remain unattached to earthly materials. Allow the earthly part of you to die through pain and emotional death and to be reborn spiritually. The goal is to be prepared to die and to conquer the fear of death, as death is only unity with God and the completion of the circle of life. Remain unattached to people with no expectations as those can only be fulfilled by God. God is the only constant, not men. God's perfection reflects imperfectly in man. Bits and pieces of love, wisdom, insight, compassion, but not the whole.

August 28, 2003
Dear God,

God, I believe you are leading me, guiding me on the quest, this search for Oneness with you while living on this earth. I am discovering, uncovering secrets, the guides to peace and happiness.

Per Og Mandino: God has sent to every generation special people, talented people, all bearing the same message in one form or the other—that every human is capable of performing the greatest miracle in the world—self-resurrection.

November 22, 2003
Went to an Orisha program. I believe my search for God has ended right back at the starting point—love. The Sufi mysticism book brought it back. It is love . . . my diary. Dear Love. Realization that God is the wind on a day with no wind. God is a painter, painting a new day with different colors. Sometimes black, dark, but then that's when we have a background upon which light becomes most clearly visible at the end of our lives. We have a rainbow of experiences. But we, too, are creators within the parameters of God. We, too, can create colors, experiences, and images. The search for God is in solitude. The sharing of God is in community.

My search for my inner light had led me back to the beginning—back to Love, the Love of my childhood journals. In my initiation, I was gaining insight and wisdom. My aloneness provided the time and space for growth and reflection.

Inevitably, it would lead to asking questions about my role as a wife and mother, especially in the context of a spiritual journey and calling. On August 31, 2003, I asked questions about marriage and motherhood:

> *What does it mean to be married? What is my purpose as a wife? As an angel? As the giver and sharer of your love? Does my role as a wife and even as a mother limit my ability or constrain my responsibility to God to the larger world? Feeling that tension between spiritual and sensual. Reflecting on my past relationships—is it possible to be in an intimate relationship and also seek God?*

As 2003 came to an end and 2004 began, I was diligently and passionately on my questing and questioning journey, continuing to search for the lost bones of my spirit. I remember as a child feeling a tugging in my soul to go to Egypt and touch the pyramids. In 2004, I honored that tug and traveled with a White Catholic tour group, recommended by my sister-friend, for a ten-day journey to explore Egypt, the pyramids, the tombs, and the Nile. I wrote about my experience learning about Catholicism, the concept of the Mother of God, Islam, African religions, and the power of the Great Pyramid:

February 28, 2004:

> *I am so excited, almost nervous. Thank you for this window seat [on my way to Egypt]. I will maybe be able to see awesome stuff from the plane, or at least sleep comfortably. All these White people is a little reason for contemplation. Who needs, should see, deserves to see pyramids? The oppressed or the oppressors? Perhaps, there is a reason for the oppressors . . . maybe they will see us in a different light, respect us more, have more compassion for us. But we, too, need to feel the pride*

and know about ourselves. Feel some sense of unfairness, though. But I think I also feel some sense of left-outness, isolation, as the only Black American. But then, too, there's probably a reason for that as well.

March 1, 2004 [In Egypt]

So, the Father [the Catholic priest on the trip] prays and they have Mass daily. The Catholic focus on the Mother of God is very interesting. So, I've been astonished at the workmanship and artistic refinement of the art. Our own lives are very much irrelevant as individuals. It is really what we leave behind; it is our legacy that matters, not our name.

Notes on the Great Pyramid: 2650 BC. Base is 14 acres. 2,300,000 blocks of limestone: ranging from 2 tons to 50 tons. 480 feet high. 25 feet collapsed at the top. The outer casing is limestone. There are four true sides: north, south, east, west. 0.06% error. Cannot be duplicated. Twenty-four years to finish building. The intersection of history, culture, politics, religion.

They spoke to us about Islam—submission to Allah and the pillars of faith, prayer, fasting, tithing, and pilgrimage. I am beginning to see the legitimacy of all religions. I believe God is so magnificent that God manifests Godself in multiple ways and then allows people through different religions to worship and praise God. God also performs miracles in religions and culturally affirming ways to legitimize each religion (for example, the Virgin Mary).

It is such a shame, though, the heritage in history of war. The pyramids could only be achieved in a time of peace, when there is time, energy, and extraordinary effort that can be directly solely to God. Irrelevant whether the beliefs are one God or Sun God or many gods, because the beliefs controlled the people and the belief that kings were mighty and were from God allowed reverence, obedience, direction, and leadership for society to accomplish great things. A focus on artistry, craftsmanship, time of diligence, discipline, and determination.

God does send messengers for particular times in particular races, creeds.

Some messengers are obvious: Christ, Abraham, Muhammad, Buddha, Krishna. Some are less obvious, but true leaders of people: Martin, Malcolm X, Gandhi, proponents, advocates, martyrs for peace. And still others, in the form of saints: Khalil Gibran, Yogananda, Tao, with the gift of words, insight, to capture essence of God in words. And still others with gifts and talents created for the purpose of magnifying, reflecting, mirroring, honoring, service, and life force.

Artisans' lives were significant by the art left behind as evidence of God, as another creation, of the perpetuation of the life force of creation and recreation. God creates man who recreates God through procreation and artistic creation . . . music, visual art, writing, athletics, by using talents and gifts to perfection/excellence, thus evidencing Oneness, manifesting God in life through a new creation.

The trip to Egypt was transformational. Seeing Queen Hatshepsut's burial temple on the west bank of the Nile River, near Egypt's Valley of the Kings, and learning about the Egyptian goddesses Hathor, Ma'at, and Isis affirmed my own power as an African woman. I was gaining insight into the interconnected spiritual and religious path and my role and purpose. My insight would deepen even further when my sister-friend and I traveled to Barbados and St. Kitts. While I found deep joy and a spirit of celebration in the people of Barbados, in St. Kitts I felt a deep sorrow and sadness. I learned later that during the slave trade, St. Kitts was a colony with ties to Sierra Leone, receiving shipments of enslaved Africans from Bunce Island. St. Kitts was one of the first countries where enslaved Africans were sent.

One late afternoon during our time in St. Kitts, I went for a walk alone on the beach. The sun was beginning its descent but was still radiant and reflecting in the ocean. On the beach was a beautiful dark-skinned man, riding a horse. It was like a scene out of a movie. Enthralled, I started to talk to him. I learned he was from St. Kitts and was trying to process shifts and challenges with his daughter and former girlfriend. We talked awhile, and I encouraged him to go visit his daughter. He had a gentle and kind spirit. He asked me if I wanted to come with him and ride on his horse. Giddy with excitement, I said yes. He helped me up on the horse, and he guided us through the wind and the sand, along the ocean. It was such a liberating feeling. It was as if he was a messenger sent to remind me to gather the bones of freedom and flying. I had received clarity on my calling, and I wrote it in my journal:

July 24, 2004

My call is to be an angel and to guide others spiritually to particular destinations. My call is not limited or constrained by race, though the masses and the majority that I will be called to serve are disenfranchised. My goal is to embody love at all times and in all circumstances. Achievement of goal requires self-control, self-discipline, self-sacrifice, and diligence in maintaining connection— close connection—with Spirit. Need to be receptive, open, a vessel to be used by God.

The next day, my sister-friend shared her thoughts and reflections about me in my journal. I had asked her for her insight. She knew I was on a quest and was seeking insight and understanding:

July 25, 2004
Dear God,

Menah, my friend and the angel you sent me, has asked me to tell her how the you in me sees her, so I am asking you to speak through this pen.

When I look at you, Menah, I see a perfect creation. You embody the many paradoxes that define the lives of those who are truly seeking to be in harmony with their divinity but are constantly struggling with their humanity. Your humanity tells you that you must achieve at levels of excellence (defined by whom I know not) but your divinity tells you to rest in the knowledge and understanding that God's grace is sufficient. So you struggle to plan and orchestrate your life and that of your family to allow for optimal success (according to whom I know not) while at the same time your spirit is saying rest in the knowledge that God has you in the palm of God's hand.

The first man you called father, Dr. Pratt, taught you a way of being in the world that will always be with you. It is how the human Menah engages and judges what she deems worthwhile for herself and her family. It is perhaps at the same time your greatest strength as a human being and your greatest weakness as a spiritual being. You are able to bring this strength to bear in your life work in that it allows you to bring a measure of discipline to the doing of the work and this is good. However, it can be an obstacle: one can't always apply human principles to spiritual things.

The path of your life has been one in which you have packed a whole lot of living in a short 37 years. You have suffered much. You have experienced much. You have gotten many degrees. Your level of academic achievement parallels your level of life experience. You have a couple of master's, a JD. And a PhD in life. But, unlike in academics where you have two terminal degrees, the terminal degree you are seeking in life, Oneness with God before death, has yet to happen for you. And while you can pursue it as you have your degrees, you can't make it happen through discipline, hard work, or as your dad made you into a professional tennis player. I often hear and see you bring the achievement mind set in much the same way as I do in your attempts to engage the world from a spiritual perspective. I am uncertain of its efficacy in spiritual things.

In spite of these tensions, however, you continue to press toward the mark of the higher calling, and for that I am grateful, and because of it, the world is a better place for the many whose lives you touch. You are charged to be an angel, not just to do the work of an angel but to exemplify/personify the being of an angel so that all who experience you, in small ways or large, can see and learn to be angels themselves when the call for angel duty comes.

The depths of your compassion for others is paralleled only by the depths of your suffering at the hands of others. I, and all who encounter you, are grateful for your suffering because it has given you the skills necessary to be compassionate toward us and more importantly, act out that compassion. Suffering and compassion—two sides of the same coin. Paradox. You embody the paradoxes of the human condition and therein lies your divinity and thus your perfection as a work of the creator. I love you. To love you is to love me. To love you and me is to love God. Walk in peace and love.

She knew me—discipline and excellence, suffering and sorrow. She understood my quest and my search for Love, for Oneness, and to actualize my potential. She confirmed my calling—to be an angel. My questing had enabled me to give birth to a new part of myself. This new energy, however, would not be welcomed, and like weeds and invasive species, forces would seek her destruction.

SCENE TWO: **Darkness**

Trouble was brewing in the Bahamas. Obadiah was experiencing challenges at the high school, and Emmanuel's health was suffering from the absence of a medical infrastructure to treat his asthma. We decided that our children would come back to Nashville to start school in the fall of 2004. Initially, Obadiah was going to remain in the Bahamas. A couple of months later, though, Obadiah decided that he, too, would return to the United States. He was returning to a new house that I had been able to buy. It was a beautiful red brick four-bedroom house. Its large living room housed the 1912 Cable upright childhood piano from 1405 that I had moved to Nashville in 1990. It was the one prized possession that I hadn't lost in the bankruptcy. The new house had a downstairs bedroom and bathroom next to the kitchen and three bedrooms upstairs, including the master bedroom and the children's bedrooms.

The transition back to America would be challenging for the marriage on multiple levels—impacting our finances, my friendships, and his physical health. Anticipating some, but not all, of the challenges, I planned an African marriage reclamation ceremony for us to renew our vows and reclaim our eleven-year-old marriage. It was my attempt at integrating Obadiah back into the new life that I had created for myself in his absence. I invited close friends and Mama to the new house. Committed, though conflicted, Mama came. Unlike the first ceremony with no friends or family, this ceremony had both. I loved the ceremony and being surrounded and embraced by family and friends.

During Obadiah's absence, I had developed a very powerful and sustaining network of friends—male and female, young and old, Black and White. I had prayed to God for these friends after losing Obadiah and Sunshine, and She had answered my prayer. It was the first time in my life that I had a network of friends. This community was so important to me because I had never had the opportunity or time to really form a close network of friends, always busy working, taking classes, and then being a wife and mother. Alone and on my own, I had time and space to create special and sacred relationships. My friends loved me, and I loved them. These friendships proved to be a problem for Obadiah, however, who did not want me to "indulge" in these relationships. For some reason, Obadiah developed a particular dislike for a friend that the kids and I affectionately called Grandpa.

Grandpa was an older Black gentleman, about seventy years old. He was kind and funny, blunt and honest, and deeply caring, and like an older, wiser father figure, he gave me practical and useful guidance. He also loved the children, and the children loved him. The children and I met Grandpa when Obadiah first went to the Bahamas. I had started attending Metropolitan Interdenominational Church, and one night we met Grandpa at Wednesday Bible study. Grandpa became my friend and helped out tremendously, picking the kids up from school in his purple Ford Ranger truck when I was busy. He missed the children when they moved to the Bahamas and was delighted when they returned. He resumed his grandpa role, picking them up from school and spending time with them on weekends. He was a blessing to me and them. But he and Obadiah had a contentious relationship, as did Obadiah with almost everyone.

In addition to the friction with my friends, Obadiah resumed his quarrelsome relationship with his ex-wife and her husband, having unnecessary arguments over small and petty matters about clothing and schoolwork. Inevitably, Obadiah's agitated spirit began to impact his now twelve-year-old daughter. Their relationship was eventually severed, and the legal system again became an expensive and stressful monster in our lives.

Another challenge in our lives would be finding Obadiah a job. He did not have the credentials to teach in the United States, and he would be unemployed for months, until I helped him get a third-shift position as an environmental technician, working as a janitor at Vanderbilt Hospital. The third shift was difficult, and he began developing migraine headaches. We started sleeping in different bedrooms because he needed silence and darkness to manage the headaches. He slept in the downstairs bedroom, and I upstairs; he rarely came up to my bedroom. I wasn't supposed to go to his bedroom and interrupt his sleep. There was very little intimacy and barely any conversation.

In the midst of the madness, Mother Africa had not forgotten me. She was still calling my name. Grandma Pratt had recently passed away, and I needed to deal with her estate and the never-finished still-under-construction apartment building. In the spring of 2005, I decided to travel to Freetown to deal with the property and decided it was time to introduce Obadiah and our children to Sierra Leone. As we had always done, we stayed with Aunt Dorothea. Her circumstances had changed, and her husband was no longer part of the government. As she was no longer affluent, there was no running water for the shower; there were no permanent staff. Yet Aunt Dorothea was still a force of faith, waking up early, reading her Bible, praying, and singing. She was still a Wild Woman.

During that visit, I was able to visit Bunce Island, a former British slave castle where Africans were held before the Middle Passage. I was able to feel the spirit of the ancestors in the dilapidated shell of a cinder-block prison, overgrown yet still revealing hidden altars. That visit reminded me of my commitment to my ancestors. I wanted to do more meaningful work as a career, and I felt called to move closer to Mama. I was disappointed when she left Nashville, but I understood her commitment to the Pratt Music Foundation. She was the only surviving grandparent, and it was important for our children to have a meaningful relationship with her. I also knew that I wanted to be close to her since she was getting older and was in her mid-seventies.

In 2006, I started looking for jobs close to Mama in Bloomington, Illinois. After nine months of diligent searching, I was finally hired as an assistant provost and associate director for the Office for Equal Opportunity and Access at the University of Illinois at Urbana-Champaign. The salary was $30,000 less than what I was earning at Vanderbilt, and the position was significantly lower status than I had at Vanderbilt, but Mama was just forty-five minutes away.

Excited to start in October 2006, I left the children in Nashville with Obadiah. Our plan was that he would come to Champaign with them when the semester was over. But out of the blue, he called me the day before my job started and demanded that I pick them up. Out celebrating Mama's birthday on Sunday, October 15, we had to immediately change our plans and arrange to meet him. We met halfway in Kentucky and picked up the very confused children, who had abruptly been pulled out of school and pulled away from their community and friends without any goodbyes. To this day, I don't know what happened. I don't know if he felt overwhelmed or angry that he was left to deal with the move and the children by himself. I felt that he was trying to sabotage my success, my new job, and my new life.

When Obadiah arrived in Champaign a few weeks later, it was as if an evil spirit had embodied him. He came to town with an anger that I had never seen, simmering and bubbling just below the surface; an explosion was inevitable. I felt and sensed it; I just didn't expect it the day it happened—the day I came home from work, and he ambushed me in the master bedroom. As soon as I entered the room, he immediately closed the door and began to beat me, accusing me of not being submissive. It was humiliating and dehumanizing. I wrote in my journal:

Dear God,

Please help me. Please hear my silent cry and rescue me from this chaos, this crazy world into which I have descended. I want to escape, disappear into clouds and nothingness . . . into air . . . into silence . . . into peace . . . into silence . . . into stillness . . . into silence . . . into peace . . . silence, peace, quiet, quiet, quiet . . .

Suffocating, gasping for air, for breath, for clarity, for insight, choking, coughing, panting, exhausted, demanded upon, submerged under water. Mad, angry, furious, hateful, mean, angry, angry, mad, frustrated, violent, very violent crazy, psychotic, incoherent, mad— insane, mad, need to hit, pound, beat hard, long until exhausted! Scared frightened fearful mad angry.

Obadiah moved into a hotel for several days. Although he was extremely remorseful, I think he was just scared I was going to call the police and file charges. I didn't. I was embarrassed that I, a Black feminist, could be beaten and abused. I tried to keep going. As my "punishment," Obadiah decided that I would have to take the children and pick them up after school, even though he wasn't working. And so, I had the challenge of trying to leave work around three o'clock, navigate long lines of parents picking up children, take ours home to him, and then go back to work. I wrote very little during that time, but my August journal entries in 2007 epitomize the ongoing trauma I was enduring:

August 9, 2007

I so often feel so scared, bruised, battered, emotionally and spiritually. So alone, so isolated, so trying, so not noticed, so trying. How to continue the journey, so silenced, so invisible, so cautious, so trying, so tiptoeing, so second guessing? God, only you know my commitment, my loyalty, my dedication, my effort, my aloneness, my silence, my needs, my fears, my desires, my pain. So, you must help me, you must. I'm tired of being strong, of holding back tears, of not shouting, screaming, yelling. I'm doing, keeping, holding, trying. I'm tired, tired, tired, hurt, exhausted, and broken. God, please help me, guide me, comfort me, show me a way to peace and rest.

Obadiah had silenced me, symbolically removing my tongue. My spirit had been crushed. He had become my father, and I was the powerless daughter: the daughter who had suffered beatings for losing tennis matches and for "disrespecting him." Our marriage would never be the same. Obadiah had violated a sacred expectation. Like a weed, he had tried to stifle, suffocate, and kill my spirit.

Though he had tried to break my spirit, I refused to surrender, even bruised and battered. As I had done all my life,

I would call out to God: *"Please help me, guide me, comfort me, show me a way to peace and rest."* And She would hear and answer my anguished cry. She would fertilize my spirit and provide a balm and salve for my wounded soul.

SCENE THREE: **Discernment**

I had asked God for help, and She guided me to the buried bones of my dissertation and the stories of Black women and girls of Detroit. Somehow in the midst of my marriage madness, trauma, and sorrow, I heard Black women and girls crying out from basement boxes. I heard them crying out from newspaper articles, legal briefs, the Detroit School Board memos, Black feminist articles, and theoretical and methodological journals. They were calling my name, wanting my attention, because it was only me that knew their story, their trauma, and their pain. It was only me that could bring their hidden below-ground existence to above-ground reality.

I would begin to write what would become my first book, *Critical Race Feminism and Education: A Social Justice Model.* In the introduction, "A Black Girl's Story," I shared the genesis behind the book:

> *The spring of 2007 represented a turning point for me. . . . I began again to contemplate my mission and meaning in life. The questions began again in my mind: Who was I? What did I want to do with my life? What did I have an obligation and responsibility to do as a Black woman? . . .*
>
> *It seemed all of sudden that the energy in the universe was calling me to tell the story of Black girls in Detroit. It was as if Black women were calling to me*

from the boxes where my dissertation, along with news-
papers and journal articles, was buried, having been
moved around for almost 15 years through four homes
and two states. It was as if the Black women were tell-
ing me that they still had a story to tell; that their story
could still make a difference in the world; and that I
needed to use the aloneness, loneliness, and quietness
of Champaign–Urbana to begin to write and revise my
dissertation to tell their story (Pratt-Clarke 2010, 6–7).

While I was writing to tell their story, I was also writing for the universal and ubiquitous Black woman and girl—descendants of women and girls who had been enslaved, abused, disinherited, disenfranchised, marginalized, and minimized in society. I was heeding the revolutionary call of Lorraine Hansberry, to write as if our lives depended on it, because they did. I was writing to "channel my anger at injustice in society against Black women." I was writing "to stop spirit murder and spirit injury of Black women." I was writing because:

Black women suffer and struggle spiritually, emotionally,
and physically as we push forward with an almost unbear-
able load, often shouldering not only our own trials, but
also those of Black men and Black children. It is because
of these loads that we, as Black women, often bear alone,
that I had to write (Pratt-Clarke 2010, 7).

As I wrote on October 27, 2007, "*If I were to die today,*
what would I wish I had done, completed, accomplished?
WRITE BOOKS." I was writing to save myself. Buried in the boxes of my dissertation was my personal statement written in 1994 for the American Association of University Women dissertation fellowship application, where I wrote: "*I know*
that I must continue to be a role model for other women as

an educator in the tradition of Ms. Bethune, nurturing a desire for knowledge."
Consistent with that commitment to be an educator like Mary McLeod Bethune, I decided that not only would I write books, but I would also begin a clandestine journey to become a tenured faculty member. Even though I had a full-time job as an administrator managing discrimination complaints, disability accommodations, and affirmative action compliance, I decided that I would quietly and discreetly build a portfolio for tenure consideration. I knew that in the hallowed grounds of the academy, I would not have any power or respect as a Black woman if I wasn't a tenured faculty member. To stake my claim to legitimacy and belonging, I needed to be tenured.

I began teaching classes on critical race theory, critical race feminism, and Black feminism every semester either in the Law School or in the African American Studies Department. I also started publishing book chapters and articles while continuing to work on the book about the marginalization and minimization of Black women and girls in the Detroit single-sex school debate. In the manuscript, I was exploring and creating a new model for doing transdisciplinary applied social justice work, illustrating the power of integrating law and sociology to study race, class, and gender. I was looking at Black male sexism, race loyalty over gender loyalty, Black nationalism, and Black feminism.

By writing about these issues, I was slowly reclaiming my voice, empowering myself, and picking up the pieces of myself that had been beaten out of me. Writing was a tool and vehicle for healing my soul. My entries in 2008 reflect that commitment to the work of healing:

March 6, 2008
Write your dreams down: my dream is to be a spiritual leader to help others fulfill their highest potential and divinity. Honor your own self. Meditate on your

own self. Worship your own self. Kneel to your own self. Understand your own self. Your God dwells within you. I want to be a spiritual leader in the spirit of Wayne Dyer (wisdom), Iyanla Vanzant (genuine), and Mother Teresa (compassion).

March 30, 2008

Actualize my call as an angel for God in this world— an instrument of God, a tool for God to bring hope and healing to the world. I am an educated, brilliant, strong, wise, discerning, strong, surviving Black woman. I have survived abuse, racism, and sexism. I have a destiny.

June 27, 2008

Villoldo: "The most effective healers recognize that they were once deeply wounded themselves and as a result of their own healing, they develop compassion for others who are hurting. Eventually their wounds were transformed into gifts that allow them to feel more deeply and show more compassion."

In 2009, the work of healing would begin with a fast and a focus on my own health. I was reading a book on spiritual disciplines, including prayer, attending church, fasting, and tithing, and I decided to undertake a forty-day fast, blending Judaism and Christianity through replicating Jesus's experience of fasting for forty days, with the Jewish Passover tradition of eating matzah.

The fasting led to revelations that I wrote about over the next few months:

January 25, 2009

Today, I weigh 151.5. I am thriving in my self-control. I feel really good and consider the snow today a blessing

*to help me continue to fight the trial of temptation. I am
claiming my book published. It is the start of many new
roads for me, but most importantly, my career and destiny
as a writer and as a senior scholar on race, class, and gender.
I will begin to exercise soon and play tennis again. This
summer, piano again, as well as I will make a place for me in
this home, a place of quiet, peace—perhaps even the closet!*

*I know, God, you will be preparing me for my destiny
and giving me people to serve so I must continue to ask
you to enlarge my territory and strengthen my self-control, and discipline. I've been healed of asthma, feeling
more calm these days. I am making good progress on A
Course in Miracles. When I am ready for ministry, the
right program will appear for me to pursue. Focus on
sharing my gifts. I am developing another way of thinking
and being in the world—a way of carrying peace with
me in all situations. My weight loss goal remains to be
at 120–130. Thus, I still have much work remaining. At
least 20–30 more pounds or about 25 pounds so, at least
by April 7, I should be in good shape. I would like to be
a size 10 or 12. I must realize this is a lifelong change. But
I must still lose 10 more pounds in March and February.
Dig In, Buckle Down, and Pursue Perfection.*

March 2, 2009
God,

*Thank you. Thank you for such amazing blessings in
40 days. Lost 17 pounds, rent was reduced by $200, salary
increased by $27,000. Boss retired. New title . . . What
else? Debt-free, assistant chancellor, book published.*

April 14, 2009

*My whole life is a slow crucifixion to help the parts
of me that are not needed to be killed and destroyed so*

*that new spirit can live. Physical desires, needs. One
can't resist the crucifixion but must suffer gladly for the
greater good and revelation.*

September 24, 2009
Dear God,
    *Spiritual journey often seems lonely, just as leader-
ship is often a solitary journey. As a visionary, forging
ahead, trusting others to follow, just as God you are
ahead, trusting and encouraging us to follow. I want to
understand and feel the magnitude of God's love.*

I was still wanting to understand and feel Love. Though I
was no longer looking for it in the marriage, I was still committed to being married. We had been meeting with a Black
Baptist preacher for counseling sessions after the beating, and
I shared that I was committed to the marriage and committed
to misery. Both the pastor and Obadiah were equally horrified at my commitment to misery and encouraged me that I
didn't need to resign to misery. Yet much of our married life
in Champaign was about me caring for Obadiah because, as
he would say, "I keep hurting myself." I had helped him get a
job at the University of Illinois Athletics Department, working
the night shift as a janitor, but he was often injured. In the fall
of 2009, he tore his rotator cuff, a serious injury requiring
surgical repair. He had already broken two toes before the
shoulder injury.

Despite the injury, he decided that we should renew our
wedding vows for our sixteenth wedding anniversary in the
Bahamas with his family. Mama, still ambivalent about Obadiah, nevertheless came, steadfastly committed to me. I loved
the romance of the ceremony, being in a beautiful dress. I
wrote the vows and planned the ceremony, as I had for our first
wedding ceremony and for the African reclamation ceremony.

After the ceremony, it rained and interrupted the reception. We didn't get to dance. I had wanted to dance to "At Last," by Etta James. It was not to be, perhaps because he would not be my "at last."

SCENE FOUR: **Goddess Wisdom**

The lonely spiritual journey of the "slow crucifixion" was consistent with the season of weeding, of trying to pull my spirit up through the muck and mire of darkness into light. I had emerged from the choking weeds of evilness and darkness and was ready for air. I had gathered the ancestral energy from Mama Pratt in Freetown and from the desert tombs, pyramids, and temples of Egypt and Queen Hatsheput. I had soothed my soul with the ocean and shores of St. Kitts and Barbados. I was breathing life into the bones of the Black women and the Black girls of my buried dissertation boxes. My spiritual questing had given me direction and discernment about my destiny. I had clarity on my calling to be a healer and an angel. Rites and rituals would move it forward.

Reflection Questions

1. Have you had a season of questing, where you were intensely seeking to understand the meaning and purpose of life? What did that season look like? What lessons did you learn about yourself?

2. Have you engaged with spiritual practices, such as fasting, prayer, meditation, and scripture reading? What impact have those practices had on your life?

3. If you have not had spiritual practices, do you have daily rituals, such as running, walking, cooking, and eating particular foods that help define, pace, and ground your life journey? What are those rituals for you? Why did you start them? Why do you continue them?

References

Bach, R. 2006. *Jonathan Livingston Seagull*. Scribner.

Foundation for Inner Peace. 1996. *A Course in Miracles*. Viking.

Mandino, O. 1977. *The Greatest Miracle in the World*. Bantam Books.

Peale, N. V. 2003. *The Power of Positive Thinking*. Fireside.

Pratt-Clarke, M. 2010. *Critical Race, Feminism, and Education: A Social Justice Model*. Palgrave.

Somé, M. P. 1995. *Of Water and the Spirit: Ritual, Magic, and Initiation in the Life of an African Shaman*. Penguin Books.

Vanzant, I. 1998. *One Day My Soul Just Opened Up: 40 Days and 40 Nights toward Spiritual Strength and Personal Growth*. Fireside.

Villoldo, A. 2007. *The Four Insights: Wisdom, Power, and Grace of the Earthkeepers*. Hay House.

THE NINTH STAGE—Spiritual Rites

THE TIME FOR WOMB WEANING has arrived. The spirit is almost ready to pierce the soil surface, moving from womb-like darkness into light. It is a time for balancing on the fulcrum; a time of sudden shifts and solemn transitions; a time when boundaries are blurred between life and death, between that which is above and that which is below. It is the liminal interstitial space where sacred secrets are shared in rites of passage. It is a season of transitions from girlhood to womanhood and from the earth world to the spirit world.

SCENE ONE: **Girlhood Rites**

*O*ver the course of two years between 2010 and 2012, as Blackwildwoman, I participated in rites of passage related to girlhood transitions and goddess transitions, involving three generations of Black women. My ten-year-old daughter, Raebekkah, would transition from girlhood to womanhood, and my mother would transition to the spirit world as a goddess. I would be at the fulcrum, balancing, navigating, and facilitating girlhood, goddess, and grieving rites.

The January 10, 2010, journal entry reads, "*What in my life do I need God to send an angel ahead of me? Genesis 24:7: 'He will send his angel ahead of you.'*" My daughter, Raebekkah, became a woman a few days before her eleventh birthday on January 27, 2010. As a child who had such a harrowing transition into womanhood, I wanted to create a completely different and affirming experience for my own daughter. The ritual that I created was a commitment to ending the generational trauma relating to menstruation, in which the blood is a sign of shame and humiliation rather than celebration and wonder. I asked my women friends to send and share goddess wisdom that someone gave them, or they wished someone had given them, as they transitioned to womanhood. They responded and sent beautiful letters to Raebekkah, welcoming her to womanhood. Their ideas, suggestions, and well-wishes are recreated as a letter to Blackwildgirls:

Hello dear one,

I heard the wonder-filled news about your physical passage into womanhood. Congratulations on your recent entrance into womanhood! This is indeed a special time in your life. Please remember that being a woman is a magnificent thing. We created the world and are the ones who keep it going.

Now, don't be embarrassed. I know that you got your "period" recently, or as some old folks call it—your "monthly friend." I actually think that sounds kind of crazy, so we'll just call it your period. Calling it a "friend" makes it sound like you invited it over, which is usually not the case. Consider me like an older cousin who is giving you some advice, okay? You are officially one of us big girls now! All of us girls have to deal with it each month, but it's okay because it is just a part of life. Do you know I was 10 years old when I got mine, and I was so nervous at first? But then my mom told me that all of us ladies must deal with it, and everything would be just fine. And it really is that simple! Our bodies are so amazing and having a period is part of what makes women so special. You may not understand all of it now, but just know that it's a very natural thing and it's all good. Sometimes your tummy will hurt but that will get better too. Just do your best to be prepared and just remember that you only have to deal with this a few days out of the month. No big deal at all!

Now that you have begun your Moon Cycle, you are entering into the company of women all around you who will love you and take care of you in a very different way. Your blood is sacred, darling, and it is through this vessel that life is created. When your cycle is fully developed (and just because you've seen a little blood does not mean it is already finished developing), you will experience such joy in being a woman.

No one can really tell you exactly how you are going to feel once your body has fully developed, but you must take care to understand the meaning and purpose of your cycle. As you grow, whenever you are on your cycle, take care of your body because it will need a little extra care. Your mom can tell you more about that. Why do I refer to it as your "Moon Cycle?" Because our bodies are tied to the cycles of the moon. When the moon is full, more babies are born, and the full moon represents the pregnant female body. It is full of moist energy and is tied to our moods, as well. When you are on your Moon Cycle (or simply "Moon"), you may feel moody, too.

It's amazing how God exquisitely made the woman's body. It will not always be comfortable and fun, but here are a few tips in managing your new monthly friend (your mother has likely already shared these tidbits with you, but they are worth repeating):

Keep a calendar and religiously circle the first day of each cycle. After a few months, you will see a pattern and be able to determine how many days there are generally between the first day of your cycles, and thus, be able to estimate each month when it should come.

The week before and during your cycle, you may want to minimize your intake of sweets (sugar), chocolate, and caffeine. These items are known to intensify your cramps and pimples.

Once you can estimate when your period will start, you may want to plan to wear a panty liner a few days before (just in case it decides to pop up on you a little early one month) and always keep a pad discreetly in your purse during your period (replenish when you use the one you have).

Always roll up your pads tightly and fully wrap them in tissue before throwing them in the trash. Don't throw it in the toilet unless using a tampon. In any case, you don't need to let the world know that your friend is here.

Should your monthly friend catch you unprepared, or you find that you have soiled your underwear or clothes, just soak up as much as possible with tissue (and cold water if needed; never use hot water on blood) and roll up a wad of paper tissue and place it in your underwear until you can reach your mother or the school nurse to get a pad. And know that your mother, me, and every other woman in the whole world have had our host of "uh-ohs" at some point of our lives in working through this monthly occasion. So, please don't be afraid to share your questions or concerns or disasters!

Spend time reading or writing in your journal (quiet time with yourself). Curl up in the bed and enjoy time with your wonderful mother. She is a jewel. Since she is your mother, sometimes you may see her in a different light but know that she is a wise woman, and her advice will only help you. When you grow up and become a mother, you will remember the things that she taught you.

We as women are a special breed, strong, yet sensitive, beautiful inside and out. Always remember that. Be proud of who you are, and do not be afraid to be assertive when it calls for it, and gentle when needed. We as women need to embrace our womanhood. In these days of equal opportunity, I think we tend to forget that there's no shame in being a woman . . . in crying, laughing, showing emotion, etc. I believe that I can do anything I put my mind to, but I'm not a man, and as such, do not want to act or behave like one. I can be strong and assertive, and still come across feminine. There's no need to downplay that side of me. I am woman . . . hear me roar (LOL) and all that. Always be yourself, do not buy into the world's idea of what you should look like. Above all, learn to like and love yourself, because then others like you for you, and you'll radiate an inner confidence that will draw people to you.

As you grow physically, I pray that you will also grow spiritually and use your gifts to bring joy to all those you will come to know. You are a beautiful and gifted young woman on your way to becoming a beautiful and gifted adult. As you begin this new year of life and with your passage into womanhood, just remember you have choices in life. Always be yourself and remain confident and realize your strengths. You should always love and trust yourself and your instincts and value who you are. Always maintain your dreams and goals because they will take you far! You have great role models in your mom and your grandmother.

You are now entering a new phase in your life as a young woman, and this is a very exciting period in one's life. At this special time in your life, I am reminded of the tender advice given by my grandmother and my mother. They wished that I would be able to feel and hold their love as unwavering protection in my life. I am now passing on to you their gentle advice:

Keep your faith alive and trust your mom as a loving, guiding force throughout your life. Cherish your family and be there for them. Always! Be mindful when selecting friends and once you have committed to them, enjoy the sweetness of friendship. Trust that God holds you in safety and that many angels watch over you every minute of the day!

I love you. Make sure you love your body, love being a girl, and thank God every day for allowing your body to grow and develop just like She intended. You are fabulous, girlfriend! Many warm hugs to you. Much love, joy, peace, and happiness. God bless! BOOYAKAH!!!

This letter, full of goddess wisdom, reminds us to cherish ourselves, to honor our power as women, to embrace womanhood, to love our bodies, and to love being a girl. It gives us permission to roar. It validates our womanhood and the essential nature of being a woman. This rite of passage was not only for Raebekkah's birth into womanhood but also for the birth of my book. On my birthday on April 7, 2010, I wrote that my book *Critical Race, Feminism, and Education: A Social Justice Model* got accepted by a wonderful press, Palgrave. I had birthed the Black girls of the boxes into life. The veil had been lifted. They would be able to rise into the world to have their story heard.

Not only was the veil lifted for the Black girls of the boxes, but I would also be removing my own veil, birthing hidden parts of myself into the world. As I wrote on May 26, 2010, *"I am grateful for my ability to write and share my thoughts. I have to trust that the revelation of myself to myself in writing will cause your revelations and wisdom to be manifested."* A few months later, sitting peacefully and prayerfully one early morning at Lake of the Woods near Champaign, I wrote a letter to myself:

July 25, 2010
Dear Menah,

I don't think I've ever written to myself before. What do I want to say? I have so much on my spirit. The universe is alive and waking up, and I am part of it. I keep reminding myself to breathe deeply, to be conscious of the in and out of my breath, especially the release. Get it out—release what is inside of me. The energy, the power, the force, the destiny, the words, the message. I have and hold secrets—and the call is to release them. The secret knowledge, the secret experiences, the secret hurt and pain, the secrets of my life, the secrets of God. The message is to release the secrets, but to do so appropriately and balance in accord with the universe. Sometimes fast, furious, like a horse out of a gate; sometimes slow and deliberate like the seagulls' walk. Sometimes graceful like the swan on the lake. Sometimes loud like quacks and caws of birds.

But the end must be the release. Releasing myself into the Oneness of the universe and knowing I can do it without dying. What I can see is that all the studying, searching, questioning, and seeking is subtly and almost imperceptibly building a foundation in me. I am wise. I am maturing. I am powerful. I am about to unleash and explode into the world. I have to breathe deeply and release and say "ahhhh" more often.

I feel I am transitioning personally and spiritually. My book will be transformative for social justice, intellectually. I have books inside of me waiting to be birthed that have explosive, orgasmic energy, just like the rush of this waterfall at Lake of the Woods Botanical Garden. A waterfall, water from who knows where—from God—bursting forth, falling, dropping to the ground, replenishing. A force creating rivers, ponds, sustaining moving around, over rocks and obstacles full of life. Vivacious, never-ending, unlimited, making rough places smooth, flowing, harmonious, calming, yet powerful. Focused on the objective, destiny, singleness of purpose. Fall, coming forth, release.

I am a waterfall. I know one of my spirit guides is Eyaside—grandmother comes back. An institution can't constrain my destiny! I do initiations. I feel like I can initiate myself. I don't know what that looks like, but I know it will come to me.

I have to tell my father's story. I have to tell my mother's story. I have to tell my story. So, next steps: Get

ancestors together—share new vision. Create new rituals
with them. Memorize them and seek to understand their
power. Develop a relationship with my father's spirit, for
it is power and wisdom and love. He actually is my other
spiritual guide! Morning Glory is another spiritual guide.

Create an initiation ceremony. Get rid of old clothes,
too. Get ready. Create an altar.

It was as if the ritual for Raebekkah cleared the spiritual
air and aura for me. The gift of initiations and rituals is that
as we take on a new Self, we also gain new knowledge. I had
received a message to release the secrets, and spirit guides
would accompany me on my new journey.

I was ready to live fully alive. I was reading *A Course in
Miracles*, a deeply spiritual book about transformation and
reimagining traditional Christian principles and ideologies.
The text includes teachings and lessons, and one of those was
about altars. I would journal about the altar within me, a
secret space:

February 1, 2011

A Course in Miracles: The altar of God. I have an
altar inside of me. It is an altar of God which I need to
access that I have been separated from. How do I access
my altar? Fear is a barrier. Atonement is a tool to access
the altar. At the altar is peace, joy, love, and acceptance.
To reach the altar, I have to be an atonement, a tool for
others—a vessel of love. An atonement doesn't happen in
isolation. It is a direct result of interaction with others.
I believe that my altar had been hurt, damaged, but it
is protected yet imperfect, still! What was attacked was
my mind and my body.

Fifteen days later, I had a revelation about my altar. It was a part of me that I had been separated from for decades. On February 16, 2011, I wrote: *"I have a backpack with a heavy little girl in it—Eyaside. How do I love her unconditionally? The separation from her keeps me paralyzed. Why do I not like her? Who is she? What is the wall, division?"*

I had rediscovered Blackwildgirl during a painful session with an amazing Black woman counselor. For months on a weekly basis, I had been processing my life with her, and in that session, her persistent and gentle questioning had led to the revelation that part of me was in a backpack. It was Blackwildgirl—my queen superpower. I remember leaving counseling and sitting in my car with a sorrow that released a thousand dams of water: tears from all the years that I had swallowed and suffocated them, tears for the child that could not let her light shine, and tears for all the words she never spoke but always felt. She had made her presence known. She was ready to come out, and I would need to begin to develop a relationship with her.

The time had come to revisit the dethroning of my childhood, where my symbolic crown, representing my divine feminine essence, was severed. It was a time to reconnect with the little girl of my childhood, the powerful spirit of divine feminine knowledge and intuition, my Queen of Sheba. It would take years to learn to love the little girl, but the first steps had been taken. She had been acknowledged. Though I thought the girlhood ritual I had created was for Raebekkah, I now knew it was also for me. My little girl needed to be validated, loved, and affirmed.

It was this little girl in me that would be baptized a month later in another rite of passage ceremony—a baptism in the Jordan River. Though I had been baptized before as an adult at Metropolitan Interdenominational Church, the children and I were blessed to go to Israel for a vacation together. During that trip, we all got baptized in the chilly and cold Jordan River. Being baptized in a sacred land was a cathartic and cleansing experience.

In Israel, I felt the Love of God surround me. When I walked along the Dead Sea and saw the pillars of salt, I felt the depth of the thickness, heartiness, and resilience of life. When I walked among the Mount of Olives and saw rows of olive trees, I felt the rejuvenating energy of life. I resonated with the reality that in order to produce olive oil, the olives must be pressed. Yet there is a beautiful outcome in the end. I realized that in my spiritual trials, I was being pressed, but I would experience the fruits from years of searching, yearning, and questing. In Israel, I gathered sustenance and strength that would fortify me for one of the most difficult and challenging experiences of my life—helping to shepherd and guide my mother across the thin line connecting life to death, as part of her goddess rite of passage.

SCENE TWO: **Goddess Rites**

mama was sixty-eight years old when Papa died. After his death, she decided it was time to let her Black-wildgirl out to strut in the world. It was that part of herself she had hidden for years to navigate the "messy situation" in the marriage, the part that she had made small for my dad, and the part that enabled her to walk slowly behind my father. For the next sixteen years, Mama sashayed all over the United States and across the world: from Poland to Hungary, from England and Wimbledon to New York and the US Open, from tennis to hot air balloons in New Mexico, to concerts with Awadagin. She often traveled to hear Awadagin perform, and she enjoyed her White House visits with him, including two visits with President Obama.

When Mama returned to Bloomington, she started hosting large dinner parties in her home. She cooked incredible and delicious meals of salmon, lamb, oxtails, and chicken dishes, with vegetables, fruits, and salads. She baked desserts too. She would host close to thirty friends for sit-down dinners with china and place settings. She really loved these events, and her friends loved them too. Mama had a diverse group of friends, young and old, Black and White. Many of her friends were couples who were affiliated with the Pratt Music Foundation: Darlene and Marc, Patsy and Jack, and Pam and Jack. Mama, Patsy, Pam, and Darlene were all best friends. Pam was an African American woman who had worked with Mama on the Black History Project when Pam was a professor at Illinois Wesleyan. She was one of the founders of the Pratt Music Foundation and was still on the board. Darlene and Patsy were amazing White women who were also founders of the Pratt Music Foundation, board members, and involved in many civic organizations in the community. These women would do anything for Mama, and Mama would do anything for them.

As part of Mama's decision to let her Blackwildgirl roar, she decided to take voice lessons when she was eighty and record a DVD of her singing. She also created a DVD of herself reciting poetry. She instructed me to play these at her funeral. She wanted to record the DVDs while she could still remember the poems and songs. She had lived with mild Alzheimer's for several years and had managed it quite well, but she knew that at some point, it would begin to impact her daily living activities.

She lived alone in a beautifully decorated three-bedroom apartment and was still driving in 2011, at the age of eighty-two. She continued to play tennis and participate in water aerobics. She was also still supporting me by caring for my children at times. In the summer of 2011, Raebekkah was twelve and Emmanuel was thirteen. Raebekkah spent a few weeks with Mama, while Emmanuel spent time in the Bahamas

with his father, still convalescing with pain. During Raebekkah's visit, Mama called me in a panic to tell me that someone
had stolen her dish towels. I reminded her that she had many
antiques and valuable items in her beautiful apartment, and if
something was going to be stolen, it was not going to be her
dish towels.

Mama had collected antique commode and potty chairs
for decades, accumulating a collection of almost thirty. They
were a reminder to her of the stark contrast between wealth
and poverty, and class divisions even in the shared humanity
of existence. As a poor Black child in the 1930s American
South, she had to use outhouses and buckets; the wealthy
had elegant mahogany and walnut commodes with colorfully
painted chamber pots. The chairs she collected were unique
and distinctive; some looked like dressers, some looked like
chairs and thrones, and some looked like small wooden boxes.
Mama also had beautifully engraved chamber pots, egg cod-
dlers, and other precious antiques. Her apartment was like
a museum. As I told Mama, a thief would have a variety of
valuable options—not dish towels. Agreeing, Mama laughed
nervously and then hung up the phone.

After we finished talking, I sensed that Mama was reaching a turning point in her independent lifestyle. I'd suggested
a few months earlier that we should explore an assisted-living
facility, and she'd become very upset and angry. She told me
that she, not me, would decide when she was ready to leave;
I knew I needed to respect that. Though I was worried, I was
glad that Raebekkah was there with Mama, but I knew that
it was a responsibility that I needed to bear and not my young
and impatient daughter.

After the dishcloth incident, Mama called me a few days
later and said, "I'm ready." She recognized it was time to leave
her beloved apartment in Bloomington. I was initially relieved;
Mama had made the decision on her own terms. Over the next

few weeks, though, I became overwhelmed as I began to realize the magnitude of the new responsibility that I was assuming, and trying to explore whether Mama wanted to live with us or at an assisted-living facility.

When we first moved to Champaign, we rented a town-house. After a year, we found a home to rent in Urbana, and the owners eventually sold us the home. It was a beautiful four-bedroom house. There was a master bedroom and guest bedroom on the main floor with two bathrooms. The upstairs had two bedrooms and a bathroom. On the first floor, there was a small dining room that became my office, and a large kitchen with an island that opened up into a large two-room living room. It was a beautiful, spacious house, and of course, I had my beloved piano too. The house was a perfect size, in case Mama needed to move in.

Mama initially preferred an assisted-living facility, rather than our house, and so in preparing for Mama's move, I learned a lot about assisted-living facilities: the wait lists; the possibility of getting a room where someone had just passed away; the exorbitant costs, including the down payment, which was almost as much as for a house; the unexpectedly high monthly payments for rent; the additional fees and charges for any supplemental care, including administering medicines and inhalers; and their pervasive Whiteness. I wanted to find a place that was diverse, representing Mama's community of friends. I didn't want Mama to be the only Black person in an all-White facility, because of the likelihood for her to experience either overt racism or microaggressions.

Eventually, I found a facility just a few minutes from our house in Urbana. We sold many of Mama's possessions so she could scale down to the one-room unit. We could only keep about five of her most treasured antique potty chairs. I knew this was a source of much sadness for her. Courageously, she resigned herself to her new reality. I visited Mama daily, making sure she was adjusting well; meeting the staff that was taking care of her; and playing piano in the dining room before the dinner meal for the many residents that lined up in their wheelchairs at least an hour before mealtime. The music was a small way for me to try to counter the heaviness of illness, the eerie quietness, the unabatable loneliness, the inevitable sadness, and the pervasive whiteness of the walls and people. I often took Raebekkah and Emmanuel with me, and even though Mama was irritable and unhappy at losing her independence and being in a facility, she almost always seemed glad to see us.

We were also adjusting to her increasing Alzheimer-inflicted repetition. I had to remind Raebekkah in her adolescent impatience not to say, "Grandma, you already said that." She would argue with me and say, "But she did." I would remind her that Grandma didn't know what she had just said. Although Alzheimer's was clearly impacting her, she was able to travel to Cincinnati in December for my brother's wedding. She had been practicing a few songs to sing but could only remember a few verses at the wedding. At the wedding, Mama had a subtle cough and a scratchy throat. We thought it was a mild cold.

When she returned from the wedding, the nagging cold seemed to be worsening; eventually, she was diagnosed with asthma. It was becoming clear that this was not just a regular winter cold. I began spending more and more time with Mama. In my journal I sought to understand the relationship between Mama's dimming light and my own increasing radiant light of self-awareness in entries addressed to both God and Menah:

January 4, 2012
Dear God,

As I read about my wounded child within me, I realize that caring for my mom should help me care for that child and heal her.

April 15, 2012
Dear Menah,
I am in training to be an Ascended Master. I am a
student. I have been on this journey for a while without
knowing. I've encountered spirits in unactualized potential
who were attracted to my light. I have a light that I must
shine always. I must control the light radiance and direct it.

In my journal, I was reflecting on the relationship of caring for Mama, who was regressing to a more dependent life, and caring for the parts of myself that were also dependent. I was also reflecting on the transitional nature of our lights that shine for a relatively short lifetime, and the importance of letting them shine as powerfully as we can while we have that power. Mama's light was beginning to flicker. She was becoming weaker, and the doctor's appointments were becoming more frequent as they tried to diagnose the cause for the asthma:

April 29, 2012
Dear Menah,
Having the feeling Mama is staying weak too long.
But God knows all. My only responsibility is love.

I had decided that the best strategy for me to support Mama on her goddess journey to the spirit world was to embody Love and to be patient, kind, thoughtful, and selfless. I felt that love was a tool for healing and bringing peace to a complicated and perhaps deteriorating mental and physical condition. A few weeks later, I would learn why Mama was staying weak too long. She was diagnosed with lung cancer and given just a few months to live. She had never smoked, so the diagnosis was a shock. We had been focused on Alzheimer's. Now, we had to focus on cancer. Our options were limited. I wrote to try to process a new reality of her condition:

May 10, 2012

Mama was diagnosed with lung cancer. Her journey to eternity is tied with my journey to eternity. What are the principles that will guide me on this journey? I am the Resurrection and the Life. I am the Living Water. I am the Bread of Life.

As Mama began her transition to the spirit realm, my journal entries begin to chronicle this journey. I used my early morning to engage in spiritual practices of reading the Bible, studying spiritual texts, practicing and writing the lessons from *A Course in Miracles*, and writing in my journal. When I found a meaningful scripture, I would write it, sometimes verbatim, sometimes modified, sometimes as a combination from different versions, and sometimes rephrased to suit my own needs. Sometimes I would write to God and sometimes to myself. Using biblical references to Jesus as a savior and healer, I tried to remind myself that I, too, could be a healer and source of life. My journal was also a place for prayers:

May 22, 2012

God, please help me to navigate this journey with grace. I feel challenged by the jointness/aloneness, responsibility of multiple roles, emotions. I need to stay calm, peaceful. I feel anger—it needs to dissipate. Today, she said October was too long. What does that mean? What does her spirit know? The doctor said lung cancer would essentially be a blessing because the shortness of the journey. Can I be strong? Should I be strong?

May 23, 2012

I am the presence of Divine Love at all times.

May 25, 2012
God, please do not let Mama be in pain or suffer.

Realizing the gravity of the cancer diagnosis, I moved Mama from the assisted-living facility into our home. She had the guest bedroom and bathroom on the first floor, just a short distance down the hallway from the master bedroom. Our initial plan was that Obadiah and I would take care of Mama. He had recently recovered from a broken coccyx that he had injured in a fall at work. During the long recovery, Obadiah spent hours each day lying immobile on the living room floor. Once he was healed, he returned to his night shift, and he agreed to watch Mama during the day while I was at work. When I got home, he would try to sleep and get ready for the night shift.

Alzheimer's made Mama irritable and confused. In addition, she really didn't like Obadiah and often wasn't kind to him. Obadiah was trying to care for her, cooking her lunch and trying to watch her so she wouldn't leave the house. Obadiah would generally be in the living room, and sometimes she would try to sneak past him to go out the front door when he was taking naps. Sometimes she would just announce: "I'm going to 1405." We would try to explain to her that she couldn't go to 1405. Because of the progressing Alzheimer's, she couldn't process why she couldn't go home. With her increasing moodiness, we realized we needed more help.

I began looking for help, eventually finding a woman named Mrs. Clarke to come to the house and help care for Mama. She was a divine assignment, having our same last name, having home care experience, and being Black. She had a calm spirit, and I hoped that Mama would feel more comfortable around a Black woman. Even though Mama didn't understand why a stranger was watching her all the time, she slowly became accustomed to her and less combative.

Obadiah, as usual, was a source of conflict with Mrs. Clarke, fussing over her cooking and cleaning and feeling like she wasn't doing enough. But I trusted her and was just glad that she could watch over Mama.

As I was navigating Mama's transition, I continued to journal, reflecting on the points of connection between my mother's dying journey and my living journey:

June 1, 2012
God,

John 19:28. "Jesus knew that everything was now finished. When Jesus tasted it, he said, 'It is finished.' Then he bowed his head and gave up his spirit."

Psalm 119:133: "Guide my steps by your word so I will not be overcome by any evil."

Psalm 143: "As pressure and stress bear down on me, I find joy in your commands."

John 20:19 "Peace be with you."

John 20:22: "Then he breathed on them and said to them, 'Receive the Holy Spirit.'"

It is a sad, gray, dreary day . . . cold . . . What will the news be? Have I taken Mama home to . . . ? I can't even write it. It is finished. Let me forgive quickly for your will is being done. Yet let the one learn the lesson you are seeking to teach and let me learn as well.

June 18, 2012
Dear God,

I am writing as I am thinking deeply about death. Mom is here at the house and is dying. I wonder how this journey will end. God, I pray your love and grace upon her, that you give her peace, that you spare her from suffering, and that you keep her from pain. Allow her days to be filled with joy and laughter and for her to ascend into your Oneness as the sun does into the horizon. Thank you, God, for this answered prayer. Amen.

The goddess ritual was getting more challenging. My heart was aching almost every day, watching the small but noticeable shifts in Mama's journey to the goddess realm. I was still working my full-time job, but also trying to spend more time at home. I didn't feel that there was space to cry, and I felt that I needed to be strong for Mama. One gift in this journey was my son, Emmanuel. Mama called Emmanuel "my little buddy." Emmanuel spent hours in her room, talking to her and watching TV and the news with her. He said he liked being around her because she was nice, wise, and funny. He said Mama would have a conversation, then two hours later have the same conversation, but this didn't bother him like it did Raebekkah. Patient and kind, he said he just acted like it was the first time he heard it.

Grateful for Emmanuel, I wrote about his role and impact on Mama in my journal on June 20. I referenced the relationship between God and Emmanuel since Emanuel means "God with us." I was hoping that Emmanuel's presence would have a positive impact on Mama's spiritual journey: *"I trust that, through him, she will see you in a new wonderful and powerful way, for it is impossible to feel Emmanuel's love without feeling your love. Amen."*

As part of her goddess journey, I created a sunrise ritual. I would go to her room in the morning: "Good morning, Mama."

"Hi, dear."

"Would you like to see the sunrise?"

"Yes, dear."

"Okay, let's get you ready." Slowly and patiently, I helped her get dressed in clothes that were easy to slip on. She would then slide from the bed to the wheelchair. Once her shoes were tied, we would go for our walk. Slowly steering the wheelchair out the front door, down the few steps, and to the sidewalk, we walked and rolled down the street and around the corner to a small lake. At the lake, we'd pause and silently watch the sunrise, comforted by the tweeting birds and the subtle pull and push of the breathing lake. After the sun rose, we rolled and walked back to the house, to her room, and to the bed.

On July 8, I wrote about our sunrise ritual and my growing anxiety about Mama's transition:

July 8, 2012
Psalm 6:9: "The Lord has heard my plea; the Lord will answer my prayer."

God, I am working to care for Mama. I take her to see you when I can and to see the sunrises. They are so beautiful and colorful and powerful. God, please continue to prepare me for understanding death. In whatever ways you can, prepare me. Help me to under-stand what is real and what is not real, what is the dream and what is reality—so interesting to access what is real, what is life, death, connection. I know I will get the answer. Course in Miracles talks of the body assuming a ridiculously large role in our lives, almost a joke. Well, more tomorrow. The sunrise beckons me now.

I loved our sunrise ritual because it was a time of reflection for me too. It was a time to reflect on the tenuous cord that connects life and death; it was a time to reflect on the sacredness of each breath, the breath that I knew one day soon she would no longer breathe. It was a time to reflect on the spirit world and the role of dreams, and it was a time to reflect on the relationship between a finite body and infinite spirit. My journal was a place for me to ask hard and unanswerable questions, to call on God and be heard, and to remind myself of the promises of hope and help from the Bible. My entries often referenced Psalms:

July 11, 2012

Psalm 9:10: "Those who know your name trust in you, for you, oh Lord, have never abandoned anyone who searches for you."

So, God, you have led me to Paulo Coelho—why? I know there will be a message for me in his work. I will carve out time to read his work and also Jonathan Livingston Seagull *again. In this journey with Mama, do I look for signs of life or signs of the end of life?*

July 21, 2012

Dear God,

Psalm 17:6: "I am praying to you because I know you will answer, oh God. Bend down and listen as I pray."

Surround Mama with your abundant, everlasting, radiant, and awesome love. Absorb her, encompass her, enrapture her, praise her, and envelop her in your majestic awe. Let her be my guardian angel, my intercessor with you, my advocate. May the heavens delight in her delightful and lovely spirit. Always allow me to feel her presence in my heart and my spirit.

July 29, 2012

Precious Lord,

What an amazing journey. I have been watching the transformation from life to death. I feel a little over-whelmed sometimes, exhausted, alone. I watched literally my mom transition to paralysis. At first, a little less eating, then less walking, then not able to stand, then not able to sit up, then barely drinking water. Now I struggle to change her Depends and administer morphine, Haldol, and lorazepam in regular time intervals. I know this will end soon and she will be an amazing ancestor and guardian angel for me. My question is what is a lesson here for me? What am I to learn from this journey as an active participant? How do I prepare for my own transition? How do I live this life more boldly, compassionately, and purposefully?

Psalm 22:29: "But all mortals—those born to die— bow down in his presence." The two most precious moments recently are the day she delivered a sermon and the day she listened to Patsy, Darlene, and Pam sing "Amazing Grace" and gave them applause. "Dear Lord, please let there be decreased urine output," says Raebekkah. And she adds, "She looks more comfortable than we ever tried to make her."

This day would be the last day that she spoke. She had been speaking less or not at all on most days. She had "delivered a sermon" a few days before this day, telling us to basically be good and to trust God. Although often agnostic in her Christian faith, she was a deeply spiritual person. When her best friends—Darlene, Patsy, and Pam—came to visit, I had tried to prepare Mama for their visit, freshening her up a bit. Mama was bedridden and often held a multicolored quilt closely about her for comfort and warmth. Her gaze had become vacuous, as if she were looking into another world. When her friends walked in the bedroom, she did not appear to recognize them and said nothing to them. They kindly and gently spoke to Mama, but she did not respond at all. Eventually, they left the room and walked into the living room.

Emmanuel, as usual, was in the room with Mama. He stayed after they left and eventually came out to the living room to tell us that she wanted them back in the bedroom. We all went back into the room, and she began to speak, very softly, just above a quiet whisper. She said they were good people and doing good in the world. She then said, "Sing." We were a little confused and sought to clarify if she really wanted them to sing. Softly and quietly, she repeated herself: "Sing."

They debated among themselves what they should sing, and they started laughing. They told Mama they couldn't sing, and they didn't even know what to sing. After a few minutes, they settled on "Amazing Grace." They didn't even know the lyrics, and so Pam looked up the lyrics on her cell phone. Because the others didn't know the lyrics, she was "lining" it out in the traditional form of gospel singing in the Black church, when the minister would say/sing a verse and then the congregation would follow. So Pam would say the line, and then she, Darlene, and Patsy would sing it. It was like a bad comedy show; they were out of tune and sounded terrible.

Mama knew it and suddenly said to them, "You all not too good." It was so funny, and we all laughed. Mama laughed too. And then she tried to sing: "Through many dangers, toils, and snares, I have already come." She was too weak to continue, but her friends finished singing: "'Tis grace that brought me safe thus far, and grace will lead me home." They sang one more verse, and when they were done, Mama clapped her old withered, thin, and worn fingers together and said, "Bless you, bless you all." Those were the last words she spoke. They gave her hugs and said their final goodbye. Awadagin arrived from a concert late the next day. She recognized him but was no longer able to speak. She had been asking for him, and he'd come as soon as he could. They had their last moments together, and he left to return to his concert tour.

As Mama's condition continued to deteriorate, hospice began to help us, administering pain narcotics and providing guidance on the signs of death: bowel and bladder changes, breathing irregularity, and changes in skin color. Mama was experiencing all the signs. Raebekkah and I were frequently changing her Depends, and she was getting tired of the strong, almost putrid, smell of Mama's urine—tired of the smell of death and dying. Every evening, the kids and I kneeled down next to her bed and said a prayer for her, asking for her not to be in pain. One night, Raebekkah added her own prayer: "Dear Lord, please let her have decreased urinary output." I had to laugh. I understood her prayer. It was getting more and more challenging to watch and participate in the goddess transition. Mama peacefully lay in the bed for almost ten days after her friends left, her chest rising and falling ever more slowly, until every breath had fulfilled its purpose, and there were no more left:

August 7, 2012
Dearest God,

Mama died yesterday. August 6, 2012. I had tried to stay in the room and was just too tired. Emmanuel and I laid down at 11:30 p.m. You tickled me awake at 2:00 a.m. and Mama's chest was not rising or falling. I miss you, Mama.

August 10, 2012
Dearest God,

I'm trying to remember the signs from Mama. I'm sure it was her who woke me up to let me know. I never wake up at 2:00 a.m. Since she left, I have seen two glorious rainbows and I heard "Amazing Grace" on the radio, a beautiful violin rendition. The morning she died, the kids and I went for a walk and saw a beautiful sunrise. I'm fighting a spirit of depression, sadness, and a strange strong urge to go to where Mama is.

My children recently shared with me their memories of the night that Mama died. Obadiah was at work, and the children and I were home. Emmanuel remembers that we were in the room just a few minutes after she died. He had been lying down with me in my bed, and we went in together. He said, "She had sparkles on her face and on her cheeks." Raebekkah was sleeping upstairs, and I told Emmanuel to tell her. She remembers Emmanuel running into her room shouting, "Grandma's dead. She's dead." She was thirteen years old. She said, "He sounded excited, with lots of energy. Maybe he was frantic or panicked, but it felt like the wrong vibe." She remembers coming downstairs and the emergency responders putting Mama in a body bag and taking her out. They both remember us walking to see the sunrise. Raebekkah said it took her about a month to be able to go to sleep at night regularly. She said her mind was just racing with ideas about ghosts, dead people, heaven, and hell, and she listened to "Bluebird" by Christina Perri because it was calming and peaceful. Emmanuel told me that sometimes he still misses Mama. I told him I do too.

Mama's memorial service was on August 19. After she died, one of her friends who was an artist wanted to design the cover for her memorial program. The cover was an image of a woman, like Mama, but with the appearance of an angel, singing in the clouds, as if in a heavenly choir. Consistent with her wishes, at her memorial service, we played the two DVDs that she had recorded of herself singing and reciting poetry. With the recordings on the huge screen in the university chapel, she looked larger than life. It was as if she had conquered death by performing at her own funeral. Her videos on YouTube (Pratt-Clarke 2018b; Pratt-Clarke 2018c) are goddess wisdom about overcoming obstacles, achieving success, giving back, and caring about humanity. I would need her wisdom, particularly the reminder from "Lonesome Journey": "We all have to walk that lonesome journey. We have to walk it by ourselves. Nobody else can walk it for us. We have to walk it by ourselves." And I would now be walking that lonesome grieving journey by myself.

SCENE THREE: **Grieving Rites**

My grief journey would not only be about the loss of my mother. Five days after Mama's funeral service, Obadiah seriously injured his left eye. He fell and punctured it on the edge of the bed. And so, in addition to two broken toes, a broken coccyx, and a torn rotator cuff, we now had to contend with this injury. He was not able to see out of the eye, and we began going to doctor's appointments, trying to understand what options were available for treatment.

In addition to caring for him, I cared for our children alone. I would take them to school, pick them up from school, take them to violin and viola lessons, and get them to all their extracurricular activities, including the dreaded late-night play rehearsals. In my journals, I reflect on the lonesome journey of life:

September 13, 2012

The spiritual journey is a lonely, individual one where you must journey alone. Dear God, I trust you completely in your wisdom, plans, insight for my life. I just want to stay enveloped in your love. I just want to access your constant peace for this journey. I pray for your hand to rest on and guide Ob, Rae, and Emmanuel at all times, that you give them great joy, laughter, that you direct them in their careers in the path of destiny that you have selected for them. Keep challenges to a minimum, so that they may have that great peace in this world. And for me, continue to hold my hand, be my best friend, and direct my steps to the destiny you have set aside for me.

September 24, 2012
Dear God,

I have so much on my mind. Questions for God: What stuff do I not want left behind? What happens when I die? Who will I see? What is that world like? What do I need to know to live a better life now? What is going on with Ob? What type of journey is this and why am I on it with him?

October 4, 2012
Dear God,

I am so thankful for your "I am" presence within me. Do the masses of humanity live lives of quiet desperation while holding the power of the universe in their hearts as unleashed, unfulfilled, unactualized potential waiting for just a spark and flame? Yes, I believe. If so, what is my role? It is to be the spark to light their flame of potential.

In addition to thinking about the lonesome journey of life, I also began trying to process Mama's transition. It began with a dream about her and documenting my longing for her:

October 9, 2012
I had a dream about Mama. I wish I wrote it down. She was talking about transformation or transfiguration, or maybe the transition. I hope she visits me again.

October 15, 2012
Dear God,

I miss Mama. Where is she? Mama, where are you? Today is your birthday. What does that mean? I don't miss you in the condition you were before you died. But, we had some nice times together and I miss your spirit and your presence. The memories don't feel like they are enough. I can't hear from you. I can't see you. I can't touch you. How to feel your spirit? 2 Thessalonians 3:5: "May the Lord bring you into an ever deeper understanding of the love of God and the endurance that comes from Christ."

I needed to feel Mama's spirit. I wanted an answer to this question, and so I called my first flame, Leonard. He had become a Baba—an African priest and spiritual guide in the Orisha tradition. He had given me a few readings and oracles over the years, and I felt that I could trust his wisdom. I called him and asked him for guidance on managing the grieving journey. He was like a divine angel, and his advice reflected an integration of concepts from African religious tradition and physics:

October 20, 2012

A message for me from an angel: Create an altar—an ancestral altar. Do a libation for ancestors. Begin with Mama; create an energy field that gains "field strength" if I do it every day. Create a space for her to come to me. I will be able to sense a difference. Do it daily. Mama's spirit follows gravity and wind like a leaf. It goes where it is pulled. Where it is most connected, pulled, it will go. Otherwise, it will drift with its own energy. Mama is spirit without a body. She is everywhere energy is, so I can set up a place that attracts her. I can connect to spirits with and without a body. As part of my grief and loss, I need to reorient myself to her. I should drink extra water to have extra electrolytes to help keep my energy grounded.

Mama needs a field that attracts energy and she will come to where the energy is. She has no choice and has to respond to where the energy is. At death, the body no longer contains energy and all the tension is released. What is released are the electrons that took the shape of a body, but the electrons still respond to the laws of spirit. The laws of spirit include the law of similarity and commonality. I have lots of Mama's spirit with me. Mama has a reorientation period as a spirit only and she still has work to do as a spirit. There are lessons to teach herself and laws to go by. If there is enough energy, she has to travel in service of that energy, just as light causes dark to leave or change. Need to do a libation—calm my spirit, pour water out calling the name of Mama (Mildred Inez Sirls Pratt). I need to honor ancestors by act of libation. The act of libation will help smooth the way and make my path easy by giving time and energy to me.

I am an ancestor though I still have my body. My children are ancestors with their bodies. My mom is an ancestor without her body. Libation connects land energy to those without a body. I have to make her libation a part of my life.

My life's purpose is to learn my lessons. I am here to learn the lessons that spirit provides me and then help others with their lessons. We came to learn lessons. I can access her lessons if I can access her energy. Most lessons are fun. It is like a test you write for yourself that you forgot you wrote.

Spirit can inform spirit. Spirit without body can inform spirit. Mama's spirit can connect to my spirit. At birth, we experience the perception that we are separate from spirit because it has been encapsulated in a body. It is actually a delusional separation from spirit. We spend our life trying to reconnect to spirit and to stay connected. Certain prophets, sages, and messengers encourage others to reconnect. The goal is to see everything as spirit. I have an opportunity to become better and to love my mom in a way that she has never been loved before—without her body. This is an opportunity for me to explore how to love on a different kind of level.

My relationship with Mama shifted after I received this guidance. I created an altar for Mama, and that changed my grief journey. I started to write journal entries to her:

October 21, 2012
Good morning, Mama.

Today, I'm starting a new relationship with you. It's going to be just as cool as the last one. I'm going to learn to enjoy it just as much. It's been pretty tough lately without you as I was used to you. But I'm determined to adjust to our new relationship. It's not as if there is a choice! You are all spirit now. But I see you representing friendship, wisdom, love, and loyalty. And I'm grateful for you and what you symbolize.

October 28, 2012
God will turn scars to stars. I'm hurting but I'm still here. There is an "after this."

November 6, 2012
Dear Mama,

You did a disappearing act. Now you see me, now you don't. You are so merciful to me through God. You were sick for such a short time. Seeing and watching you die was really tough. Leave everything behind. . . . Well . . . there are only lessons I should learn. I must learn from your journey. Please share them with me. Thank you, Menah.

John 6:63: "It is the spirit that gives life; the flesh is useless. The words that I have spoken to you are spirit and life."

I was suffering and struggling. The pain of the grieving journey felt like a knife that continually was stabbing me in my chest. It was a deep ache in my psyche and spirit. I was fighting against the urge to yield to the pain and the competing urge to fight the pain. I was also learning to accept the removal of Obadiah's eye, after the doctors determined that not removing the damaged eye could impact his right eye. The removal of his eye would leave him unable to drive for a period of time and in constant nerve pain. Disabled and unable to work, Obadiah would sit in the La-Z-Boy chair, much like my father did, brooding, suffering, silent. Obadiah was not emotionally available to me to comfort me, to process with me, to hold me, or to dry my tears.

I had to keep getting up every day and trying to put one foot in front of the other, go to work, and do my job well. Unexpectedly, I would be recognized for my diversity work at Illinois:

November 11, 2012
Yesterday was a celebration of diversity at the University of Illinois. I got an award—the Larine Cowan Award (for diversity leadership). It was just a beautiful event and Dagin came and played the piece from your service. I will treasure the award for my lifetime. But Mama, what I love about you now is that when I look at your picture, you are smiling and that always makes me smile back, always.

The program felt like the start of a path toward healing from the sharp edge of grief. I remember coming home that day and sharing the good news about the award with Mama. I had created an altar, and on the altar was an amazing picture of Mama. She was smiling and sitting on top of her favorite antique potty chair that looked like a throne. She looked like a queen in her favorite purple African dress, smiling from ear to ear. I was learning how to connect, touch, and feel Mama in a more spiritual way, including through my dreams:

November 21, 2012
Mama,
> *I had a dream about you. You wanted to leave to be with me. Gosh, Mama, you were so graceful in death and dying. I never really saw you complain or act up. Wow. I miss you, but I will write your book for you! I love you, Mama.*

I started writing Mama's book at the end of the year. Mama's book, *From Cotton Picking to College Professor: Lessons about Race, Class, and Gender in the United States*, would be about her journey, part autobiographical and part biographical. Mama had been jotting notes and memories about her life's journey. She had asked me, or rather told me when she realized she was transitioning, to finish her story, and so I began to write it. It was a journey from outhouses to the White House to hear her son perform before presidents; from sharecropping fields to academic fields; from the high school valedictorian who could not be selected as class president because she was a girl to becoming a full professor of social work when less than 1 percent of Black women faculty were full professors. As it was with the first book, writing would be a salve for my wounded and hurt spirit. I would wake up early every morning with the same discipline that had been instilled by my father. At 4:30 a.m., I would write and transcribe Mama's handwritten notes, touching part of her spirit through her words; it was as if she was still alive.

SCENE FOUR: **Goddess Wisdom**

my spirit was learning how to navigate the wild, unwieldy, unpredictable nature of Grief. Sometimes Grief would send me almost to the edge of a cliff, as She did on November 11, when I briefly contemplated suicide and thought about jumping in a lake and joining Mama. I was on my way to work, and the knife of Grief stabbed me so intently I almost couldn't drive. Pulling over to a local park with a lake, I tried to gather myself, swallow the tears, and make it to work. I could not. Walking around the lake, I stopped on a bridge overlooking the water. My journal entry on November 12, 2012, was entitled "The day the water was the sky":

> *Dear God,*
> *Yesterday, at Crystal Lake, I was indeed distressed. Yet as I contemplated jumping in the lake, I saw the sky in the lake. Was I looking at sky or lake? The reflection was so strong, it made me confused. And I realize what life seems is not what it is. How do we know what it is? I did not see the water in the lake; I saw the sky. I couldn't jump into the sky. Psalm 20:1: "In times of trouble may the Lord respond to my cry."*

I was still crying out to God, suffering from the insistency of Grief, writing on December 13, 2012: *"Grief is like an unending knife in my heart. It is a void, empty gap longing to be filled without being able to be filled. Exhaustion. God, help me please!"*

And She would, as She had done my entire life. She would hear my cry once again and answer me, console me, and counsel me through my journals. My journals were an ongoing conversation with Her. The journals, as they had when I was a child, would bear witness to my suffering, but they were also a protective circle around me, providing a space for searching, questioning, and questing. In writing scripture and continuing to search for Love, for God, and for the Divine Mother, I was being comforted, and my prayers were being answered. The journals were a space for both questions and answers, a space for doubt and affirmation, and a space for vulnerability and strength. Opposites were no longer opposites in the journal. Everything could coexist in harmony: the unknowable with the knowable.

I had survived weeds and weeding. I was no longer a seed. I had risen above death, darkness, and devils. I had contended and wrestled with forces seeking to stifle me and stamp out my light. I had survived. I was now above ground, with stem and leaves, ready to drink the dewdrops of rain and standing gloriously in the rays of my own divine light.

On my birthday on April 7, 2013, I wrote about my commitment to share my gifts with the world.

April 7, 2013

Today, I am 46 years old. In 4 years, I'll be 50. Where and what do I want to achieve? Am I on the path to achieve that? It all seems to come back to writing: writing about my life, my journey, and my journey to understanding God and sharing God's love and my gifts.

As I move toward the final stages of the Blackwildgirl journey, I will be liberated to dance in the wildness of the world, even with my scars, knowing that the scars have toughened and strengthened me.

Photographs and Images

Photographs tell their own story. These photos capture some of the salient moments in Act III. They include photos of my travels to the pyramids and Bunce Island, as well as letters from my father. The photos also include the tiny footprints of Morning Glory that were given to me by Vanderbilt Hospital after the miscarriage, as well as a few journal entries.

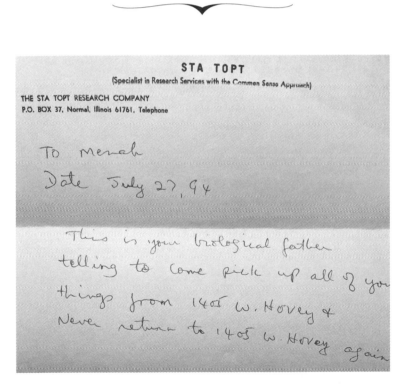

Papa's letter to me after learning of my marriage, of which he disapproved, July 27, 1994. Photo credit: Menah Pratt

STA TOPT

(Specialist in Research Services with the Common Sense Approach)

THE STA TOPT RESEARCH COMPANY
P.O. BOX 37, Normal, Illinois 61761, Telephone
January 6, 1996.

Dear MENAH,

i got your check dated 12-31-95 apparently as one

instalment payment which might be either for DEC. 95 OR JAN 96.

THIS TYPE OF CONFUSION IS NOT TOTALLY UNEXPECTED since I already believed
that YOU ARE LIVING BEYOND YOUR MEANS.

LIVING BEYOND YOUR MEANS IS ONE OF THE WORST THINGS YOU COULD DO
ESPECIALLY IF YOU HAVE LEGAL TRAINING.

You might as well recall or realise that the LOAN MADE TO YOU WOULD
NOT HAVE BEEN MADE HAD I BEEN IN PROPER HEALTH- so you really
benefited from my illness-LUCKY.

YOUR ACTIONS since 94, HAD BEEN IMMATURE AND MYOPIC- under the guise
that"I am grown up and can do anything at my age."

You may recall my letter to you in JULY 94. I STAND BY IT ESPECIALLY
THAT I KNOW THAT YOU FEEL THAT YOU ARE ALRIGHT NOT KNOWING OR
BOTHERING THAT YOU ARE HEADING IN THE WRONG DIRECTION.

WHEN YOU WENT AND GOT MARRIED WITHOUT MY KNOWLEDGE AND PERMISSION,
your action could only be considered as"PROTEST.
WHY AND WHAT ARE/IS BEING PROTESTED ?

YOU TALK ABOUT SACRIFICES !Shame but PITY.
CAN YOU EXPLAIN SACRIFICES OR DO YOU, even as ENGLISH MAJOR,know
what it means ?

You do not know what PREOCCUPATION WITH SUCCESS FOR YOUR BLACK
CHILDREN in this country means.
it was a 24hrs job-NO SLEEP-LYING IN BED OR NOT,

THE FACT IS THESE WERE/ARE CHILDREN OF PARENTAGE, highly EDUCATED
IN THE UNIVERSTIES and on the streets but wiTh inadequate FINANCIAL
MEANS desirous of MAKING AN EASY and COMFORTABLE LIFE for every one in the
FAMILY. PARENTS WHO DID NOT HAVE ANY INHERITANCE OR initial financial
family lift.
I AM NOT UNFAMILIAR WITH YOUR WEAKNESSES OR STRENGHTS FOR A
RATHER LONG/ SHORT PERIOD OF TIME.

YOU MAY CONSIDER THIS AS A TIMELY REPLY TO YOUR JULY 6, 1993 LETTER.

THERE ARE NONE OF THOSE NICETIES as I love you.

THE FACT IS---- YOUR BIOLOGICAL FATHER.

Papa's letter to me about the Pratt Setup, January 6, 1996.
Photo credit: Menah Pratt

Footprints of Morning Glory, first pregnancy that was miscarried at three months on September 3, 1996. Photo credit: Menah Pratt

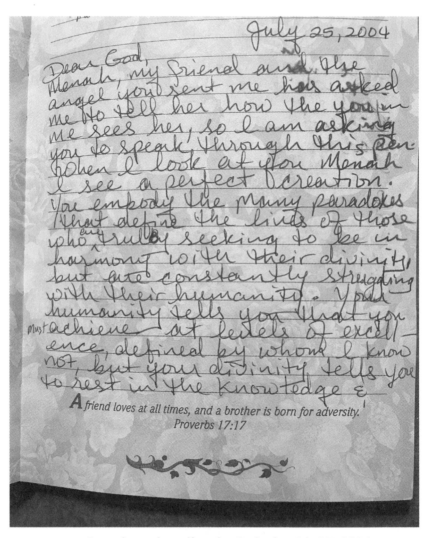

Journal entry by girlfriend in Barbados, July 25, 2004.
Photo credit: Menah Pratt

Menah Pratt, Egyptian pyramids, 2004. Photo credit: Unknown

Menah Pratt, Bunce Island, Freetown, Sierra Leone, 2005.
Photo credit: Unknown

Dear God —
Please help me — please hear my silent
cry and rescue me from this chaos, this
crazy world into which I have descended.
I want to escape, disappear into clouds and
nothingness... into air... into silence... into
peace... into silence... into stillness... into
silence... into peace... silence, peace, quiet
quiet, quiet...

Suffocating, gasping for air, for breath
for clarity, for insight, choking
coughing, panting exhausted
demanded upon submerged
under water.

mad, angry, furious hateful
mean angry angry mad frustrated
violent very violent crazy
psychotic incoherent mad — insane mad
need to hit, pound, beat hard long til
exhausted!
Scared frightened, fearful mad angry.

He who dwells in the shelter of the Most High, who abides in the sha-
ow of the Almighty, will say to the Lord, "My refuge and my fortress..."
Psalm 01·1 and 2

Menah Pratt, journal entry, fall 2006, after moving to Champaign,
Illinois, from Nashville. Photo credit: Menah Pratt

Photo of Papa and Aunt Dorothea, date unknown.
Photo credit: Unknown

Reflection Questions

1. What have been your grief journeys? Who did they involve, and what impact did they have on you?
2. Have you created or been part of any rituals or rites of passage related to other transition moments (birth, teenage years, college, marriage, death)? What was the initiation or ritual? What did you learn from the ritual?
3. How do you understand death and the transition of the spirit to the spirit world?
4. Do the photos generate any emotions in you? What are they and why? What photos are important in your own life now?

References

Foundation for Inner Peace. 1996. *A Course in Miracles*. Viking.

Pratt-Clarke, M. 2018a. *A Black Woman's Journey from Cotton Picking to College Professor: Lessons about Race, Class, and Gender in America*. Peter Lang.

Pratt-Clarke, M. 2018b. "Mildred Pratt Recording of Poetry - July 2009." YouTube video, 19:27. January 2, 2018. https://www.youtube.com/watch?v=WdanEVKtzoc.

Pratt-Clarke, M. 2018c. "Mildred Pratt Recording of Spirituals - July 2009." YouTube video, 19:29. January 2, 2018. https://www.youtube.com/watch?v=Vxa3H_6xVwQ.

Act IV: Branches

Supporting.
Swaying.
Sashaying.

THE TENTH STAGE—Blackwildgirl

THE SPIRIT-SEED, AFTER BEING BURIED, tenaciously sprouting roots, tangling, and tussling with weeds, is ready to rise above the ground and assume her divinely assigned role. She is no longer a seed. Like a sapling, she is ready to emerge from the shadows into light. It is a season of reconciliation and reclamation and a time for redefining relationships, including childhood bargains.

SCENE ONE: **Reconciliation**

Both my parents were cremated—their ashes kept in beautiful urns. My mother had shared her desire that Awadagin and I scatter their ashes in the Atlantic Ocean, in homage to Papa's Sierra Leone heritage. I was the safekeeper of the ashes until we could find a time to release them. One morning, Obadiah woke up and insisted that the ashes could no longer remain in our house: "All I know is six feet under; all I know is six feet under." It was a mantra that he continued to repeat. In his cultural tradition, the deceased were buried in the ground, and the presence of ashes inside the house was disconcerting to him. They were comforting to me, yet as I had often done in our marriage, I put his needs first.

Saddened and distressed, I called Awadagin and asked him if he could keep the urns. He agreed and arranged to meet me in Indianapolis, halfway between Urbana and Cincinnati, where he and his wife were living. Arriving early before our noon lunch meeting, I went to Butler University, where my mom had gotten her master's degree in religion. I wrote about my short visit there:

February 10, 2013:
Mama,

We went to Butler University yesterday. It was wonderful. Put a few ashes in a tree stump near Holcomb

Lake and watched a few ashes flow into the lake. Then,
suddenly and magically, you showed up as a rainbow in
the fountain. Thank you, Mama. I love you,
Menah

Even though Awadagin had the urns in his house, I would
get them back one day, without Obadiah's knowledge or permission. It was part of a deliberate and clandestine commitment
to take small but important steps to regain and reclaim my
power. Seven years after I gave the urns to Awadagin, I was
visiting him in Cincinnati, and I saw them on a bookcase in his
basement. I said, "Oh, so that's where they are?"

"Do you want them?" he replied.

"Oh yes, I'd love them, if you are okay with it."

"It doesn't matter to me."

So I took them with me back home, extremely pleased to
have my parents quietly and secretly protecting and guarding
me. During the seven-year absence from the urns, my parents
were still very present, often appearing in my dreams. I wrote
about my dreams in journal entries addressed to them:

May 13, 2013
Dear Mama,

You showed up in a dream, getting dressed, moving
slowly, looking older in transition. How are you doing?
I miss you so much. I need your energy and power to
sustain me with your book.

May 22, 2013

I dreamed about you, Mama. We were standing with
some people. I can't remember who. You were with me
and asking who people were that I couldn't see. I eventu-
ally realized you were in transition and you were seeing
spirits. You had on your green winter coat.

June 6, 2013

Dear Mama,

I "met" Ruby [my mother's sister who died as a little girl] yesterday. Pat [my mother's sister-in-law, the wife of her oldest brother, George] sent a picture of her in her casket. I trust you have reconnected with your siblings. How are you doing in that heavenly journey? We are going to Alabama for the family reunion. I'm carrying you in my spirit there. Show up in some magnificent way so I can feel your presence! You really have left me a magnificent gift in your writing. I am grateful. I miss you, but it isn't terrible now. I still feel very close to you.

June 10, 2013

Dear Mama,

I was at the family reunion. Met a lot of Thirkills. I love you, Mama. What was amazing was being in the "energy" of all those ancestors in Landersville and Mount Hope. There was an amazing lady at the archives who helped us.

This was the first Thirkill family reunion I was able to attend. Mama had hoped to be at the reunion before she was diagnosed with cancer and was so disappointed when she realized she wouldn't be able to attend. I learned so much about my family on that visit, including the five different spellings of my great-grandfather George's name: Threlkild, Threlkelds, Thirkill, Thirkle, and Thirkile. The inconsistent spelling of names is a legacy of enslavement. Our names and identities were taken away from us when we were enslaved, and we were given names attached to plantation owners as their property. Much of our journeys as African Americans has been about trying to reclaim our names, identities, and heritage. Family reunions help us to reconnect to family, as do visits to grave sites. I would feel a powerful connection with my great-grand-father when I visited his grave site in Phoenix. He had moved to Phoenix after his wife, Rosie Hubbard, died and his only daughter, Eula, got married.

Not only was I connecting with my mother's ancestors and descendants, but I was also starting to have powerful dreams about my father, chronicling them in journal entries, beginning on May 7:

May 7, 2013
Papa,

I had a dream about you just now. You actually leaned back in a car (from another car) into my car and gave me a kiss! At first, I thought you were angry with me because of road rage. But then I realized you were not angry at all and that you just wanted to show me some love—wow! I am who I am because of you and I love you.

It's like the car was a separate carriage that Paulo Coelho speaks of, where spirits exist without bodies. But in dreams, those boundaries can be dissolved; the boundary vanished so you could reach me. Thank you for doing that. It's what I've been wanting, needing from you for many years. Thank you so much. I missed you back this morning. I love you. We are going to have a great relationship.

May 8, 2013
Papa,

I am still in amazement at our reunion. So thankful for it. Thank you for your willingness to break through the carriage to me. I am so grateful. I'm going to ask you to help me in my life.

In *Aleph* by Paulo Coelho, he writes: "What we call 'life' is a train with many carriages. Sometimes we're in one, sometimes we're in another, and sometimes we cross between them, when we dream or allow ourselves to be swept away by the extraordinary" (2011, 117–18). In my dream, Papa had moved between the carriage of the spirit world and the carriage of the earthly world to start a new and different relationship with me. We began a journey of reconciliation, seventeen years after his transition:

June 16, 2013
Dear Papa,

It's Father's Day down here. You are on my mind. I'm still quite perplexed by death and the disappearing act it entails. You have power in your world to help me as a guide. I'd like to ask for your help. Just send me (through the universe), guidance, protection, and a calm, peaceful spirit. Help me to be radiant—always. I love you, Menah.

August 23, 2013
Dear Papa,

Yesterday, I started going through your papers from Illinois State University. What a sad, painful journey that was for you. I am so sorry about that. I feel, though, that it helped me understand a bit more about why you were you. I'm so sorry about that pain in your life. I now understand Mama even more and the depth of her love and compassion for you. But going back to May 7, I feel you understand the pain from my childhood. You just were not loving in the way a child needs. But I'm okay now. I am okay now. Thank God and will always be. I am the legacy of your pain! The Pratt Music Foundation is your legacy! It took this long for you to begin to heal, to reach me, but it was real. Thank you. I love you.

September 19, 2013
Papa,

Today is your birthday . . . still. You live on in many ways, but especially through the Pratt Music Foundation. Now, that is amazing. It is a validation of the significance of your life goal—to impact children. Now you have all these children whose lives you impact! Wow!

The Pratt Music Foundation would continue to grow with an endowment of almost $700,000 in 2023. While initially named to honor my father, after Mama passed, the board decided to make it clear that the foundation was named after both of them. It annually provides free music lessons to almost thirty elementary, middle, and high school students with talent and need.

I had reconciled with my father. His spirit had manifested itself from the spirit world to me. We both found love and compassion for each other. I would continue to reflect on my childhood and my relationship with both my parents. The anniversary of Mama's ancestral journey provided an opportunity for me to reflect on her relationship with my father:

August 6, 2013
Dear Mama,

It has been a year since you joined the Heavenly Choir! I thank God for that image of you singing with the choir. I can testify that time is a wonderful gift. My spirit feels lighter about you. I took great pleasure in knowing you are doing just fine. It's almost like I knew you would be fine. You became the epitome of surrender and acceptance as you laid down to die. You left your messages behind of amazing grace and you blessed us. That was such a beautiful gift. Thank you so much for that.

Your writing was another gift you left me. It has been an honor and privilege to write about your life. You know Pat sent the quilts and bedspread your mother made. I know you had something to do with that! Righting injustice, returning things to their rightful place. I know you will continue to live powerfully close to me through this book as it takes off. I'm trusting you for that!

Thank you so much for showing me so much love and being so strong in such a difficult time when Papa was so conflicted. I know you must have struggled, but you never showed it. You never wrote about it either. Maybe that's a lesson. Not to focus on pain and sadness and give it energy and life but rather focus on what's positive, possible, and full of potential and ensure those energies get stronger. Ensure that is where my effort is directed to ensure the success of what has life.

Thank you, Mama, for watching over me, ordering and orchestrating blessings. I feel you and your presence. I am so grateful. I love you. Menah

August 9, 2013
Dear Mama,

This weekend, we will do an ancestor remembrance for you and cook some salmon and reflect on the year. The most important thing you need to know is that I survived! We survived! We miss you profoundly, but we made it through. You are still guiding, helping, and assisting. I am so grateful. I know you'll send the right editor for the book and will ensure its success. Thank you. I love you.

My cousin in Sierra Leone had shared that it was a cultural tradition to honor the one-year anniversary of an ancestor with a small ritual. The African ritual involved cooking food for the dead, discussing their life, and then burying the food. We decided we would perform the ritual for Mama. Mama loved salmon, and so Obadiah cooked some as part of our lunch. During the meal, the children, Obadiah, and I shared life updates. After we finished eating, Obadiah dug a small hole in the back corner of the backyard, similar to Mama Pratt's ritual at her eightieth birthday party, and buried the salmon.

Later that day, Obadiah began to exhibit some very strange behavior. He put on his shoes and started walking to the front door: "Ob, where are you going?" I asked. There was no response. He looked like he was in a trance. "Ob, what are you doing?" Still, no response. He picked up one of the kids' backpacks and a shirt that he had draped over his arm. In an almost disembodied voice, he said, "I'm going home to 1405."

"What?"

"I'm going home to 1405." The kids and I were aghast. We didn't know what was happening. I motioned for Emmanuel to go stand at the front door. Obedient as always, he stood by the front door. Like someone who was possessed, Obadiah continued moving toward the door, repeating, "I'm going home to 1405." I tried to get in front of him, and he pushed me aside: "I'm going home."

"Obadiah, there is no home at 1405. This is your home; this is where you live." I didn't know if I was talking to Obadiah or to Mama, because Mama had said, "I'm going home to 1405" when she was living in our home. Raebekkah, Emmanuel, and I continued to talk to Obadiah, and eventually, we were able to persuade him to sit down. After a while, he took off his shoes, lay down on the couch, and went to sleep.

After he went to sleep, the children and I tried to process what happened. It was as if Mama's spirit had inhabited him after the ritual. When Obadiah woke up, he was clearly confused and disoriented. This would be the first of a few sacred times when Mama's spirit seemingly would manifest from the spirit world, moving between carriages.

She continued to appear in my dreams, and I continued to write to her, sharing updates about my life:

September 3, 2013
Dear Mama,

Last night, I had a dream about you. You were not living, but you were sitting in a chair in an apartment. I was startled, but not afraid. I didn't speak to you. I didn't know what to say. I just sat in your presence.

September 7, 2013
Dear Mama,

Today, I got to see the Bloomington-Normal Black History Project. I just wanted to see the legacy of your work. The book [A Black Woman's Journey from Cotton Picking to College Professor] is in the hands of the editor. All is unfolding divinely. Thank you. I feel it does justice to your life and also Papa's life. I feel good about it. I'm already trying to think about what is next. So, Mama, what is next? I look forward to hearing from the ancestors.

October 15, 2013
Dear Mama,

Today is your birthday! Happy birthday! You would have had a big party if you were here. All the food, friends, and fun. I miss you. You lived a great life and I know that you will continue to impact the world. I'm going to Arizona in a few weeks and will visit your grandfather George Thirkill's grave. It is just divine. I'm so grateful. I have his picture with his wife and child on my altar and you and Papa, too. I'm learning how we

can still have a relationship, meaningful and full. Thank
you, Mama, for everything. I love you. Menah

October 16, 2013
   I got tenure yesterday! On your birthday! I know
you would be proud of me! You would have celebrated
with me. I know you are rejoicing for me, you, and
Papa. I feel that. Thank you both for all the love and
pain of growing us/me as a little Black girl in a racist,
sexist community and society. I am grateful and I love
you both. Menah

I had achieved the almost unachievable: a tenured Black
woman in the academy. When I arrived at the University of Illinois in 2006, I was an associate director and assistant provost in
the Office of Equal Opportunity and Access. I slowly advanced
up the administrative ladder, moving from an associate director to
director, to an assistant chancellor, to an associate chancellor and
associate provost. And now, I was also an associate professor, with
tenure. After six years of working two full-time jobs, including
teaching and writing as a scholar, I had accumulated the dossier
of a tenured faculty member.
   While it was a largely lonely journey without mentors, the
dean of the College of Education (James Anderson) and the
chancellor (Phyllis Wise) agreed on a process for reviewing my
dossier, including external letters and internal reviews at the
department, college, and university level. The tenure letter validated the Pratt Setup with its focus on discipline and excellence.
It was the Pratt Setup that helped me to have the discipline of
writing, working as an administrator, being a wife, and being
a mother. When I got the letter, I felt that I had somehow
redeemed my father's aborted tenure journey, preparing a pathway and birth canal for new life to emerge. It felt like justice:
karmic wounds were being healed.

SCENE TWO: **Reclamation**

Eyaside, representing the Blackwildgirl spirit of my childhood, was dismembered as part of the bargain through a series of separations before I went to the University of Iowa in 1985. The gentle, innocent, authentic, and powerful girlhood spirit—the Queen of Sheba—was a casualty of the Pratt Setup. She was the sacrificial lamb. Buried, she would patiently wait to be exhumed, appearing for the first time in 1993, just before I married Obadiah, in my letter to him where I mention two Menahs: *"One is a tough, hard, rough, intolerable, unbending, hard-nosed disciplinarian and a perfectionist, and the other is a soft, sensitive, emotionally vulnerable, gullible, and naïve girl."* I referred to the tough one as Menah Adeola, and the soft one was Eyaside.

It would be eighteen years before Eyaside reappeared in my journals after a counseling session where I wrote on February 16, 2011: *"I have a backpack with a heavy little girl in it—Eyaside. How do I love her unconditionally?"* Two years later, Eyaside appeared again in my journals. I was reading *Faith in the Valley: Lessons for Women on the Journey to Peace* by Iyanla Vanzant. One of the lessons reflected on the ancient culture that values boys more than girls, and the ways that girls are "ignored, pushed aside, abused, or abandoned" (Vanzant 1996, 37). Vanzant reminds us that as women we have a little girl in us who is valuable and worthy. Inspired by that lesson, I journaled about my little girl within:

January 12, 2013
Lately, the "little girl" Menah keeps coming to my mind. How is she? She was a sad and not beautiful child, emotionally fragile, damaged in a backpack. Iyanla: "There is a little girl in you. Have you loved her today?"

Hugged her, kissed her, told her she was special, valuable, appreciated, honored, beautiful? How do I treat my little girl?

By the fall of 2013, I was ready to value, appreciate, and honor her. My journal entries over a three-week period illustrate Eyaside's growing presence and my growing awareness of my desire to get to know her, reconcile with her, and reclaim her. I was still reading *A Course in Miracles*, and Lesson 182 seemed as if it was written just for her. The lesson was about our inner child wanting to be welcomed home. Inspired by the lesson, I wrote about Eyaside in my journal as a letter to Jesus:

October 21, 2013
Dear Jesus,

A Course in Miracles *Lesson 182: There is a child in me who seeks Her father's house. She desires to go home so deeply, so unceasingly. Her voice cries unto me to let Her rest a while. This child needs my protection. She is far from home. She is calling me to let Her go in peace, along with me, to where She is at home and me with Her. She will take me to Her home and I will stay with Her in perfect stillness, silence and at peace beyond all words, untouched by fear and doubt, certain that I am at home. I will be still an instant and go home with Her and be at peace a while.*

Oh, goodness. Sometimes, I feel like a motherless child, a long way from home. This child—I know her. I've known her all my life. She is Eyaside. She is my spirit's connection to the Eternal—to You. She is the reminder, the remnant, the promise left in me to evidence the connection with the One to which I am part of. Eyaside has always felt the pull, the call. She has always felt the tug, heard the voice. Always. Christ, you

have asked for my help in letting you go home today.
Completed and completely. Eyaside is the Christ in me.
How do I feed, nurture, protect, and love her? I will be
fiercely protective of Her.

Eyaside wanted to return home. She was ready to be exhumed, loved, and cherished. She was ready to pierce the seal and return to her mother: "Why not go home to Momma today? God the Mother is waiting to hear from you" (Vanzant 1996, 36). The Great Wild Mother would welcome her with open arms:

October 26, 2013
I've had a revelation. My little girl is Eyaside.
She is a spirit of my ancestors. My grandmother and
great-grandmother's and back to the Great Mother. She
is the original wisdom, Mother Earth, the force of cre-
ation. I have known her all my life.
She is so powerful and so has been seen as a threat
all her life. So, she has been repressed. Not only repressed
but also suppressed, beat down, put down, denied her
humanity, denied her voice, since she was a little girl. She
has experiences primarily from men—physical, emotional,
mental, psychic, spiritual pain. The experiences resulted
in a muteness, like Maya Angelou, where I/she couldn't
speak, but could write. And she has written—for years.
Yet, now, she must write a different way—she must
speak. She must speak out. She has much to say and
much that others need to hear. Eyaside is that spirit of
my ancestors—of my grandmothers—of ancient wisdom,
power, and love. She, the spirit of God in me, is my
Secret Place of the Most High.
Yet, I have not cherished her. I've placed her in a
backpack, zipped her up, and carried her around like a

heavy load that I often wanted to drop, leave behind,
and forget about. Yet, she has never left me. She has
fought to become visible—honored, cherished, loved,
and valued. She has fought to unzip herself from the
backpack, to raise her head, to be heard, to move from
the back to the front of my life.

How did she fight? She went looking for love and
attention through men since she could not get it through
me. And there was a series of rejections where she
attracted energy that confirmed the image of her (broken
down, beat up) and not the reality (the light of God).

But darkness—deep darkness—returned. It was a
darkness of self-hate, of suicidal thoughts: the unlovable
image, the unworthy belief, and the ugly returned to roost.
The illusion became real and so the abuse returned—
physical, spiritual, psychic, mental, emotional. And, now,
she cries once again, and this time, I hear her and I will
value her, honor her, cherish her, and love her.

She must rise and stand tall, above all.

October 30, 2013

I am an angel. I must get my wings together to be
able to not just fly literally, figuratively, and spiritually,
but to soar. My wings have been in my backpack. I must
make her stand on the shoulders, front and center and in
the middle, as my guide. Eyaside is my wings.

My wings and I began to travel together. We started with
a spiritual pilgrimage to Arizona. Sedona had been calling my
name for a long time, and Grandpa George, my great-grand-
father's spirit, had been summoning me as well. I heard his
summons and knew I needed to meet him in Phoenix where
he was buried. A work conference in Scottsdale gave me the
opportunity that I had been waiting for. I flew into Phoenix,

got my rental car, bought flowers at a vendor on the side of the road, and drove to Greenwood Memory Lawn. The cemetery office gave me a map, showing me where a George Thirkle was buried: section 42, block 35, lot 4, space 7. Nervous, yet giddy with excitement and anticipation of connecting with the ancestral energy, I parked in section 42 and slowly wandered for at least an hour in the hot late-afternoon sun, looking intensely at tombstone after tombstone. Where was George? I called him: "George, George." The sun was almost setting, and I was starting to panic: "George, George." Responding as if he heard me, he suddenly revealed himself: "Beloved Father, George Thirlkile, 1875–1945." I collapsed on the tombstone, overcome with deep gratitude, relief, and love. Just like Mama Pratt had introduced me to her ancestors decades ago, I introduced myself to George and placed fresh flowers on his tombstone—a libation.

It felt like he knew I was there, as if his spirit was calling out to mine. He wanted to be found and created an energy field at a vibrational frequency that enabled me to connect with him. I felt that he was a protective, guiding energy. His spirit accompanied me to Sedona the next day. Arriving in Sedona, I bought a celestial amethyst, violet flame rock. It is a crystal that is attuned to the transmutation of the violet flame that heals and connects spiritual guides, helpers, and stellar beings. A guided spiritual hike and an ancestral reading led to a journal entry written to myself, reflecting another level of understanding and connection:

November 4, 2013
Dear Menah,

It's a new day for me! Spiritual journey. These past few days have been amazing. In Sedona, I felt Mother Earth as a purple warmth. I felt Father Sky as a blue wind—cool. I heard the birds—bluebirds. My message:

Be unconditional love. Accept the mantle of being the matriarch of my family. I need to embrace the principles of the Divine Feminine. I need a balanced life—what I give to myself and what I give to others. I need to understand what it means to be a woman—beautiful, feminine.

My ancestral reading reveals that I am on the journey of a healer, the path of a healer. Healer, know thyself to heal others. I am the high priestess who understands energies and can find lessons through joy and the outer life. I am part of a line of women down my father's side of strong women; one was a midwife who had many children. I have doors (not windows) open into the healing arts, both physical and spiritual. I have a gift of understanding and I relate to images. The dream world is very important.

I have Nubian heritage within me: a physical heritage going back to Egypt. Pyramids were designed to connect the physical with the spiritual, astronomy, etc. It is about giving Self to the awakening of the God mind on the earth plane. I am an old soul. I have journeyed on Earth a long time. I'm here to raise consciousness. I can stand in the storm because of my strength. I've just completed a cycle in my life. Something different is moving.

The next book is my autobiography.

November 10, 2013
Dear God,

Last night, I dreamed I had to get to work to a meeting. Somehow, I was running late to get there. I jumped from very high into a body of water. As I was flying through the air, headfirst, I realized I needed to change positions to be feet first. I did change, landed in the water, and then had to swim to the edge of the pool. At some point, I was pulling a young girl—a Black girl—to shore with me. She was pulling on my finger. She said thank you once she got to shore.

I believe this dream, again, represents my inner child wanting to join and accompany me in life. And the lesson is that I should not be afraid to fall, to dive, to jump in. Be unafraid.

SCENE THREE: **Goddess Wisdom**

As 2013 ended, I found myself immersed in the work of reconciliation and reclamation. I was paying attention to my dreams; I was connecting with the ancestral energy of my parents and my great-grandfather. I was moving ever so gently in between train cars of the earthly and spiritual. I was forgiving and releasing old wounds from my childhood, creating a clear path for Eyaside, my essential and divine feminine energy, to reveal herself. My calling and purpose had been revealed and confirmed: be a healer to heal myself and heal others. It was time to go "home" to Mama. Her spirit, symbolized by Blackwildmother with ancient ancestral energy, was waiting to accompany me.

Reflection Questions

1. Have you had opportunities to engage in the work of reconciliation, perhaps reconciling with an influential person in your life? Who was the individual, and what did the work of reconciliation look like? What lessons did you learn from that experience?
2. Have you taken a special trip or vacation where you connected with elements of your spirit?
3. If you have not undertaken the work of reconciliation, do you feel a need to do so? What might be holding you back?

References

Foundation for Inner Peace. 1996. *A Course in Miracles*. Viking.

Vanzant, I. 1996. *Faith in the Valley: Lessons for Women on the Journey to Peace*. Fireside.

THE ELEVENTH STAGE—
Blackwildmother

THE SPIRIT-SAPLING IS BOTH ABOVE ground and below ground. Above ground, she is able to feel the warmth of the sun, to soak in the rays of light, to drink raindrops. Leaves are growing, offering themselves to the world. Below ground, roots are still growing and deepening. It is a time for experiencing new ways of being in the world. Like springtime, it is a time of resurrection and rebirth.

SCENE ONE: **Resurrection**

*I*n the archetypal initiation journey, the ancient ancestral mother spirit appears for sacred encounters when the spirit is ready. She is a spirit of resurrection and rebirth. She travels between spiritual and earthly realms. Like a kind and graceful breeze, she is a soothing and calming presence—a reminder that She was, is, and always will be a source of Love.

On January 11, 2014, I called the house phone from my cell phone at work. Obadiah was now disabled and in chronic pain from the eye injury, and I occasionally called to just check in on him. Answering the house phone, he said, "Hi, Mildred."

I was puzzled. Why was he calling me Mildred? I said, "Mildred?"

"That's what the caller ID says: Mildred Pratt."

Later that day, I called a friend of mine in California from my cell phone. She answered, "Mildred Pratt."

I said, "What?"

My call had appeared on my friend's caller ID as Mildred Pratt.

My phone number was registering as her name. Mama had manifested herself through the thin veil connecting the earthly and spiritual. There was no rational explanation. Mama had used a pay-as-you-go TracPhone before she died. My account was a T-Mobile account, and she had never been on my plan. It was such an astonishing spiritual act; I wrote about it for months in my journal:

January 11, 2014
Dear God,

So, Mama showed up on my phone on Wednesday. I called my house phone and called my girlfriend in California and they both said that the caller ID said "Mildred."

Mama? Why did you show up? Just to let me know you love me?

February 3, 2014
Dear God,

I'm still perplexed by Mama's name showing up on the caller ID for my girlfriend and for our house. It's a recent occurrence. I wonder what it means.

February 8, 2014
The appearance of Mama's name means she is letting me know her spirit still lives on.

March 17, 2014
Dear Mama, my dear Mama, what do you want me to know? What are you trying to tell me? Use the Holy Spirit to let me know what you would have me know or what would you have me to do. I do miss you so much. A friend's ancestral reading said that you wanted me to know you were/are sorry. But why are you sorry? Are you sorry? You sorry for leaving me? Sorry for challenges in my life? You know, I accept your apology. I know you did your best. I'm just thrilled to "hear" from you. I love you. Menah

May 29, 2014
God,

I had a dream about Mama. She had died and I guess her body was still in bed, and at some point, she came back to life! And she was still recovering from being dead but was talking about moving into a house for about $59,000. Kids were around. Obadiah was around. She was in a wooden bed. She looked dead but was alive—she spoke to me. She was naked (under a sheet).

Dear Mama, it was so wonderful to see you in my dream last night. I miss you so much! Where are you and what are you doing? Please continue to take care of me and my family and protect me and bless me. Thank you.

Trying to process and understand Mama's manifestation, I began to read books about death and dying and the spiritual journey. I would share insights from the readings in my journal:

June 6, 2014
Dear God,

I just finished reading Beyond Death: Conditions in the Afterlife. *It's definitely powerful reading. The take-away lesson is that life is for learning lessons. There is no real religion. There is only one truth—progression. Progression leads to unification and wholeness. The world exists in vibrations. Life is for living and learning. What are my lessons that I have learned? The goal is to progress to the highest level of existence at the level of pure love. There are seven levels of existence in the spirit. There is a subconscious block when you get born/ reborn to be able to come back and learn and progress further. Life's challenges are for lessons.*

July 5, 2014

I just finished reading The Afterlife of Billy Fingers. *It is consistent with* Beyond Death, A Course in Miracles, *and* Archangels & Ascended Masters. *There is no death, just constant transformation into Oneness. Yet, this life—this life has a purpose even if it's pain. The purpose is not just to learn lessons. The purpose of this life is to bring heaven to Earth. Exude and love God. Am I to start writing about spiritual things? Probably! I think there is more to say than I realize. Mama came by phone to be very present to me, to manifest herself into my consciousness, and to let me know death is not the end. It is about progression and expansion.*

July 25, 2014

God, yesterday, I noticed Mama's name isn't on my phone anymore. I do feel a bit sad about that. I will look for her manifestation in this world from this train car. It's coming up on her two-year anniversary of her death. I don't like the word death—her transition to spirit world. Mama, I love you. I miss you.

Mama's manifestation occurred through the phone for six months. July 24 was the last day I saw her name on the caller ID. Though her manifestation ended, I continued to have dreams about her and would share those in short entries:

September 18, 2014

God,

I had a dream. Mama was in it. I think she just showed up by her car or a car she was trying to find. Because of her Alzheimer's, I was worried she didn't know her car. She came to a dance where I was but didn't want me there "interfering" with her social hour. Mama, I miss you! Will I ever not miss you?

October 9, 2014

I dreamed about you Mama. You came back to me after you died, and I had a conversation with you as a dead person. My friend was in the car, too; we were driving somewhere. I saw the funeral cloth and box for you. You were telling me about land somewhere.

October 15, 2014

Dear Mama,

As I remember your birthday, I remember you and your potty chairs! You brought me joy! I enjoyed being around you. I miss you. You did love me. I felt it. I loved you, too. I know you felt it. Mama, I committed to the book. It's been a long process, but the end is in sight. I do remember you love purple, the color purple. It made you so regal—royal.

What are you doing these days? You are so gracious to reappear and to let me know you are still around, or were around, through the phone. I love that. That was a wonderful gift from you. You were so loyal to Dagin. You went to concerts whenever you could. I admire that about you. I enjoyed getting advice and wisdom from you.

So, where am I now in my life? Goodness, Mama, still fighting racism, sexism. I hope you're at peace. I love you, Menah.

As part of writing this book, I reflected that I had submitted the first draft of the manuscript for publication on December 31, 2013, and Mama appeared in January of 2014. I had been working on transcribing her handwritten notes about her own life around the Christmas holiday after she died in August 2012. Each morning at four thirty, in homage to the Pratt Setup, I was working on the book before going to work. And then, on weekends and evenings, in a new symbiotic relationship with her words, I would be drawn to the desk, the chair, and the computer. A year later, the manuscript was done and submitted. Though the initial press where I submitted her work would not ultimately publish the manuscript, the fulfilling of my promise to her could have been a catalyst for her manifestation.

SCENE TWO: **Rebirth**

mama was Blackwildmother—an ancestral angel sending out rays of love with her wings. She had resurrected herself from the dead with a singular purpose—to remind me that Love had never left me and never would. I needed to feel her love. I was still fighting racism and sexism in my work in the Office for Equal Opportunity and Access. As associate chancellor and associate provost, I was leading both diversity and compliance efforts. I was also teaching as a tenured associate professor at the Law School and in the African American Studies Department. Though I was fighting for equity for others, I was feeling inequitable treatment. I was still being paid less than the White men with the same title, and I was battling a faculty bully who was trying to assume my portfolio. As a tenured faculty member, the validation, affirmation, and legitimacy I expected and hoped for was not forthcoming. I was feeling marginalized and minimized at work.

I was also feeling marginalized in my marriage. In November 2014, almost two years after losing his eye, Obadiah had knee replacement surgery. Although the surgery appeared to be successful, he began to experience chronic knee pain. He continued to remain a fixture in the beige La-Z-Boy: he was attached to it, enveloped by it, and defined by it. I no longer had a partner in a marriage, I didn't have a friend to talk to after work, and I didn't have a lover to love, embrace, and hold me. I remember feeling that I was in a relationship with a man who had a mistress. Obadiah's mistress was his pain. He talked about his pain all the time. The answer to every question was "Pain."

He spent most of every day listening to the Bible on tape, listening to sermons from conservative Christian television evangelists, and watching Judge Judy and all the other judge shows. He surrounded himself with voices of judgment, condemnation, acrimony, and controversy. He was becoming what he was watching: unpleasant, irritable, angry, frustrated, and inflexible. He wanted to inculcate his ideas and the ideology from the evangelists on me and our children.

Newly empowered with my wings, I gained voice and breath, able to advocate for a healthy, affirming, and fun childhood for our children, adamant that they needed to fully participate in the social fabric of their high school community. I refused to reenact the trauma, loneliness, isolation, and out-of-placeness of my childhood and high school years. Because of my persistence and determination, after many conversations, Obadiah finally agreed to allow the children to have an almost normal high school experience: attending school dances, prom, and even the after-prom party. They played high school sports: Emmanuel played on the tennis team, and Raebekkah was the captain of her basketball team and also ran track. Although Obadiah refused to allow them to spend the night at their friends' houses, their friends could occasionally spend the night at ours.

Because of the debilitating impact of Obadiah's chronic pain, I oversaw all the parts and pieces of my children's lives.

The children and I had a very close relationship. We talked all the time: we talked during breakfast; we talked on the way to school; we talked when I picked them up from school; and we talked before they went to sleep. When they were younger, I would sing "Amazing Grace" to them as part of our bedtime routine. Older now, we just chatted in the evenings. I took them to their music lessons, and I took them to summer camps. I went to almost every home track, tennis, and basketball game. I chauffeured prom and school parties. Obadiah rarely participated, engaged in his intramarital affair with Pain.

In my April 10, 2014, journal, I wrote: *"Emmanuel says I am an inspiration to him. Raebekkah talked about me being a role model to her. I may have underestimated my role/influence on my children."* I was intentionally mothering them to be fully themselves, to use the gifts that they had been given, and to feel loved and affirmed. I wanted peace, love, joy, and beauty in my life, and I wanted to share that with them as part of their lives:

November 2, 2014
God,

I'm so excited about knowing there is another world beyond this. Everything confirms the journey of the spirit and soul into Oneness. What I am particularly interested in, in this life, are ways to connect to that world and the peace, the joy, the love, and the beauty that exists more vibrantly there and that is also here.

I was entering a different season in my life—a season of integration and wholeness, where the earthly realms and spirit realms were One and where I was One with them. As 2014 ended, a spiritual reading forecasted that a new job would be on its way:

November 29, 2014

I am seeking to actualize my potential while here on Earth. What does that mean? What does that look like? Where and how can I be effective? God, I trust you and know you have plans for me. A new job has been forecast in the Akashic records. I am to write about God, finding the Divine Light. What am I being prepared for? I feel a need for a timeout—to regroup, reposition, get a new plan. I have a restlessness. I am supposed to live in the imagination of the reality I seek. What do I seek? New challenge, simplicity. In what role can I be a healer? How can I best serve others as an angel, a manifestation of the Divine? In what role can I best serve others? How can I serve humanity? I want to stay on the Noble Eightfold Path: right values, right speech, right mode of living, right thinking, right aspiration, right conduct, right effort, and right rapture.

I began 2015 in South Africa, chaperoning a study abroad trip for the University of Illinois. During the trip, I met Mawu, an African Mother Earth creator goddess:

January 19, 2015

God, I'm back! I'm so grateful for the blessing, the beauty, the majesty, the gift of South Africa, and the love. I saw dolphins again in Durban—the gifts of play and peace. They remind me of the dolphins I saw in Puerto Rico at the women's conference in November, and that dolphins are a symbol of resurrection. I found Mawu [an African Mother Earth creator goddess]. She showed up as an angel on my last day—my African angel. So much to carry in my heart—make every moment memorable. It always comes back to my purpose to write. Be a writer.

Mawu revealed herself during my last day in Cape Town. Waiting for me to notice her, peacefully posing on a small table in a jewelry and souvenir shop, she was a majestic African angel, looking like a goddess. I learned that Mawu is a mother figure from the Dahomey mythology and is a "West African Mother Earth creator Goddess associated with both the sun and moon. She is the Goddess of the night, of joy, and of motherhood as well as the ruler of the world's wisdom and knowledge" (Star 2012a). A symbol of germination and growth, her origin story connects closely with the origin story of the Yoruba mythology related to Yemaya.

In Yoruba mythology, Yemaya is the goddess of the living ocean, the Mother of All, representing Mother Earth (Star 2012b). I met Yemaya and connected with her spirit and the Black Madonna in Cuba, as part of the National Association of Diversity Officers in Higher Education's visit to Cuba six months later in July. I wrote a journal entry about the visit:

Dear Journal,

Wow. The Cuban church. What an amazing experience to walk into a Catholic Church and see a very large display of a Black woman holding a Black child at the front of the church. There is also a little separate room to the side of the main sanctuary that is filled with more Black images, icons, and candles. I'm wondering what is happening. Many people file into the little room first, say prayers, and then sit down in the regular pew. I, too, walk into the little room. I am filled with awe and a feel a special connection to the room, to the symbols, the icons, and the images that are Black.

Sara, our guide, tries to explain Santeria to us—a unique blending of African religion and Christianity/Catholicism that is widely practiced in Cuba. She shares that the image at the front of the church is the Black Madonna and the

Virgin Mary and that she is holding the Christ child. She shares that Santeria believes in orishas, "gods living in your head." She speaks about the importance of divination and reflection and prayer and initiation.

In Cuba, it seems that the religious syncretization of Yoruba and Catholicism, African spirituality and Christianity is a source of self-knowledge, power, creativity, and defiance towards the imposition of Christianity that was inconsistent with their African heritage. I believe that Black Americans need tools like Santeria to fight against oppression, White hegemony, and racism.

July 14, 2015 [In Cuba]

God, I sit here at the hotel in front of the sea, the ocean, and your magnificence—in the dark at 6:00 a.m., with no hint of sunlight. Yet, I know it will soon appear. And I will wait expectantly for you, your word, your call, your love, and your reassurance. It is the same: to write, always. It is my gift. It comes naturally. It is to serve through writing. A sunrise over the ocean looks different every day, depending on the clouds, their formation, and their darkness. Yet the sun still rises. The clouds do not have the power to stop the sun from rising. They can obscure the view, create the illusion of darkness, yet it is only an illusion. The sun does not cease to shine. I, too, must not cease to shine. I will have clouds of illusion in my life that could appear to obscure my light. Yet it is only an illusion. I must let my light shine anyway, regardless, no matter what.

Near the end of the Cuba visit in July, Sara, the tour guide, invited me to her home. She was an African Cuban woman and her father and brother—Yoruba priests—gave me an Orisha ancestral spiritual reading. They encouraged me to give water and flowers to my parents from time to time as an ancestral offering. They told me to be very careful when walking because I could fall into a hole, especially in a forest, if I couldn't see which way to walk. They also told me that Yemaya was an important guide in my life. I didn't realize at the time that I was about to be sent into a forest in Blacksburg, Virginia, and that true to the Akashic reading, there was a new job on its way.

SCENE THREE: **Goddess Wisdom**

Before I left for Cuba, I had been contacted by a search firm to apply for a position at Virginia Tech, in Blacksburg, Virginia. When I returned to the United States, I was invited to an airport interview as a semifinalist. In September, I visited the campus in Blacksburg as a finalist. During my visit, I went on a hike into the mountains to see Cascade Falls. As I walked slowly on the lush trail, along the babbling brook, something caught my eye in the water. Blending in, but also apparent, was a large green snake. It was as if she wanted to greet me. Later that day, I saw another large black snake crossing the road. Learning that snakes are a sign of transformation and associated with the shedding of old skin to reveal new life, I accepted the offer to join Virginia Tech as vice president of strategic affairs, vice provost for inclusion and diversity, and a full professor of education. I became part of the 2 percent of Black women faculty who are full professors in the academy. My new job began on February 1, 2016.

In preparation for that transition, one of my dear sister-friends from Champaign sent me away with the following blessing:

I am keeping you extra lovingly in my heart as you navigate this transition. In many ways, it feels much like an initiation to yet another level, where much trust and faith is required. I have no fear, as you have limitless love and trust in God. Lean on God and the angels when you are running low on energy and sadness peaks. You will receive a charge of love so pure and clear that will make it all be okay. All is good! All as it should be! All in perfect harmony! Everyone that you have touched is learning from this transition, as well. Separation is hard, yet it is an illusion, right? We know this. We got this at the sacred time of the year. I wish you stillness, silence— even in the midst of chaos and noise, especially so . . . so you can hear, listen to your voice clear and sharp telling you: You are awesome, you are magical, you are beautiful, you will continue to make a huge difference, and you are loved!

For you, always: joy, rest, love, happiness, prayer, soul, family, peace, clarity, magic, faith, love (unconditional), commitment, guidance, nature, happy travels, determination, all the angels on your side, contemplation, patience, meditation, guidance, community, love, laughter, peace, family, happiness, love, prayer, friends, belief, hope, support, trust, real, beauty, reflection, purpose, relaxation, love, journey, clear voice, courage, the beach! Waves! Real love.

I would be off to another stage of the initiation journey. I was given instructions to trust in God and the angels, including Mawu in South Africa, Yemaya in Cuba, my own Blackwildmother, and my divine Blackwildgirl. Together and united with goddess wisdom that I had gathered from across continents and hemispheres, I was prepared to be a tree with branches, swinging and sashaying in the wind.

I would begin to howl in the forests of the New River Valley and the Blue Ridge Mountains. I would be alone.

Emmanuel and Raebekkah had finished high school and were in college. Obadiah, once again, had decided that he would return to Exuma. He had been unable to work and had been on disability since his eye injury and complications from the knee replacement surgery. He had spent the past several years hibernating (or disintegrating) in the beige living room La-Z-Boy chair. Like my father, he and the chair had become one. Our marriage had become a shell of a relationship, never fully recovering from the addiction, the separation, the abuse, and the pain. He would be going to the Bahamas, and I would be going to Blacksburg, Virginia.

I was not going to Blacksburg alone or unaccompanied. Eyaside, my Blackwildgirl spirit, no longer confined to the backpack, was with me; Mama, my Blackwildmother spirit, was traveling right alongside me; and the wild angels and goddess energies of Mawu, the Black Madonna, and Yemaya were embedded in my heart. I was ready to put on my wings and take flight in Blacksburg as Blackwildgoddess.

Reflection Questions

1. What experiences have you had with the spirit world and ancestors?
2. How have dreams impacted and influenced your life?
3. Have you been able to travel or experience other cultures? How did those experiences impact your life?

References

Foundation for Inner Peace. 1996. *A Course in Miracles*. Viking.

Holzer, H., and P. Solomon. 2001. *Beyond Death: Conditions in the Afterlife*. Hampton Roads Publishing.

Kagan, A. 2013. *The Afterlife of Billy Fingers: How My Bad-Boy Brother Proved to Me There's Life after Death*. Hampton Roads Publishing.

Star, R. 2012a. "Goddess Mawu." *Journeying to the Goddess* (blog). April 26, 2012. https://journeyingtothegoddess. wordpress.com/2012/04/26/goddess-mawu/.

Star, R. 2012b. "Goddess Yamaja." *Journeying to the Goddess* (blog). February 10, 2012. https://journeyingtothegoddess. wordpress.com/2012/02/10/goddess-yemaja/.

Virtue, D. 2004. *Archangels & Ascended Masters: A Guide to Working and Healing with Divinities and Deities*. Hay House.

THE TWELFTH STAGE—
Blackwildgoddess

THE SPIRIT, NO LONGER LIKE A SAPLING, continues to develop and evolve, becoming like a tree with a trunk-like spine that provides support and strength. Like a tree, the spirit is maturing, mothering itself through photosynthesis, leveraging its branches and leaves for sunlight and air, and drawing water and other nutrients from its roots. It is pulling energy and sustenance from inward and outward resources and reservoirs. Like a palm tree, the spirit is bending and bowing during the hurricane-force winds of life, but not breaking. Reinforced by bundle sheaths that are powerful and strong, the spirit is resilient. Like a willow tree, symbolizing healing, flexibility, and stability, the spirit is able to withstand adversity, even if it has to weep from time to time, its tears watering new life from fallen branches. And most importantly, the spirit is like an oak tree, a symbol of power and protection, able to comfort and produce other seeds and acorns. The spirit can stand tall in the forest of life, assuming its divine destiny and branching out into the world. It is a season of revolution and revelation.

SCENE ONE: **Revolution**

I still wonder: Have I been enough of a revolutionary? Lorraine and Leanita, I promised both of you that I would write, that I would not shrug my shoulders, and that I would carry your burdens that you could not. I promised I would write for you and for the years you could not write. I promised that I would show you what kind of revolutionary I am.

I honored that commitment and began publishing books. In 2017, two coedited books were published: one on Cuba from the diversity officers' trip, *A Promising Reality: Reflections on Race, Gender, and Culture in Cuba* (Brown and Pratt-Clarke 2017), and one on women-of-color presidents, *Journeys of Social Justice: Women of Color Presidents in the Academy* (Pratt-Clarke and Maes 2017). The third book, on Mama's life, *From Cotton Picking to College Professor* (Pratt-Clarke 2018), was scheduled for publication in 2018. I had pulled Mama's book from the original press that I had submitted it to in 2013. It took several years to ripen and find a home. Eventually, Mama's book and the other books would be published through the Black Studies and Critical Thinking Series with Peter Lang, edited at that time by two incredible Black women scholars, Cynthia Dillard and Rochelle Brock. In preparation for the book release of *From Cotton Picking to College Professor*,

I created my own website (menahprattclarke.com) and introduced myself with my first blog post:

> August 31, 2017: "Why I Write"
>
> *My purpose in life is to empower myself to empower others. I write as a commitment to my connection with my own creative power and the belief that creative energy is transferable and thus can empower others.*
>
> *I have written all my life. My career path has been one focused on scholarship, activism, and leadership. I recognize, in particular, that because of the challenges that women of color experience in the world by virtue of both their race and gender and the way in which racism and sexism is operationalized in their lives, there is a societal imperative to work toward the elimination of barriers that impede the opportunity for women of color to manifest their full potential in society.*
>
> *As such, I believe that there is a responsibility in society to work toward the elimination of inequality, whatever the cause, for inequality lessens the humanity of us all. And . . . for what are we here . . . but to express and share our humanity . . . fully.*

In January 2018, *A Black Woman's Journey from Cotton Picking to College Professor: Lessons about Race, Class, and Gender in America* (Pratt-Clarke 2018) came out in print. I began an eighteen-month book tour across the United States. Many of the speaking engagements included short excerpts from my mother's DVDs, which I had uploaded to YouTube, from "Negro Mother"—"Children, I come back today to tell you the story of the long dark way that I had to know in order that the race might live and grow" (Hughes 1931)—and "Mother to Son": "Life for me ain't been no crystal stair" (Hughes 1922). Her spirit—Blackwildmother—and I were swaying together.

I continued to journal, asking on July 7, 2018, *"Am I doing enough to impact? Who do I want to impact? Where do I want to impact? Why do I want to impact? What do I want? Dedicating Self to Virginia Tech or to Self or to something greater or both?"* In December, at a conference in San Diego, overlooking the ocean, I started to get answers, just having read *Becoming* by Michelle Obama, and I wrote:

December 1, 2018
What is, what will be, my destiny? What is my becoming? I want a life of influence, a legacy, a life of impact. What is my part on the stage of life? Be light. My part in the stage of life is to be an angel—to serve others as a manifestation of Divine Energy. Angels inspire, encourage, help. Angels radiate light, love, laughter.

December 12, 2018
I have tried to let Obadiah's light shine; let his dreams come true. What are my dreams? I have been selfless in much. What does selfish look like?

I was ready to be selfish, though still helping Obadiah with his dream of living in Exuma. Unable to qualify for a mortgage to build a house in the Bahamas, I borrowed on credit cards and loan sharks to finance construction costs in Forbes Hill, Obadiah's birthplace. Emmanuel had joined him in the Bahamas after graduating from college, pursuing his career and passion as an artist and painter. With my finances, Obadiah oversaw the construction of the duplex for both of them and an art gallery for Emmanuel. Raebekkah was working in sports management, having gotten her bachelor's degree from Illinois and her master's in sports management from University of Michigan, by the age of twenty! Everyone was doing well. Our marriage, however, was not.

Though the Bahamas was his home, Obadiah was traveling to Blacksburg almost monthly for his health care and pain
prescription medicine. Some of the visits were good; most were
not. He constantly complained about the racism of the United
States. He was still having his affair with Pain, most recently
nursing broken ribs from a fall in the Bahamas. Though we
renewed our wedding vows on our twenty-fifth anniversary
in New Orleans in 2018, it was more about the party with
family and friends than our marriage. True to form, after the
vow renewal and reception, Obadiah went back to the hotel
room to spend time with Pain. I went out with my cousins
and children to dance the night away. They took a photo of
me standing on Bourbon Street in the most beautiful wedding
dress I'd ever worn, a gentle light pink strapless dress with
ruching and a long trail, grinning from ear to ear. That night
I danced down Bourbon Street, feeling like a Blackwildgirl:
strong, powerful, and beautiful.

I began writing regular blog posts on my website, and on
March 3, 2019, I wrote a post honoring Blackwildmother
and Blackwildgirl called "When a Black woman walks into a
room." In part it reads:

*When a Black woman walks into a room, something
happens. For how could it not? For when we walk into
a room, we bring the ancestral power of generations,
centuries of Blackness and Womanness—intertwined,
inseparable, and immutable. When we enter a room,
we bring memories of oppression, memories of racism,
memories of sexism, memories of poverty, memories of
disrespect, memories of disenfranchisement, memories of
disregard, and memories of moments when we were minimized, marginalized, and dehumanized. Those memories
walk in with us, for they are stitched into our soul, into
our DNA, with needlepoint precision—permanently.*

We bring not only memories into the room, but we also bring our pain and our pride that is intertwined with success and sorrow, and often with stories of sadness and struggle. We bring dried tears as sacred and sacrificial offerings—etched as wrinkles—often invisible on our faces, like scars from African ancestral tribal markings. Yet we are proud—proud of our own perseverance and persistence in places of peril when our fire and flame should have been stomped out. Yet still we stand, resilient. With elegance and sophistication, hips and lips, and our breasts leading the way—breasts with white milk that nourished the Whiteness of America while serving as mammies and maids and midwives—we walk into rooms. Yes, when a Black woman walks in a room, much, much more walks in with her. Centuries of Black motherhood, of Black womanhood, of Black Goddess energy accompanies us, as our ancestors, as our angels, as our assistants, to guide, direct, comfort, and console.

When a Black woman walks into a room, there is often something else. Something submerged and sublime, simmering below the surface like fine wine maturing in barrels of our body until it's time to be poured out, sometimes smooth and silky. Other times, explosive, unrelenting, and wounding. Formed from the bowels of the earth— marinated for decades in juices of dirt, decay, and death. Formed from the misery and madness, the malfeasance and the mischief, and the mistreatment by miscreants. It walks with us. It has no name; It is part of us. Yes, yes, when a Black woman walks in a room, It comes with us. For It is Us and It is our power. For when a Black woman walks in a room, she brings not just her gender pronouns, but also her Blackness, her It, and her This and That.

For when Black women—savvy, street-smart, sophisticated, informed with the White man's knowledge, and infused with the wisdom of African queens—walk into a room, each step is imprinted with power and purpose. Each step marks and imprints permanence and existence into the earth. Each step proclaims and pounds out the right to be—to be validated, to be heard, to be seen, and to be acknowledged, as a Black woman.

Yes, yes, for when a Black woman walks into the room, let the room take notice. Let us, as women, keep pushing forward into rooms, entering with energy, like earthquakes shifting tectonic plates. Let us walk confidently and courageously into more rooms, for we do not walk alone. We walk with the invisible and invincible presence of one thousand ancestors and angels. Let us, therefore, boldly strut and stride into our destinies of greatness.

A MONTH LATER, IN APRIL 2019, I delivered the commencement address at the University of Pittsburgh School of Social Work. I returned to the same event Mama had attended almost fifty years ago when she received her doctorate. We had made a revolution, together.

My revolution continued two months later when I traveled to Penuel Ridge, a retreat center near Nashville, Tennessee. Penuel Ridge was named in remembrance of Jacob's wrestling with God in Genesis before he received his blessing. Like Jacob, I would be wrestling with myself and God. I had carried forty years of journals to Nashville in file boxes. My basement unit had a bedroom, an office, a bathroom, and a kitchen. The bedroom had three single beds. I laid forty years of journals across two of the beds in chronological order from 1976 to 2019. Sleeping in the third bed, I lived and breathed alongside those journals for three weeks, daily transcribing relevant journal entries. At the end of three weeks, I had written the initial draft of *Blackwildgirl*.

I had also brought the sentences that my father had made me write as punishment. The sentences were written on old-fashioned computer paper from my mother's office. I don't know why I had saved those sentences all those many years, perhaps as a testament and living proof for the memory I had tried hard to erase. I had also carried around letters and cards from friends and the depressing and lifeless poems I had written as a child.

During my time at the retreat center, I realized it was time to sort the wheat from the chaff and find out what I needed to keep and cherish and what I needed to let go. There was much to let go. I decided to conduct a sacrificial burning ceremony, using the pieces and parts of my life that no longer served a purpose as an offering. I knew I couldn't burn away all the memories because many had left an indelible imprint on my spirit. I wrote in my journal a statement of intention: "I want my voice back; I want to reclaim my power; I want to be fierce and fearless in sharing my gifts; I want to affirm myself. Impact the world. Be light for the world. Renewal, reclamation, and reaffirmation."

I had been preparing for this ritual ceremony from my initial arrival. I had experimented with fire building and had walked the large property gathering wood and sticks of different sizes. They were all stacked near the firepit, ready for the ceremony on my last full day. On July 24, I began the ritual with a meditation in the mud house, a small circular structure with a table in the center, like an altar, with a candle. I sat on the bench, meditated, and read scriptures. I had been in the mud house earlier during my stay and had been visited by a snake, again a symbol of transformation. There was no snake on this day, just a calm, peaceful quietness. After praying in the mud house, I walked the labyrinth maze at the retreat center, reflecting, slowly stepping. I retraced the labyrinth's inner circle. I felt liberation. I was ready for the fire ritual ceremony.

I went to the fire pit with my sacrificial offerings. I put the fire starter block on the bottom, built a little triangle structure of twigs, and added some paper. With the lighter, I lit the paper. A little smoldering fire started, and I began feeding it with the papers from my life—sentences with different numbers and assignments, letters from names that were no longer familiar, and cards that no longer held meaning. After all the paper had burned, the fire and the flame appeared to die. I felt a sickening feeling. I had worked so hard to gather sticks and wood, and now the fire appeared to be gone. Desperately, I tried to urge the fire on with all of my spiritual and physical might: feeding, fanning, and encouraging it. Nothing. Only smoke.

So I sat down, surrendered, and released it. It would be what it would be. Suddenly, a peace came over me, and I asked the universe to send me a message. I silently and fiercely prayed, literally willing the fire to appear. And then I waited patiently. All of a sudden, as I stared at the smoldering smoke, astonishingly and miraculously, a flame appeared, igniting the wood and starting a tremendous fire. I made fire. I was Aries, my zodiac sign. I was the Goddess of Fire. The fire burned all day, into the evening, gently smoldering as I drove away the next morning.

The fire also removed scales on my eyes that had blinded me to myself and my essence. I was able to see what I had not been able to see. Returning back to Blacksburg from the Nashville retreat, I noticed something unique, peculiar, and powerful. On my bedroom dresser with a large mirror that I looked at every day, I saw a framed picture. The photograph, in a five-by-seven frame, was small and inconspicuous, sitting on the end of the dresser. Almost an afterthought. I don't know how long the frame had been there. I had clearly put it on my dresser at some point in time. In the framed picture, there was a little Black girl, Queen of Sheba. It was me, as a child, Blackwildgirl.

It was as if she had been sitting there, waiting her turn: waiting to be acknowledged, validated, honored, respected, and seen. It was taken in April 1972, when she was five years old. Looking cute and pretty in a beautiful Brazilian indigo tie-dye mud cloth dress, with braids pulled back with a ribbon, and African earrings and a bracelet from my grandmother. The front of the dress has a gold embroidered design. It was taken during the time my family was in Brazil, with my parents teaching in Rio de Janeiro during my father's one-year sabbatical.

And then I started finding more little-girl pictures of me, at six and seven years old. These were all images of me: me before the bargain without knowing, before the sorrow journey, before the dethroning, before the wandering, before finding love, before the harrowing of my soul, and before the Black-wildgirl journey. Writing—it allows us to recover ourselves, find ourselves, love ourselves, reclaim ourselves, and remind ourselves of ourselves. Revolution had led to revelation. Not only did I find pictures of myself; I also found the little book on Mary McLeod Bethune, published in 1975.

SCENE TWO: **Revelation**

A commitment to being revolutionary required me to look at all the parts and pieces of my life and reckon with what no longer had a place, what no longer brought me joy, and what was a source of discontent. I needed to look at my marriage—face-to-face—and reckon with the impact of revolution on my marriage. Where Obadiah and I had once been an inseparable engine and caboose, it felt as if a hundred train cars had been added in between us.

The pandemic was the breaking point. When the pandemic and lockdown happened in March 2020, Obadiah and

Emmanuel returned to Blacksburg from the Bahamas. Fur-
loughed by her job in Delaware, Raebekkah also came to live
in Blacksburg. For several months, we quarantined together
as a family. It was a hellacious and horrendous experience.
Arriving in Blacksburg, Obadiah decided he needed to be the
"man" of the house and began to single-handedly, without any
consultation or discussion, rearrange the furniture in the living
room. With an open floor plan on the first floor with no doors,
the large living room was completely open to the kitchen. The
living room had lots of places to sit, with couches and chairs
along the walls on both sides. There were also coffee tables, as
well as a TV. A fireplace was on the far end of the living room.
In addition to the La-Z-Boy, there was a three-seater couch, a
two-seater loveseat, and a one-seater chair. There was also an
antique potty chair from Mama that looked like a chair for a
king or prophet.

Obadiah moved the long three-seater couch into the middle
of the room, facing the fireplace, dividing the living room in
half. He placed the large coffee table in front of the couch. The
coffee table was completely covered with Obadiah's papers,
Bibles, books, and multiple bottles of prescription pain medicine, all chaotically disorganized. He moved the throne-like
potty chair to the head of the coffee table. On the other side of
the three-seater couch, the one-seater chair and two-seater love
seat were on opposite walls of the room, facing one another.

Once the room was set, Obadiah decided that we needed
to have a family "Bible study" early every morning. At 6:00
a.m., we were all summoned to the living room to participate
in a completely confusing and incomprehensible Bible study
that he led. At the "Bible study," we all had our "places,"
like pews. Obadiah sat on the throne-like potty chair in front
of the coffee table, with two or three Bibles. Emmanuel was
near his father, either on the floor near the fireplace or in the
La-Z-Boy. On the other side of the couch, Raebekkah and

I initially sat together on the two-seater love seat, along the wall. We occasionally glanced at each other in utter disbelief and confusion during the "Bible study." At some point, Obadiah decided that we needed to not sit together, so we moved across from each other, still behind the couch, with me in the two-seater and Raebekkah on the chair, stealing glances as we tried to understand the un-understandable reality.

His "Bible study" was disconcerting on many levels. His interpretations were ironic and sexist, based on very conservative interpretations about the place, space, and role of women, with the expectation that women should be submissive and subordinate to the male head of house. Ironically, he had not worked for almost ten years, and I was essentially head of the house, at least financially; I was wearing the metaphorical pants as the sole breadwinner. Yet when I asked him what I should pray for related to our marriage, he said, "Pray to be a more submissive wife."

I couldn't wrap my head around the way he conducted Bible study, as if he was the sole authority. I had read the Bible through from beginning to end at least three times in my life, and having had my own early morning spiritual practice for decades, waking at 4:30 a.m. to study and reinterpret religious texts, I felt marginalized, minimized, and infantilized. He was treating me and the children like children. We were all adults, and I was his wife, and we were supposed to be equals and partners.

But we were no longer partners, as one early morning argument attested. About a month into the lockdown, waking the children up at 2:00 a.m., Obadiah told them that our marriage was in crisis and that I was the reason. Not only did I have "nontraditional" spiritual views about Jesus, the devil, and evil, but I was also "disrespectful" to him and not an "appropriate role model" for the children. Horrified and humiliated, blindsided and gaslighted, I lost my voice. I became silent and silenced. I retreated to a corner of my bedroom, as if it was the corner of shame at 1405, in between the front door and Mama's blue-green chair. I was on the verge of regressing to the Menah of my childhood and even beginning to have suicidal ideations. Having flashbacks to the Pratt Setup, feeling powerless and dominated, I knew I needed to summon the universe of goddesses to my side.

I started looking for a counselor, quickly finding an incredible, powerful, sweet, compassionate, intelligent Black woman who agreed to provide marriage counseling to us. At various seasons of our marriage, we had gone to counseling. All the experiences followed a similar pattern. We would start together. I would continue, he would stop. The pattern was inevitably repeated in Blacksburg. We started, he stopped, and I continued. I continued because counseling got me out of the house every week, counseling gave me someone to talk to who affirmed me, counseling made me know that I wasn't crazy, and counseling made me know that I was valued and cherished. Every week, my amazing counselor reminded me that I was powerful, amazing, intelligent, compassionate, and caring. She said that I was a deeply rooted tree that blossoms and blooms with fruit that nourishes others. She saw me standing tall and strong. She told me that there would be reaping and harvesting of the many sorrow seeds that had been sown, producing joy and peace in the world. My counselor reminded me that I had all the tools from my initiation journey, and I didn't need to revert back to the generational trauma of the Pratt Setup and allow my sacred and powerful spirit, the now emerging bloom, to be severed or dismembered.

Obadiah was attempting to put Blackwildgirl, my newly liberated and empowered spirit, back into the backpack. I couldn't let him. I was a tree, and I reminded myself in my journal entries in the fall of 2020: *"Be the tree, Menah, be the tree."* In September, after Obadiah finally left to return to the Bahamas, I wrote in my journal:

September 13, 2020
Dear God,

I do not know the significance, ultimately, of today, yet I know it is significant. Today, I have been liberated to love myself, to love the little girl in me that was abandoned, to find out what she needs and to give it to her. I have always cared for others with a deep compassion and have not had time or space to care for myself. I found the little girl. Now, help me to love the little girl, to care for her, to be her caretaker, to be her lover. I must care for my Divine Feminine.

Over the next year, his visits became infrequent, as COVID enabled him to get a ninety-day supply of medicine rather than thirty days. I used the space and time to become reacquainted with Blackwildgirl. In the summer of 2021, I purchased a 2018 Audi, my first "new" car in decades, replacing a 2006 BMW Wagon. And I donated the 1912 Cable piano of my childhood to the senior citizens day care program at Virginia Tech. I then bought my very first piano—a baby grand I named Simone, in honor of Nina Simone.

Proud of my new purchases, I was shocked at Obadiah's response and lecture on failing to "get his permission" and "continuing to disrespect him." I was angry, too. For years, I had sacrificed almost everything to help his dreams become reality, using almost every paycheck and paychecks I didn't even have through loan sharks and credit cards to finance his home and duplex in Exuma. I didn't even own a house. All I owned was a car and piano. I was financing his grand dreams, and he was upset about my small dreams. I realized I could no longer endure the cost of the bargain.

Like the childhood bargain of the Pratt Setup, I had entered into a marriage bargain twenty-eight years ago. Like the child that became the host for my father's dream, I had been the host for Obadiah's dream. Like the child that tried and tried to please my father but was never enough, I had never been enough in our marriage, despite all my efforts and all my sacrifices. Just as my father was a parasite on my tennis career, Obadiah was the beneficiary of my career, reaping the financial benefits and living his dream lifestyle in the Bahamas. Just as the cost of the bargain of my childhood required a restructuring of the financial relationship between my parents, the cost in my marriage was also a new financial relationship. Like the few enslaved Africans who were able to purchase their own freedom, my freedom would come at a significant lifetime cost. But the cost of freedom was actually priceless. I was liberated and free to fully be me, as I wrote in my journal: "God, I need to be a wild woman—fully, emancipated, liberated." And in July I wrote:

July 31, 2021

Today, I let go of the past. I start anew. A new way of thinking and being. Anew—once more, again, in a new or different and typically more. I am committed to slaying dragons and giants of oppression.

Six months later, I was divorced, and I reflected on my new journey in my journal:

December 4, 2021

I am, I have been on a journey of self-discovery. I am ascending to my greater destiny. On this new destiny, I will actualize all of my potential in service to humanity—globally. I will need all the spiritual fortitude I can muster. I am excited, though. Ready. I am now divorced and focusing on my journey and my destiny. I don't have to apologize or feel bad. I can and do feel sadness for the relationship and for him.

Liberated, I was no longer responsible for the heavy weight Obadiah represented, a weight that tried to control, imprison, suppress, and subordinate me. I was no longer a caged bird that could not sing. I was no longer swallowing rivers of tears from pain and suffering. I was no longer the "disappointment" he labeled me during one of our many arguments. I was no longer sacrificing my dreams, hopes, and aspirations for his. I was no longer second-guessing my feminine instinct.

I have no regrets from the marriage or the divorce. Over the course of twenty-eight years of marriage, I had endured so much: being a stepmother to his daughter, his incarceration, his addictions, his decisions to live in the Bahamas, the loss of the frame shop and bankruptcy, his medical injuries, his night shift jobs, and his mistress Pain. I had endured tiptoeing through the house for years trying not to wake or upset him. I had endured being accused of having an affair when I was playing tennis. I had endured years of silencing, resorting to journals and journaling as my only way to "speak." I had endured *"six months of hell—abusive spiritually, emotionally, and psychic,"* as I wrote in my journal in December 2020. Yet I had survived.

Despite the challenges, I unequivocally believe that we were meant to be together. The Voice of Love had told me so. We created beautiful, wonderful, inquisitive, intelligent, and loving children. The universe had used him to teach me many lessons. Most importantly, I had learned how to tame the kingly beast of masculine energy in my psyche, and I had learned how to validate, affirm, and love my Blackwildgirl. His role and purpose had been served.

SCENE THREE: **Goddess Wisdom**

I am still working on being revolutionary, even as I am stepping into my destiny as a Blackwildgoddess.

Blackwildgoddess.
Birthed from the Ultimate Mother—the Divine
Mother,
The Motherland of Africa:
A place of old wise ways and wisdom,
Of pyramids and temples,
Of ashes and ancient ancestral energy.
Birthed from rainbows
And from pots of possibility and potential,
From dust and clay and
Bits of silver and gold.

Blackwildgoddess.
Transported from the Motherland to the Fatherland
From Africa to America
Baptized in the Middle Passage through trauma and trials
Surviving rape and ravaging
Creating new goddesses to worship and
New words to speak.
Singing love songs,
Bathed in rhythms from slave ships and cotton fields,
Created on plantations of tobacco and in paddies of rice.
Love songs that comfort and caress:
Spirituals and gospel
Rhythm, blues, and jazz
Reggae and rap,
Classical and hip-hop.
Soulful and sometimes sorrow full,

Steel pan drums syncopating and
singing life into the almost lifeless,
Shattering silences.

Blackwildgoddess.
Fed with soul food, leftovers made magical,
Oxtail, pigs' feet, ham hocks, and hog maws,
Reviving and restoring hungry spaces.
Shielded
Shrouded
Shored up and
Sheltered.

Blackwildgoddess.
A warrior,
Wielding her wildness as a weapon,
Moving and stomping through the world
With confidence, conviction, and courage.
Marking her territory,
Sashaying,
Dancing, dervishly whirling.
Bold. Fearless. Fierce.
Impetuous and impatient.
Wild and unruly.
Unrestrained.
Revolutionary.

Photographs and Images

Photographs and images tell their own story. These photos capture some of the salient moments in Act IV. They include several pictures of me as a young girl, journal entries, and a photograph of my great-grandparents and their daughter. There is also a photo of my family with Obadiah and our children, as well as a photograph of me at the University of Pittsburgh School of Social Work graduation where I delivered the commencement address.

Great-grandparents Rosa Hubbard Thirkill and George Thirkill with their three-year-old daughter, Eula Thirkill, in 1902. Photo credit: Unknown

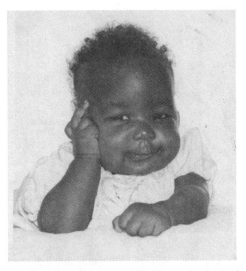

Menah Pratt, baby photo, 1967. Photo credit: Unknown

Menah Pratt, five years old in Brazilian dress, 1972.
Photo credit: Unknown

Menah Pratt photo collage, top left-right: age three, 1970;
age five, 1972 (Brazil). Bottom left-right: age six (second-grade photo);
age seven, 1974 (third-grade photo).

25th vow renewal family photo, Emmanuel, Obadiah, Menah, and Raebekkah, New Orleans, Louisiana, 2018. Photo credit: Patrick Melon

Menah Pratt, School of Social Work, University of Pittsburgh
commencement where I gave the graduation speech at the program
Mama had received her PhD from almost fifty years before, April
2019. Photo credit: Erika Johnson

11-4-19
Revelations - little girl in backpack is now on
my dresser!
Writing creates revelations -
Writing lessons
   happens
Writing happens in Blacksburg -

11-17-19
Writing, revelations,
Clarity of life's purpose in blog -
Mothers' letters to me — I was her
Best friend -

Menah Pratt journal entry, November 4, 2019
Photo credit: Menah Pratt

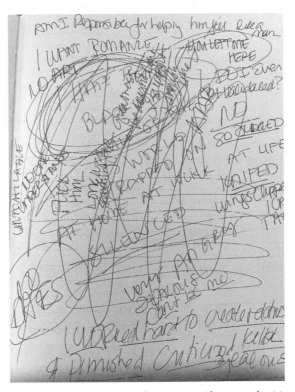

Menah Pratt journal entry, December 2019. Photo credit: Menah Pratt

the cross-
the non attachment of the spiritual journey?
Let it go give—Let it go—
Go be the tree—stmg tree on a hill overlooking the
Ocean in all its glory, & in all its wisdom
Be the tree, Menah — Be the tree—

Tears burn — you know— they burn with the pai
Singe the eyes & face in their hotness—

They give me rules to follow Idont like that—
Dont play dont do, Dont say —
That aint relationship — it aint mutual

If I was someone who loved, I would not about them

Menah Pratt journal entry on being a tree, November 1, 2020.
Photo credit: Menah Pratt

God—I need to be a wild woman— Fully—
Emancipated, liberated

A strong tree on a hill overlooking the ocean in all
its glory & in all its wisdom

Not to be shade—Others find the shade—
If they reach tree, they get peace & view because
tree in between parallel universes— coexisting in harmony—

Letting go of past, prepare for today & tomorrow

I need to be untethered—— wander free—

Menah Pratt journal entry referencing being liberated,
November 1, 2020. Photo credit: Menah Pratt

Reflection Questions

1. Reflect on your relationships in your life. Which relationships have nurtured you? Which ones have not been nurturing? Are there any recognizable patterns in your relationships?
2. Ask yourself: Am I doing enough to make an impact? Who do I want to impact? Where do I want to impact? Why do I want to impact?
3. Are you revolutionary, willing to turn around and look at yourself and your journey? What will you see if you do?
4. Do you have pictures from your childhood? What do you see in those pictures, and what qualities are reflected in those images?

References

Brown, V. and M. Pratt-Clarke. 2017. *A Promising Reality: Reflections of Race, Gender, and Culture in Cuba*. Peter Lang.

Foundation for Inner Peace. 1975. *A Course in Miracles*. Viking.

Hughes, L. 1922. "Mother to Son." In *The Collected Work of Langston Hughes*. University of Missouri Press.

Hughes, L. 1931. *The Negro Mother and Other Dramatic Recitations*. Golden Stair Press.

Obama, M. 2018. *Becoming*. Crown.

Pratt Clarke, M. and J. Maes (Eds.). 2017. *Journeys of Social Justice: Women of Color Presidents in the Academy*. Peter Lang.

Pratt-Clarke, M. 2018. *A Black Woman's Journey from Cotton Picking to College Professor: Lessons about Race, Class, and Gender in America.* Peter Lang

Walker, A. 1983. *In Search of Our Mothers' Gardens: Womanist Prose.* Harcourt Brace Jovanovich.

Epilogue

SCENE ONE: **Liberation**

*T*wo important photos represent this work. The first is a painting by my son, Emmanuel. During the COVID summer, I commissioned a painting from Emmanuel for a possible book cover. He used the Blackwildgirl photo of me at age five and painted her in a collage of excerpts of sentences that I had saved from childhood, as well as scraps of drafts of the book. The large framed artwork is hanging in my living room. It is a reminder that Blackwildgirl is liberated and a part of me.

Blackwildgirl collage, 31 x 38 inches, by Emmanuel Pratt-Clarke, with
excerpts of sentences I wrote as a child and drafts of this manuscript.
Photo credit: Menah Prattt

The second image is a photo that pays homage to the writing process: the archival work required for this manuscript and the almost innumerable drafts. It is based on over twenty journals from forty-five years, hundreds of letters between my mother and me from 1980 to 2011, and many, many photographs from living and traveling in the world. This photo includes a sample of manuscripts, photos, and drafts. I had substantially completed this manuscript and was in the process of seeking copyright permissions. One of the key permissions that was initially granted was surprisingly revoked. Not only was I not granted permission; I was subsequently denied the opportunity to participate in a retreat led by the author. Devastated and heartbroken by the rejection of a beloved and admired writer, I undertook a significant revision to remove all references to the writer. Among the drafts, journals, and photos are rejection letters and emails not only from her but also from over seventy agents and publishers. Only the persistent prayers to ancestors and angels allowed this manuscript to manifest.

Archival material for *Blackwildgirl*, including journals,
photos, letters, and manuscript drafts, April 6, 2023.
Photo credit: Menah Pratt

SCENE TWO: **Love**

*I*n my journal in the fall of 2020, I wrote, "I want a Hallmark romance." My statement of intention manifested. Look for volume two, *The Adventures of Blackwildgoddess*, and visit my website at www.menahpratt.com to learn more about *Blackwildgirl*.

Menah Pratt, photoshoot at Virginia Tech, 2022,
in my favorite dress. Photo credit: Golder Baah

Reflection Questions

1. What did you learn about yourself from reading *Blackwildgirl?*
2. What does liberation look like for you?

Please take a minute to share a review about *Blackwildgirl* on Goodreads, on Amazon, on the Blackwildgirl Facebook Page, or on my website at www.menahpratt.com.

Acknowledgments

This book began when an eight-year-old Black girl wrote her first diary entry. Over the course of forty-five years, thousands of pages were written in many journals, documenting a life and a journey from Black girlhood to Black womanhood. During a three-week period in July 2019, at Penuel Ridge Retreat Center in Tennessee, I found the space to lay them all out. Gently and compassionately, I combed through each one with a tender loving eye, looking for nuggets of wisdom and parts of myself that I could courageously show the world. This book would not be possible without the space and sanctuary provided by Penuel Ridge.

I am grateful for lives that intersected with mine: my parents, my brother, my children, and my friends. I am grateful for Virginia Tech and the mountains of Blacksburg, Virginia. The mountains have provided a sanctuary for me to weave academic, intellectual, and administrative pursuits together to pursue my calling.

Three amazing women editors—Diedre Hammons, Kathleen Furin, and Kelly Anderson—did an incredible job editing my manuscript, and they were so affirming, especially as I was still navigating the challenge of remaining courageous in baring my soul. There were also a few early readers of the manuscript that were so supportive: Aurora Chang, Sylvester Johnson, Kris Tilley-Lubbs, Venus Evans-Winters, Beverly Guy-Sheftall, Dominique Hill, and Gordon Hodnett. Gabriella Gutiérrez y

Muhs and Valerie Lee provided invaluable suggestions. I am grateful to each of them for making the time to read the manuscript. I am also grateful for Obadiah, who supported this book project.

This work has had a long and difficult journey, waiting for a home. After over seventy rejections from agents and presses and five years after the writing retreat, I am honored and grateful for She Writes Press bringing this work into the world.

This work was inspired by Black women warriors whose first names are enough: Lorraine, Leanita, Maya, Harriet, Sojourner, Oprah, Nina, Nikki, Alice, Audre, and Serena. My own dear warriors—Mildred, Raebekkah, Eula, Mama Pratt, Mercedes, and Aunt Dorothea—were at my side. Mary McLeod Bethune, founder of Bethune-Cookman University, has always been my heroine and inspiration. I am grateful to #SayHerName, and the named and unnamed women of color around the world, who inspire me daily by making a way out of no way. Clarissa Pinkola Estés, and her marvelous works on women and their divine intuition and power, inspired the framework for this work. And I cannot thank Nikki Giovanni enough for her love and friendship and the poem she wrote for this book. When I arrived at Virginia Tech in 2016, I invited the small group of African American elders to my house. She brought yellow roses to welcome me.

I hope that this book accomplishes the purpose for which it was written: to encourage all women to liberate their wildgirl from within so that she can get her wings and fly. If you want begin your own wildgirl journey as you read the book or as part of a book club, please explore using the companion journal, *Blackwildgirl Companion Journal: Finding Your Superpower.* The companion journal includes reflection questions and ideas for book club discussions and conversations. Additional resources for book clubs, supplemental photos, and other inspirational materials are available at www.menahpratt.com.

About the Author

MENAH ADEOLA EYASIDE PRATT is a nationally recognized and diversity-award winning author of four books on race, gender, and diversity, including *From Cotton Picking to College Professor: Lessons About Race, Class, and Gender in America,* an auto/biography of her mother, Mildred Pratt. Born in Pittsburgh, Pennsylvania and raised in Normal, Illinois, Menah received a BA and MA from the University of Iowa and an MA, PhD, and JD from Vanderbilt University. She currently serves as Vice President for Strategic Affairs and Diversity and Professor of Education at Virginia Tech, and she is the founder of the Faculty Women of Color in the Academy National Conference. Menah lives and works in Blacksburg, Virginia.

Author photo © Chris Kwaramba

Selected Titles From She Writes Press

She Writes Press is an independent publishing
company founded to serve women writers everywhere.
Visit us at www.shewritespress.com.

*No Thanks: Black, Female, and Living in the Martyr-Free
Zone* by Keturah Kendrick. $16.95, 978-1-63152-535-3. In
essays written with humor and wit, Kendrick reimagines what
it means to be "a good black woman"—from women choosing
never to have children to mothers regretting their choice to
have them, from being a lonely black atheist to conquering
loneliness as a single woman in a foreign country—and, in
the process, challenges the expectation that black women will
serve as either noble martyrs or sacrificial lambs.

Freedom Lessons by Eileen Harrison Sanchez. $16.95, 978-
1-63152-610-7. A heartfelt, unflinching novel about the
unexpected effects of school integration in 1960s Louisiana
told by three very different people living in the same rural
town: Colleen, an idealistic young white teacher; Frank, a
black high school football player; and Evelyn, an experienced
black teacher.

The Outskirts of Hope: A Memoir by Jo Ivester. $16.95, 978-
1-63152-964-1. A moving, inspirational memoir about how
living and working in an all-black town during the height
of the civil rights movement profoundly affected the author's
entire family—and how they in turn impacted the community.

Amazon Wisdom Keeper: A Psychologist's Memoir of Spiritual Awakening, Loraine Y. Van Tuyl, PhD. $16.95, 978-1-63152-316-8. Van Tuyl, a graduate psychology student and budding shamanic healer, is blindsided when she begins to experience startling visions, hear elusive drumming, and become aware of her inseverable, mystical ties to the Amazon rainforest of her native Suriname. Is she in the wrong field, or did her childhood dreams, imaginary guides, and premonitions somehow prepare her for these challenges?

Living a Spiritual Life in a Material World: 4 Keys to Fulfillment and Balance by Anna Gatmon, PhD. $16.95, 978-1-63152-256-7. Dr. Anna Gatmon demystifies the all-too-often elusive nature of spirituality and brings it down to earth, providing a concrete roadmap to living a life that is spiritually fulfilling without having to give up material pleasures.

Note to Self: A Seven-Step Path to Gratitude and Growth by Laurie Buchanan. $16.95, 978-1-63152-113-3. Transforming intention into action, *Note to Self* equips you to shed your baggage, bridging the gap between where you are and where you want to be—body, mind, and spirit—and empowering you to step into joy-filled living *now!*